# ART IN THE LIGHT OF CONSCIENCE

**Angela Livingstone** read Russian and German for the Modern Languages Tripos at Cambridge (Newnham College). She became a lecturer in the Department of Literature at the University of Essex in 1966, and taught there for more than three decades, ending up as Professor. She published a biography of Lou Andreas-Salomé in 1984, but her main interest was always in Russian rather than German, and she has written much on 20th-century Russian literature, concentrating on the work of Boris Pasternak, Marina Tsvetaeva and Andrei Platonov. Her publications include a study of *Doctor Zhivago* in Cambridge University Press's Landmarks of World Literature series (1989); an annotated translation of Marina Tsvetaeva's *The Ratcatcher* (Northwestern University Press, 1999); a transposition of fifty passages from Platonov's novel *Chevengur* into English verse (Gilliland Press, 2004); and *The Marsh of Gold: Pasternak's Writings on Inspiration and Creation* (Academic Studies Press 2008), which she translated and edited. She is now translating longer poems by Tsvetaeva and parts of her correspondence with Pasternak.

First published in 1992, her edition of Marina Tsvetaeva's *Art in the Light of Conscience* was reissued by Bloodaxe Books in 2010.

# MARINA TSVETAEVA

# ART IN THE LIGHT OF CONSCIENCE

## EIGHT ESSAYS ON POETRY

TRANSLATED WITH AN INTRODUCTION & NOTES BY
### ANGELA LIVINGSTONE

## BLOODAXE BOOKS

ISBN: 978 1 85224 864 2

This edition published 2010 by
Bloodaxe Books Ltd,
Eastburn,
South Park,
Hexham,
Northumberland NE46 1BS.

**www.bloodaxebooks.com**
For further information about Bloodaxe titles
please visit our website or write to
the above address for a catalogue.

Supported using public funding by
**ARTS COUNCIL
ENGLAND**

Cover design: Neil Astley & Pamela Robertson-Pearce.

Digital reprint by Lightning Source.

*To the memory of my dear friend Valya Coe*

# ACKNOWLEDGEMENTS

For the first edition of this book I was helped with innumerable questions of Russian language by Valentina Stefanovna Coe, whose undying delight in Russian poetry has inspired me for some forty years and to whom the book is again dedicated. Celia Hawkesworth and Dragan Milivojevic advised me on Serbian and Alexandra Smith commented usefully on the Introduction and on aspects of translation.

My thanks again to Donald Davie for having allowed me to reprint his translations of the quoted verse in 'Downpour of Light'; my translation of that essay was first published in *Pasternak: Modern Judgements*, ed. Donald Davie and Angela Livingstone (Macmillan, 1969) and was considerably revised for this book. My translation of 'Art in the Light of Conscience', first published in *Russian Literature Triquarterly*, 11 (Ardis, 1975), was also greatly revised. The translations of twelve poems have also been revised.

The original edition of this book was published by Bristol Classical Press in the UK in 1992 and by Harvard University Press in the US. Thanks are due to David Marshall of Duckworth Publishers for his kind assistance.

# CONTENTS

I have followed the usual British transliteration conventions, representing ы as y and и or й as i; e stands for both e and э. Well-known names are given in their familiar form.

Except for those on pages 21 and 136, all footnotes are Tsvetaeva's own.

# LIFE OF MARINA TSVETAEVA

A brief chronology, mentioning her main collections of verse and her other works referred to in this book. (The best biography is Simon Karlinsky's *Marina Tsvetaeva: The Woman, Her World and Her Poetry*, Cambridge, 1985.)

| | |
|---|---|
| 1892 | Born in Moscow. |
| 1894 | Birth of sister, Anastasia. |
| 1902 | Mother develops tuberculosis. |
| 1902-4 | Living in Italy, Switzerland and Germany. |
| 1906 | Death of mother. |
| 1908 | Published her first poems. |
| 1909 | Visited Paris. |
| 1910 | First volume of poems published, *Evening Album*. |
| 1912 | Married Sergei Efron. |
| | Second volume of poems, *The Magic Lantern*. |
| | Birth of daughter, Ariadna. |
| 1913 | Death of father. |
| 1915 | Met Osip Mandelstam. |
| 1917 | Revolution. Efron with the White Army. Tsvetaeva stranded in Moscow. |
| | Birth of second daughter, Irina. |
| 1920 | Death of Irina. |
| | Wrote *Swan's Encampment* (poems) and *Tsar-Maiden* (long poem). |
| 1921 | Wrote the long poem *On a Red Steed*. |
| | Publication of volume of poems, *Versts*. |
| 1922 | Left Russia. Joined her husband in Berlin. |
| | Wrote the essay 'Downpour of Light'. |
| | Publication of *Versts II*. |
| | Moved to Czechoslovakia (to a village near Prague). |

| 1923 | Publication of several collections of poems, including *Psyche*. |
| | Wrote long poem *The Swain*. |
| 1923-4 | Wrote first neo-classical play, *Ariadne*. |
| 1925 | Birth of son, Georgii (called Mur). |
| | Wrote long poem *The Ratcatcher*. |
| | Moved to Paris. |
| 1926 | Correspondence with Pasternak and Rilke. |
| | Wrote the essay 'The Poet on the Critic'. |
| 1927 | Wrote play *Phaedra* (this and *Ariadne* are verse-tragedies, |
| | referred to by Tsvetaeva as her *Theseus*). |
| | Moved to Meudon. |
| 1928 | Publication of *After Russia*, last volume of verse in her lifetime. |
| | Wrote long poem *Perekop*. |
| | Met Mayakovsky in Paris. |
| 1930 | Wrote cycle of poems to Mayakovsky upon his suicide. |
| 1931 | Wrote the essay 'History of a Dedication'. |
| 1932 | Wrote the essays 'The Poet and Time', 'Epic and Lyric of |
| | Contemporary Russia', and 'Art in the Light of Conscience'. |
| 1933 | Wrote the essay 'Two Forest Kings'. |
| 1934 | Published the essay 'Poets with History and Poets without |
| | History'. |
| 1935 | Sergei Efron began working for Soviet secret service. |
| | Met Pasternak in Paris. |
| 1938 | Returned with son to Moscow, where husband and daughter |
| | had already returned. (Anastasia was sent to prison camp the |
| | year before.) Ariadna and Sergei both arrested that summer. |
| 1941 | Soviet Union entered the war. Tsvetaeva evacuated from |
| | Moscow. Hanged herself in Elabuga. |

# INTRODUCTION

## I

'Good poetry is always better than prose,' Tsvetaeva wrote. Prose as good as hers, however, is very rare. In the Soviet Union as in the West, Marina Tsvetaeva is now generally acclaimed as one of the four great Russian poets of this century. But she has yet to be acknowledged as the consummate writer of prose that she also was.

The three poets whose names are sometimes bracketed with hers – Osip Mandelstam, Boris Pasternak and Anna Akhmatova – also wrote excellent prose; the prose of Mandelstam and Pasternak, written mainly in the 1920s, ranks as high as their work in verse. The 1920s were in fact a remarkable decade in Russian literature. The renascence of poetry at the turn of the century was followed by an efflorescence of prose that had the concentration and power of poetry, whether its writers were actual poets (such as Belyi, Kuzmin, Mandelstam, Pasternak, Sologub) or solely prose writers (Babel, Olesha, Pilnyak, Platonov, Remizov, Zamyatin). Roman Jakobson called it the 'prose peculiar to an age of poetry'.[1]

Although she lived abroad from 1922, Tsvetaeva remained creatively in touch with the best literary work being done in Russia, and her prose can well be compared with Pasternak's and with Mandelstam's (who stayed there). It is as carefully wrought as theirs is, as demanding and as rewarding of effort from the reader. It is, however, unlike theirs in its overt and personal passionateness, its dialogic orientation, and its intent focus on etymology.

Much of Tsvetaeva's prose, like much of Pasternak's and Mandelstam's, is centrally concerned with the subject of poetry. Collected here in English translation are eight essays by Tsvetaeva on poetry, along with some poems, mostly written much earlier but thematically related. Some parts of her memoirs – of her childhood and of poets who had been her friends – would contribute to our theme but I have not included them, as they are, in the main, already available in English, in a collection

1

translated by Janet Marin King.[2] For reasons of space I have left out one other piece that I would like to have included, an essay entitled 'The Poet Mountaineer' (about a young émigré poet, N. Gronsky). The purposes of my collection are to make Tsvetaeva more widely known as a writer of prose (only one short piece overlaps with J. M. King's book), and to help communicate to English-readers her thoughts about what it means to be a poet. Few have done as much as she has to explore the processes of creation and the feelings of the exceptionally creative person in the ordinary world.

A short chronology of Tsvetaeva's life is given on pages ix-x. Here I will mention only three aspects of that life which it will be useful to have in mind as one reads her work. These are: plenty, poverty and exile. Each of them furnishes a metaphor for an aspect of Tsvetaeva's relation to poetry.

Daughter of a highly accomplished musician and a highly successful scholar; 'inundated' with lyricism in her childhood; given a good classical education (largely at home); speaking fluent German and French from childhood on, and acquainted with the best literary works in those languages as well as her own; travelling in Italy, Switzerland and Germany (albeit forced to by the needs of her consumptive mother); spending a year in France at the age of sixteen; publishing a volume of her poems at her own expense at seventeen; easily meeting poets, artists and scholars during her adolescence: Tsvetaeva started life in conditions of not indeed wealth but a certain cultural and material good fortune.

At the Revolution, nearly all her family property was seized. For five years she experienced desperate poverty, living in Moscow with her two small children, unable to earn her keep, her husband away in the Civil War with the White Army and completely out of touch for two years; her younger daughter died of starvation. Later on, in émigré life, she again lived in less dire but still hampering poverty, in an endless struggle to keep going.

Most of Tsvetaeva's works were written in exile, 'in the emigration'. From about 1925, when most post-1917 émigrés from Russia had come to realise that there would be no going back, 'the emigration' became a distinct category within Russian literature. Its largest and most active centre was Paris, and it was there that Tsvetaeva settled in November 1925. She was welcomed and noticed, she gave readings of her work, and she was able to publish most of what she wrote during the fourteen years of her life in Paris. But she also acquired hostile critics, particularly when her essay 'The Poet on the Critic' appeared soon after her arrival. In the essay she quite deliberately offended émigré writers' and readers' sensibilities with attacks on their obsession with the past and with her assertion that real creative force was to be found not amongst them but 'over there' in Russia. She earned a further onslaught of criticism when she repeated this judgment two years later with reference to Mayakovsky. *Émigré* Russians were, for the most part, as dismissive of Soviet literature as most Soviet critics and publishers were of *émigré* literature, and they especially hated Mayakovsky for his loud support of the Soviet regime. Tsvetaeva stood out among the *émigré* writers for her conviction that her true readers had remained in Russia. She was neither pro-Soviet nor pro-communist, any more than she was pro-capitalist: her arguments against government interference in the arts, and against any 'command' or 'demand' whatever from the 'time' to the poet, make it clear enough that she was far from favouring the Soviet system, and she did not wish to go back to Russia where she knew she would not be published. 'There, I wouldn't be published, but I would be read; here I'm published – and not read,' she wrote in 'The Poet and Time',[3] and a few years later she wrote to a friend: 'Everything is pushing me into Russia, where I cannot go. Here no one needs me. There I'm *impossible.*'[4]

Each of these three experiences had a metaphorical significance for her poetry. Emigration was the physical counterpart to the spiritual condition of being a poet. 'Every poet is essentially an *émigré*,' she writes in 'The Poet and Time', '*émigré* from the Kingdom of Heaven and from the earthly paradise of nature.' And, in the same paragraph: 'Next to that emigration, what is ours?' Struggle with material hardship was a counterpart, perhaps even one that she needed, to the labour of writing and struggle with its material, which she repeatedly insists on. And the comparative plenty of her early life is a counterpart to the spiritual wealth and 'fullness' of being born with a talent, with 'genius', as she did not hesitate to name it (honouring not her self but genius *itself*).

Tsvetaeva knew herself to be extraordinarily gifted, and felt she shared this with very few; in 1935 she told a friend: 'The only equals in strength to myself that I have met are Rilke and Pasternak.' 'Strength', in Russian *sila*, translatable as 'power' or 'force' or even perhaps 'energy', is a central concept for Tsvetaeva, as it was for Pasternak. Tsvetaeva conceived an intense admiration for Pasternak when she read his book *My Sister Life* (see the essay 'Downpour of Light'), and just as intensely admired Rilke, whom she never met but with whom she corresponded in his last year of life. (The relations between these three poets can, to some extent, be studied in their now published correspondence[5] of the year 1926.) It was in the mental company of those two, above all, that Tsvetaeva lived while writing the essays presented here. As we see from them, Pasternak was the poet she most often turned to, wrote about, and compared others with; I am making him the chief reference point in my discussion of her own work in this Introduction because of his importance to her, and because his prose too, in one way or another, is largely *about* being a poet.

All the essays translated here were written in the period of Tsvetaeva's emigration – the first of them in Berlin in 1922, the rest in France between 1924 and 1933. In her earlier years she had been primarily a lyric poet; during the 1920s she turned to writing long narrative poems (*poemy*); in the 1930s she became mainly a prose writer. The question as to why Tsvetaeva turned to prose may be answered in several ways. Because it was better paid and she was poor, and anyway *Volya Rossii*, the journal which had been publishing her poetry, closed down in 1932 – this is the reason she herself gave in a letter, adding to the word 'prose': 'which I love *very* much, I am not complaining. All the same, it is somewhat forced on me.' Because she found she could extend poetry into prose, win prose's space over for poetry's activity: Joseph Brodsky speaks of her 'transferring the methodology of poetic thinking into a prose text, the development of poetry into prose';[6] and she herself said 'A poet's prose is something other than a prose writer's prose; in it, the unit of effort, of diligence, is not the sentence but the word, sometimes even the syllable.'[7] Perhaps too, because, in Pushkin's words, 'the years incline us toward severe prose' and, growing older, she preferred a medium that could give shape to her past and extent to her thoughts.

## II

Marina Tsvetaeva's writing about poetry consists equally of celebration and defence. She writes in praise of poetry. And she writes to explain poetry to the mistrustful; to protect it from misuse and calumny; to insist that not everyone can judge it. In these essays she is often didactic, corrective, polemic, angelic (message-bearing), constructive – of almost unbuildable bridges. She is at once exclusive and welcoming, as if saying: 'Don't cross this bridge if you lack the courage and the wit, but if you have them, *come!*' The essays seem written to make the matter both easy and difficult, to make readers select themselves and arrive with pounding hearts. Brodsky says (differently): 'she tries, often against her will, to draw the reader closer to her, *to make him equally great*' (my italics). It seems that Tsvetaeva will do everything possible to make us like, read and live with poetry. She will do nothing that might reduce, dilute, undermine, popularise it. Essential to her thought is that poetry is *not* a continuation of the ordinary and the commonplace, but is the opposite of what the 'philistine' supposes it to be; something other, yet, at the same time, not marginal or distant, but of the essence; a kind of knowledge, and a kind of event, *not* a technical learnable craft; 'elemental', not formal – she loathes all formal or formalist approaches.

I have quoted twice from Joseph Brodsky's essay 'A Poet and Prose', and perhaps the best I could do, in introducing Tsvetaeva's prose, would be to point to the whole of that essay. What Brodsky says there – about a 'crystalline' growth of thought, the energy of her style, an instinctive laconicism and how rare Tsvetaeva is in this, being 'fenced off from her contemporaries by a wall composed of discarded superfluity'; as well as his description of her 'harsh, at times almost calvinistic, spirit of personal responsibility' – can surely not be bettered. But I shall try to put stress on the sheer intelligence he has noted in Tsvetaeva's writing, and on her 'dialogic' manner; and to point to certain recurrent figurative usages in her accounts of poetry-writing.

\*

Many poets write very good prose, but few take one's breath away, as Tsvetaeva does, by their mental energy, their skill in pursuing a thought to its furthest and clearest conclusion, and their analysis of a concept for all it both denotes and connotes. Energy of mind, a kind of laconic thoroughness, also enables her to give new vitality to old concepts:

> Equality in gift of soul and of language – that's what a poet is. So there are no poets who don't write and no poets who don't feel. If you feel but don't write, you're not a poet (where are the words?). If you write but don't feel, you're not a poet (where is the soul?). Where is the essence? Where is the form? Same thing...[8]

Comparison with Pasternak may be instructive here. Pasternak was as concerned as Tsvetaeva was to describe the moment of 'what is called inspiration', and a good deal of his work attempts to do this. Probably the main difference between his view and hers is that he regards that moment as one of change in the world itself, in the very surroundings, while her emphasis is on the person (the creating mind) of the poet, its invasion by other forces. In a poem of 1917,[9] Pasternak writes that poetry

is the peas grown wild and sweet,
it's tears of the cosmos in pods,
it's Figaro hurtling down
from flutes and from music-stands
like hail onto planted beds.

Meanwhile Tsvetaeva (1923) uses the universe to explain the poet:

> ...for a comet's path
> is the path of poets: burning, not warming,
> tearing, not tending...[10]

Another difference is in the ways they make the reader work. Pasternak is difficult because he leaves things unclarified, presents dense image clusters which feel right but which have not been cerebrally thought through; he rarely comments on his own statements. But Tsvetaeva sets out to clarify everything, makes explicit the meanings hiding in every ambiguity, thinks everything through, offers abundant commentary on what she has just stated. Yet she too is hard to read because the commentaries often introduce further complexity, and because she is able to be brief and sudden even while being expansive. Reading Pasternak's prose, one tends to search underneath it for hidden patterns and pressures, for the sunk forms causing the rising shadows. In Tsvetaeva's, everything is brightly lit and outlined – so brightly that far more angles, curves, juxtaposed and counterposed shapes and bulks show up than one had ever suspected expository thinking could be composed of.

I will quote a passage by each poet about the moment of 'inspiration'. In his autobiographical work *A Safe Conduct*, Pasternak describes what first prompted him to write. There was, he says, a kind of race going on between nature and love, which carried him onward in a fast movement, and:

> Often I heard a whistle of yearning that had not begun with me. Catching up with me from behind, it provoked fear and pity. It issued from the point at which everyday life had become torn away and it threatened perhaps to put brakes on reality, or perhaps it begged to be joined to the living air, which in the meantime had got a long way ahead. And what is called inspiration consisted in this backward glance.[11]

It sounds definite, yet is strangely obscure. What is actually going on? Is a train hidden here? What is the 'living air'? How can he say 'this backward glance' when no glance has yet been mentioned? It seems that inspiration consists in looking out from oneself, from absorption in some intense feeling, to the neglected ordinary world. But we have to guess and be content with probability. By contrast, Tsvetaeva writes:

> To let oneself be annihilated right down to some last atom, from the survival (resistance) of which will grow a world. For in this, this, this atom of resistance (resistivity) is the whole of mankind's chance of genius. Without it there is no genius – there is the crushed man who (it's the same man!) bursts the walls not only of the Bedlams and Charentons but of the most well-ordered households too. [12]

She too, working hard to describe the inspirational moment, keenly distinguishes the poet from the rest of the world. But her idea, while not transparent, does yield to visibility: a force threatens to crush you; if you are crushed, you're the one we call 'mad' or 'depressed' or 'lost' in everyday life; but if you survive – by opposing to it (as she says in the next paragraph) a single unit of will, like a one to a row of zeros, thus (in a marvellous numerical metaphor) converting them into millions – you are the one we call 'genius'. Inspiration consists in almost wholly submitting to an onslaught, in just resisting it. Typical is her threefold repetition of 'this', calling attention to what is extraordinary; typical too the explanatory shout in brackets, indeed the use of brackets altogether, suggesting that there are always further ways of developing an idea.

Pasternak seems carried away, along, by feeling which generates ardent thought; Tsvetaeva – upward by an ardour of brainpower which generates equally ardent feelings. Pasternak speaks as if to himself, as indeed Tsvetaeva has pointed out ('thinking aloud – speaking in his sleep or his half-sleep'),[13] while Tsvetaeva, except perhaps for her meditative work on word-stems, sounds and affixes, which is like a lyrical address to language itself, speaks declaratively and to us.

*

No less than at the monumental pairs of ideas that form the basis for many of her essays, Tsvetaeva is gifted at close analysis within a narrow range. We find her taking to pieces – tenderly – a poor poem by some unknown nun (in 'Art in the Light of Conscience') or – ferociously – a solecism committed by one of her critics (in 'The Poet on the Critic') and tirelessly scrutinising the implications of lazy, or just common, parlance. Both, grand vision and close scrutiny, are her forte. Meanwhile, much of the prose consists of something in between these: a wrestling with, shaking of meaning out of and into, such concepts as poet, genius, time, conscience.

Intolerant of cliché and of wordiness, Tsvetaeva has developed a style in which heady lucidity is produced by the contradiction between two feeble commonplaces. By juxtaposition she will annihilate both 'poetry is inspiration' and 'poetry is craftsmanship' ('The Poet on the Critic'), both 'only modern poetry is any good' and 'all poetry is good except the modern' ('The Poet and Time'); or write a commonplace herself either to transform it or to make it crackle against its immediate contradiction: 'Everyone is free to choose his favourites. No one is free to choose his favourites' ('The Poet and Time'). (She would never consider expanding this into 'while in one sense it is true that everyone...yet in another sense it could also be said...'!)

Close to the device of rapid contradiction is the exercise of looking at something from a position exactly contrary to the usual: 'The opposite shore had not yet reached the ferry'; or, 'seen from the future, the child is older than its father'; and why should not the bass notes be called 'high' and the treble ones 'low'? – a reflection developed in the 1935 memoir 'Mother and Music'. These examples have a ludic, amiable quality which called to my mind two formulations by Paul Celan in which, too, the opposite of a common view is tried out: 'Spring: trees flying up to their birds'; 'Bury a flower and put a man on its grave'.[14] However, they are not of this kind. Celan's sayings are pictures, made for the sake of the shock of sadness or delight and, above all, of sight: a surreal renewal of vision. He jolts and charms. Tsvetaeva jolts and provokes. Her 'other-way-round' ideas, as all her attacks on fixed habits of mind and speech and her readiness to embrace their contrary, at least momentarily, are contrived for the sake of a renewal of *thought*. They are an attempt at conceiving, however slightly touched on, some fundamentally different order of things – almost in the manner of Nietzsche, like whom she is very aware of the conventionality of language – and distantly echo some of the language-work done by Russian Futurists such as Kruchonykh or Khlebnikov.[15]

*

The reader of this obstacled and uncompromising prose has to be as agile and vigilant as a rock-climber. But the rocks do have summits. For all its digressions, this style conduces to climactic summations, often to epigrammatic statements or even proverbs. In 'The Poet and Time', a muscular journey through notions of time culminates in a proverb both cited and revised: 'However much you feed a wolf, it always looks to the forest. We are all wolves of the dense forest of Eternity.' A tendency to the epigrammatic and the antithetical or paradoxical informs the whole style: 'to lose oneself in the alien and find oneself in the kindred' ('Epic and Lyric'); 'having given everything, it gives everything once again'; 'valleys fight, peaks unite' ('The Poet and Time').

Climbing towards a summit, and reaching it, is a characteristic pattern and can be noted on the scale of the phrase, of the paragraph and of the whole essay. On the scale of the essay, Tsvetaeva will approach the top of her investigation or exposition with words like: 'Now, having cleared my conscience of all omissions…having acknowledged my dependence upon time…I finally ask: Who is my time that…I should…serve it?' ('The Poet and Time'). The journey to the desired point is often experienced almost as a physical walk and climb (as in 'Downpour of Light': 'having worked my way out from the dreamy eddies'). Similarly, the analysis of the poems in 'Two Forest Kings' is presented as a movement up toward the most vital moment ('we come now to the peak…of the ballad' and a little later, 'And at last, the last – an outburst…') from which she can only go down, to a valley of strongly exhaled 'conclusions'. On the scale of the phrase, characteristic is such a sequence as: 'not this, not this, not this – *this*' (thus about the dream-door in 'Art in the Light of Conscience', and the train carrying Mandelstam in 'History of a Dedication'); or: 'not only this, but *this* too' – a way of presenting the thing indicated as a pinnacle as well as appearing to take us beyond some expected limit. And on the scale of the paragraph, here are seven sentences from 'The Poet and Time':

> Everything is point of view. In Russia I'll be understood better. But in the next world I'll be understood even better than in Russia. Understood completely. I'll be taught to understand myself completely. Russia is merely the limit of earthly understandability, beyond the limit of earthly understandability in Russia is an unlimited understandability in the not-earthly. 'There is a land which is God, Russia borders *with it…*'

We climb the paragraph by ledges that go: better – even better – completely – myself completely – limit – unlimited – God; or by ones that go: Russia – next world – Russia as limit to the earthly – the unlimited non-earthly – Russia bordering with God. And other such upward paths can be traced; for example, one leading from 'I' to others (the quoted words are Rilke's).

\*

Tsvetaeva's style is vocal and dialogic. The vocative case alternates frequently with fast-moving indicatives and interrogatives. Statements are made through dramatised interchanges between two persons. Or other persons are visualised (auralised), joining in with the author, countering, inquiring, reminding her of something she has forgotten – voices of others or variant voices within herself. Others' rejoinders are fitted in to the text of her own voice, so that the reader has to pause and work out who is speaking; and words mid-sentence may be put in quotation marks or emphasised as if quoted, a method much used by Dostoevsky; and indeed there is something in Tsvetaeva's polyphonic monologue, with its digressions and disquisitions, yet with its single underlying passion, that recalls something of the speaker in 'Notes from Underground', a comparison which makes noticeable the absence, in Tsvetaeva, of any neurosis or negativity. She is all sane – if complex – affirmation. (It is curious that Tsvetaeva did not particularly value Dostoevsky's work.)

Tsvetaeva will sometimes introduce a counter-argument to, even a refutation of, the argument she is about to propound, as if to forestall someone's saying 'but what about *this*?' Setting out, for instance (in 'The Poet and Time'), to claim that no one worthy of respect ever denies the importance of the past, she'll start with Mayakovsky, whom she admires and who did just that. This tendency of Tsvetaeva to provoke herself by offering disproofs of her own argument, to surmount or to incorporate them, accounts for much of the vitality of her style. Another quasi-dialogic form is what might be called her rhythmic paragraphing. A proposition, developed as far as possible in one direction, is followed by its restatement in the initial form, to be taken now to its extreme in another direction, as if it were from someone else's point of view. The word 'dialogue' could also be applied – on a larger scale – to the way the dual constituents of a given essay's theme are played against each other, since each side is usually given its full say, full validity: time and timelessness, the moral and the elemental, Pasternak and Mayakovsky, even Zhukovsky and Goethe. At the same time we are generally led to accept one point of view, for Tsvetaeva's is not a manner that sets us free to choose, to diverge or to add. We will agree with her that 'time' is less than timelessness, that the elemental (to those who experience it) is greater than the moral, that Goethe is more elemental than Zhukovsky. Only in 'The Poet on the Critic' is one side not given a full voice; and only in 'Epic and Lyric' are the two sides held in lofty balance.

\*

Even more than with poetry, Tsvetaeva is concerned with poets or, more exactly, with the poet. While her memoirs[16] portray poets as the individual persons she knew, the present essays (except for the first section given here of 'History of a Dedication') discuss them solely as creators of poetry. She does not often analyse particular poems, although she quotes from those she admires with a readiness that suggests a fellow-creative sympathy. She does analyse a poem by Mandelstam in 'History of a Dedication', does look closely at parts of poems, for example in 'Poets with History', and there is her marvellous comparison of Zhukovsky's 'Erlking' with Goethe's (though these are not exercises in formal analysis, which she despised as much as she despised the pedagogic method of 'paraphrase'; what she points to in poems is the quality of feeling, degree of originality, the words' meanings, derivations and connotations). But her main concern is with the poets – their common experience, their difference from one another and their difference from non-poets; from critics, readers,'philistines', workmen, scholars.

\*

The poet is no initiator or inventor, but a medium, and in the way Tsvetaeva conceives of this there is again a certain – albeit incomplete – coincidence with Pasternak. According to him, the poet merely makes a faithful copy of the inspirationally changed world, of the strange 'new category' in which reality has arisen. According to Tsvetaeva, whose account of creativity is less visual, more aural, the poet, overwhelmed by the *stikhiya*, the elemental, seems to hear or half-hear an already written poem which she must work immensely hard to recapture and write down. This process is described in 'Art in the Light of Conscience' and in 'The Poet on the Critic': 'To hear correctly is my concern. I have no other.' The Lutheran tone is not random: it is a declaration of lonely faith and of will. But Tsvetaeva's stress on the poet's will is unlike anything in Pasternak.

Tsvetaeva rejects any link between art and ethics. She would not call a book, as Pasternak once did, 'a cubic piece of burning smoking con-science – and nothing more'. Yet her idea of an 'SOS' from the world's phenomena does bring a compassionate note into the creative process (somewhat like Pasternak's 'whistle of yearning'), and there is something burningly moral in her thought that art, regarded ethically, is wicked, just as there is in the loudness and anguish of her insistence not merely that it does not, but that it *cannot*, care whether it harms its users. The artist's fidelity to 'the essence' she calls his 'sin before God'. Thus 'the book' itself is not conscience, but Tsvetaeva's *discussion* of 'the book' contains a good deal of conscience. Moreover, it is not because of any virtuous message, but because of its sheer elemental force, that she predicts for Pasternak's *My Sister Life* a good effect on a very large scale: 'And no one will want to shoot himself and no one will want to shoot others!'

\*

One of Tsvetaeva's main metaphors for poets is 'fullness': being too big for the surroundings, excess, overflow. A poet is not just presented with answers, but is 'outgalloped' by them. He is 'brimful', 'overfilled', has more than he needs. Of what? Not of feeling (this is not Wordsworth's 'overflow of powerful feeling'), but of power itself: 'an excess of power, going into yearning' ('Mother and Music'). This explains his strengths, faults, joy and grief. Thus, in Tsvetaeva's view Pasternak's 'chief tragedy is the impossibility of spending himself – income tragically exceeds expenditure' ('Epic and Lyric'). Likewise, in a fine essay on the artist Natalya Goncharova (written in 1929) she explains why Pushkin married a thoughtless young beauty, in the following terms: 'the pull of genius – of overfilledness – to an empty place...he wanted the nought, for he himself was – everything'.[17] Poets who, as persons, were physically large, fascinated her: one of the main things we remember about Voloshin from her account of him in the memoir 'A Living Word about a Living Man',[18] is that he seemed too stout to get into her tiny study; Mayakovsky's tallness is related to his being, as a poet, too large for *himself*. Whether things fit within themselves, whether there is room, how filled or empty a thing is – this range of ideas is important to Tsvetaeva. In 'Mother and Music'[19] we read that the reason there cannot be 'too much' of the lyrical is that it itself *is* the 'too much'. And a poignant instance of imagery of size is Tsvetaeva's conviction that over there, in spacious Russia, 'if they'd let people speak', there was, as in the West there wasn't, room for her.

## III

What follows is a brief account of each of the essays included in this volume, with a glance at the circumstances of its writing and an indication of its main content.

'A Downpour of Light' (1922) – 'the first article of my life' – is the dis-
covery, celebration and communication of a fellow-poet, Boris Pasternak,
whose volume of verse *My Sister Life* Tsvetaeva received from him shortly
after leaving Russia; Pasternak did not leave. *My Sister Life* was to mark
the beginning of his fame, 'A Downpour of Light' the beginning of a long
correspondence between the two poets. Although she feels that Paster-
nak, as poet of nature, is unlike herself, Tsvetaeva feels sufficiently alike
in 'strength' to be able to 'speak for' him to the world outside Russia. So
the first essay in this book expresses a creative kinship, with which all the
accounts of difference in the subsequent essays stand in contrast.

*

'The Poet on the Critic' (1926) – 'the work in which Tsvetaeva found herself
as an innovative prose-writer' (Simon Karlinsky)[20] – contrasts sharply with
'A Downpour of Light': instead of acclamation, there is demolition; in-
stead of speaking for another, she now defends herself; she demonstrates
how a poet works, discusses – announces – how a critic should work. The
essay earned her enemies in the Russian community in Paris for its sharp
*ad hominem* attacks on writers venerated there, including Zinaida Gippius
and the 'Olympian' Ivan Bunin (who was to win the Nobel Prize in 1933),
as well as for its fierce attacks on certain prevalent categories of critic and
on the tasteless 'mob' of readers. Along with 'The Poet and the Critic', she
published a selection of sentences by the critic G. Adamovich (object of
her scathing analysis in the opening section) to prove his incompetence.
People were offended, articles were written against her, the influential
Gippius sought to organise a hostile press campaign. We though, far from
the fray, may see the work as a powerful defence and description of the
poet in society and a liberating devastation of all pretentiousness, in the
tradition of Pushkin's 'Poet and Crowd' (1828) and of a kind with
Alexander Pope's 'Essay on Criticism' (1711). 'Let such teach others who
themselves excel/And censure freely who have written well' is exactly her
opening argument, and we can hear her too in: 'Some have at first for Wits,
then Poets, past/Turn'd Critics next, and proved plain fools at last', or (her
disdain for the 'formalists') in: 'Some drily plain, without invention's
aid/Write dull receipts, how poems may be made.' Thus two great poets,
in different lands and times, rather similarly turn their sharpest critical
light on contemporary critics of poetry; and when we find Tsvetaeva being
called 'captious' or 'aggressive' we should remember that her 'aggressive'
writings belong in an honourable tradition.

\*

'History of a Dedication' (1931) offers another attack upon falsehood, as well as, like 'Downpour of Light', an instance of the relation between two poets, this time less unmixedly celebratory. It differs in form from the other pieces in this volume: an affectionate, humorous recollection of an episode in her friendship with Mandelstam is followed by the sarcastic analysis of a dishonest 'recollection' of the latter which another *émigré* poet, Georgii Ivanov, had published a few years earlier. It is a good example of Tsvetaeva's use of prose to defend a fellow-poet; she was also defending the Russian past she had known against distortions of it. Unluckily, the defence did not reach its public; it was not printed until long after her death.

The two sections of the essay presented here are the second and third parts of a three-part memoir. I exclude the first because it does not contribute to our subject: she describes there how one day in 1931, in France, burning old manuscripts with a friend's help, she came across something in print containing a poem Mandelstam had addressed to her. She then withdrew from the flames what turned out to be the untruthful memoir – and consigned it to the flames of her criticism.

\*

'The Poet and Time' (1932) is described by Brodsky[21] as 'one of the most decisive' of her essays for understanding her work, and as making 'a semantic frontal attack on the positions held in our consciousness by abstract categories (in this case, an attack on the idea of time)'. What matters, says Tsvetaeva, is not whether a work is modern or not, but whether it is genuine or not; and genuine art is always 'contemporary' – it cannot but show its time since it is what actually creates the 'time'. Not to be contemporary, in this sense, is to go backward. The essay makes a sustained assault on the general esteem for certain *émigré* writers, but its main theme is the timeliness of poetry, its 'contemporality' – a word I have formed by analogy with 'temporality', in order to avoid the clumsy and diffuse sound of 'contemporariness', the 'momentary' sense of 'contemporaneity', and the inapposite connotations of 'modernity'.

\*

'Epic and Lyric of Contemporary Russia' (1932/3) is a comparative exposition of the poetic personalities of Pasternak and Mayakovsky. Implicitly, it is a defence of these two 'Soviet' poets against *émigré* antipathy, particularly of Mayakovsky who, as leading Soviet poet, was much disliked 'in the emigration'. Tsvetaeva had published a cycle of poems to Mayakovsky after his suicide in 1930, and she dedicated numerous poems to Pasternak. (Pasternak too had been a passionate admirer of Mayakovsky before the latter put his oratory at the service of the Bolsheviks, so that there are some elements of a threefold relationship here, except that Mayakovsky, who felt warmly towards Pasternak, was, for political reasons, somewhat cold to Tsvetaeva.)

The essay is a tremendous *tour de force*, which one would like to be able to memorise whole and quote: a series of lapidary formulations of differences between the two poets. Some of them, perhaps, are not hard to discern: Mayakovsky to be read in chorus, Pasternak against all choruses; Mayakovsky a giving out, Pasternak a taking in. Others, though, are the product of a rare insight and grasp: how people 'follow' Mayakovsky but 'go in search of' Pasternak; Mayakovsky – a collective noun, Pasternak – adjectival; and neither of them able to depict human beings, Mayakovsky because he exaggerates them, Pasternak because he dissolves them. Even someone who does not know the work of Mayakovsky or of Pasternak can enjoy the essay – for its conjuring up of two fundamental ways of being and writing; and for the large, finely handled balances of material throughout it, amounting to something like a choreography in which the two poets meet, diverge, feign approach, grow distant, look across the distance. A prominent feature in this patterning is that the essay begins by invoking unity ('all poets are one poet'), thereupon opens out into the world of differences, and concludes in a new, now tensely equilibriated unity by quoting in full a poem by one of these poets (Pasternak) in praise of the other (Mayakovsky).

*

'Two Forest Kings' (1933/4): Zhukovsky's translation of Goethe's 'The Erlking' is one of the best-known poems in Russian; schoolchildren learn it by heart. Tsvetaeva offers a close reading of it based on her analysis of its departures from the German original. This essay is, in fact, the only example included of her going systematically through a text, looking at its every word. She is once again laying siege to a reigning cliché, to a canon she does not wish to abandon but wishes to make its maintainers conscious of. She writes with perfect knowledge of German and with justified confidence. The ineffable, 'terrifying', 'more-than-art' quality which she finds in Goethe's poem, but not in Zhukovsky's, provides an illustration of what the 'elemental' means to her.

*

'Poets with History and Poets without History' (1934) is, like 'History of a Dedication', given here in incomplete form – these are the first two parts of a six-part essay. There are two reasons for this. One is that parts 3-6 are again about Pasternak and tend to rehearse what is said about him elsewhere. The other is that the original Russian text is lost: the essay was written for a Belgrade journal and was published in Serbian, so that we do not hear her voice in it as strongly as in the other works.

It is natural to ask where Tsvetaeva places herself in the classification she proposes – with the epic poets who have 'a history', forever walking ahead to something new, or with the lyric poets who dip again and again into the same 'sea'. Her deliberately failed attempt to cast Alexander Blok as the sole exception – that is, as belonging to both categories – suggests that the vacancy for such an exception remains unfilled: does *she* fill it? In 'The Poet on the Critic' she insists that her poetry changes with the years, and that no one has the right to judge it who hasn't read all her work: a poet 'with history' then. At the same time, her understanding and prolonged defence of the lyrical, here, as well as her being able to 'speak for' that pre-eminent lyricist Pasternak, give her a very close affinity to those 'without history'; moreover, her own 'epic' poems, though long, remain essentially  lyrical. (In several letters, however, Tsvetaeva declared she did not like the sea. She preferred mountains: 'The ocean is a dictatorship...A mountain is a divinity.')[22]

*

'Art in the Light of Conscience' (1932) is placed last – despite being written in the same year as 'The Poet and Time' – both because I wished to end with its final paragraph, Tsvetaeva's powerful, conclusive statement about herself as a poet, and because, being about art generally and ranging over a number of writers, it opens out and away  from the concentration on a single poet in our first piece. It was initially meant to be part of a book which would have had this title and would have contained 'The Poet and Time'; but nothing came of this. Tsvetaeva complained to the editor of the journal which printed it about excisions he had made, saying he had shortened the essay by a half and 'made it unintelligible by depriving it of its links, turning it into fragments'. No omitted sections, however, survive, and we are not obliged to find it fragmentary, at any rate not disturbingly so.

Tsvetaeva's liking for puns and homonyms is fundamental in this essay. The word for art, *iskusstvo*, is related to words meaning temptation, *iskus* and *iskushenie*; and enticement and seduction occur throughout the essay – art is a seduction away from matters of conscience. But *iskus* also suggests artifice, as well as meaning a test, or even a novitiate (period of testing), and the text brings to the surface these notions submerged in *iskusstvo*. The main point of the essay is that art is not 'holy' as people think, but is power and magic: 'When shall we finally stop taking power for truth and magic for holiness?' Art is not virtuous, but elemental, coming upon the poet in a *naitie*: I have translated this word as 'visitation', but it means a 'coming upon' – no personal being is implied.

As always, Tsvetaeva puts strongly both sides of the debate, thinks herself into the opposite position to her own. Thus she acknowledges the absolute rightness of conscience and morality, giving all honour to priests and doctors, to Gogol who burned his writings in case they were harmful, to Tolstoy who demanded the destruction of the world's best works of art because they lacked moral lessons, and to 'artless' poems by unknown folk with visions of goodness. Whereupon she declares that she elects the life in art, in 'full knowledge' of its amorality and dangerousness, and in a spirit of choosing at once damnation and Heaven.

# IV

It is almost as difficult to translate Tsvetaeva's prose as it is to translate poetry. Everywhere there are rhythms, rhymes, half-rhymes, echoings of vowel or consonant or word-structure, which just don't happen in the English words required to carry the meanings; everywhere there are expressive idiosyncrasies of punctuation (such as the frequent use of the dash) which often don't work in English. Here are just three examples of sound-repetition from 'The Poet and Time' (examples can be gathered from every page of every essay). 'A great work...reveals all that is not-place, not-age: for ever': the last four words suggest, through their phonic weft, much more than can be conveyed – *ne-vek/navek*. One could change 'for ever' to 'for all ages', but only at a high price. She writes of service to 'change – betrayal – death' (*smene – izmene – smerti*): the second and third words repeat different elements of the first one; I thought of trying to emulate the pattern with a slight mistranslation, 'change – exchange – extinction', but decided it was more important to be semantically faithful. 'Over here is – that Russia; over there is – all Russia': this reads like a short, dancing poem in the original: *zdes' tá Rossíya, tam – vsyá Rossíya*. Tsvetaeva's many lexical inventions, or near-inventions, cannot be reproduced, and above all, her exhaustive permutations on a given word-stem rarely find an English equivalent. One translation-elusive sentence (in 'Art in the Light of Conscience') runs: 'Art is that through which the elemental force holds [*derzhit*] – and overpowers [*oderzhivaet*]: a means for the holding [*derzhaniya*] (of us – by the elements), not an autocracy [*samoderzhavie*]; the condition of being possessed [*oderzhimosti*], not the content [*soderzhanie*] of the possessed condition [*oderzhimosti*].' Similarly difficult are her permutations on some common idiom. Thus in 'Mayakovsky is endlessly trying to climb out of his skin', the idiom *iz kozhi lezt'* means to try one's hardest, do one's utmost, go hell for leather; and both the transferred and the literal meanings serve Tsvetaeva's argument. For the multiple elaborations of this idiom I have used the English 'to go all out for…', which at least keeps the essential concept 'out' but is far from rendering the full physical and tragic quality of the Russian.

Certain words central to Tsvetaeva's thinking elude satisfactory translation. I have rendered *obyvatel'* as 'philistine', which is roughly the way it is used nowadays, but *obyvatel'* comes from the verb 'to be', used to mean one who 'was' in a given place, namely a 'resident', the common resident of a town, and is probably closer to 'man in the street' or 'provincial', in the insidious sense these can have of narrow-minded, with cramped horizons, reluctant to exercise intelligence. *Bol'shoi, krupnyi*, and *vysokii* mean 'big', 'large' and 'high', and are commonly used of artists and poets, with reference to both worth and reputation. The English adjectives cannot easily be used like this and so I have substituted 'major', 'important' or 'significant', and 'lofty', well aware of failing to do justice to the simplicity and concreteness of the original.

A less frequent but important word used by Tsvetaeva is 'formula'. The Russian word sounds the same as the English; however, in Tsvetaeva's use it often means not a dry or fixed piece of language, but language which has successfully caught and preserved something elemental. Thus in the poem on page 189 she writes affirmingly of 'the flower's formula', and once, in 1919, she jotted in her diary: 'Two things I love in the world: song – and formula', adding a note to this, two years later: 'that is to say, the elemental – and victory over it!'

# NOTES TO INTRODUCTION

1. Roman Jacobson, 'Marginal Notes on the Prose of the Poet Pasternak' in *Pasternak: Modern Judgements*, ed. Donald Davie and Angela Livingstone (London, 1969) p. 135.

2. Marina Tsvetaeva, *A Captive Spirit: Selected Prose*, ed. and tr. J. Marin King (Ann Arbor, 1980; London, 1983).

3. See p. 93.

4. Letter to A. Tesková, 25 February 1931, in Marina Tsvetaeva, *Pismak Anne Teskovoi* (Jerusalem, 1982) p. 89.

5. Boris Pasternak, Marina Tsvetayeva, Rainer Maria Rilke, *Letters: Summer 1926*, ed. Yevgeny Pasternak,Yelena Pasternak and Konstantin M. Azadovsky, tr. Margaret Wettlin and Walter Arndt (London, 1986).

6. 'A Poet and Prose' in Joseph Brodsky, *Less than One: Selected Essays*, (Harmondsworth, 1986) pp. 176-194.

7. Quoted from Viktoria Shveitser, *Byt i bytie Mariny Tsvetaevoi*, (France, 1988) p. 408.

8. See 'The Poet on the Critic', p. 48.

9. 'Definition of Poetry' in the cycle *My Sister Life*, first published 1922.

10. See p. 192.

11. Quoted from 'A Safe Conduct' in *Pasternak on Art and Creativity*, ed. and tr. Angela Livingstone (Cambridge, 1985) p. 76.

12. See 'Art in the Light of Conscience', p. 152.

13. See 'Epic and Lyric...', p. 108.

14. Paul Celan, *Collected Prose*, tr. R. Waldrop (Manchester, 1986) pp. 11-12.

15. See especially the chapters entitled 'Hylaea' and 'Decline' in Vladimir Markov, *Russian Futurism: A History* (London, 1969).

16. See, for example, her very fine essays on the poet Maksimilian Voloshin ('A Living Word about a Living Man') and the poet Andrei Belyi ('Captive Spirit'), also the essay about the poet Mikhail Kuzmin ('Otherworldly Evening'); translations of all these are included in *A Captive Spirit* (op. cit.).

17. M. Tsvetaeva, *Izbrannaya proza v dvukh tomakh*, ed. A. Sumerkin (New York, 1979) p. 301. The essay has not been translated.

18. In *A Captive Spirit*.

19. ibid.

20. Simon Karlinsky, *Marina Tsvetaeva: The Woman, Her World and Her Poetry* (Cambridge, 1985).

21. Joseph Brodsky, op. cit.

22. Letter to Pasternak of 23 May 1926, in *Letters: Summer 1926* (op. cit.) p. 119.

# DOWNPOUR OF LIGHT [†]

## POETRY OF ETERNAL COURAGE

Before me is a book by Pasternak, *My Sister Life*. In its khaki dustcover, recalling at once the free distributions of the South and the scanty alms of the North, bleak and boorish and covered in a kind of funereal bruising, it could be an undertaker's catalogue or the last gamble of some croaking publisher. But only once did I see it like that: in the first moment of getting it, before I'd time to open it. Since then it's not been closed. My guest of two days, I carry it with me round all the spaces of Berlin: the classic Linden, the magical Underground (no accidents, while it's in my hands!), I've been taking it to the Zoo (to get acquainted), I take it to dinner at my boarding-house, and – finally – I wake at the first ray of the sun with it lying wide open on my chest. So, not two days – two years! I've the right of long acquaintance to say a few words about it.

Pasternak. Who is Pasternak? ('Son of the artist' – I'll leave that out.) Not quite an Imagist, not quite…Anyway, one of the new ones…Ah yes, Erenburg is strenuously proclaiming him. Yes, but you know Erenburg with his there and back rebellion!…And it seems he hasn't even any books to his name…

Yes, ladies and gentlemen, this is his first book (1917)[1] – and isn't it telling that in our time, when a book that ought to be written in 1927 is already squandered in 1917, Pasternak's book, written in 1917, arrives five years late. And what a book! As if he'd deliberately let everyone else say all they had to say, then at the very last moment, with a gesture of bewilderment, he takes a notebook from his pocket: 'Well actually I… though I can't guarantee anything…' Pasternak, let me be your guarantor to the West – for the moment – till your 'Life' appears here. I declare I'll vouch for it with all my non-demonstrable assets. Not because you need it, but from sheer cupidity: it's a precious thing to take part in such a destiny!

[†] [All translations of quoted verse in this essay are by Donald Davie. Translation of quoted verse in the rest of this book is my own. – A.L.]

*

I'm reading Pasternak's poems for the first time. (I have heard them, orally, from Erenburg, but thanks to the rebellion that is in me too – no, the gods forgot to drop the gift of all-embracing love into my cradle! – thanks to an age-old jealousy, a total inability to love in twos, I quietly dug my heels in: 'Maybe they're even works of genius, but I'll do without them.') With Pasternak himself I've no more than a nodding acquaintance: three or four fleeting encounters. Almost wordless ones, as I never want anything new to happen. I heard him once, with other poets, in the Polytechnic Museum.[2] He spoke in a toneless voice and forgot nearly all the lines. The way he was out of his element on the stage reminded me strongly of Blok. There was an impression of painful concentration, one wanted to give him a push, like a carriage that won't go – 'Get a *move* on...' – and as not a single word came across (just mutterings, like some bear waking up), one kept thinking impatiently: 'Lord, why does he torment himself and us like this!'

Pasternak's outward being is splendid: there's something in his face of both the Arab and the Arab's horse – alert, watchful, listening, ready to break into a run at any moment! His eyes' enormous sideways glance, again horse-like, wild and shy. (An orb, not an eye.) An impression of always listening to something, incessantly watching, then suddenly he'll burst out into speech – usually with something primordial, as if a rock had spoken or an oak. When he speaks (in conversation) it's as if he were breaking an immemorial silence. And not only in conversation – I can say the same of his verse, and with far more experience to back me. Pasternak doesn't live in his words, as a tree doesn't live in its obvious foliage but in its root (a secret). Beneath the whole book – like some vast passage beneath the Kremlin – lies a silence.

Silence, you are the best thing
Of all that I have heard...[3]

As much a book of silences as of chirpings.

Now, before I speak of his book (this series of blows and rebounds), a word about the wires which carry the voice – his poetic gift. I think: this gift must be enormous, since the enormous essence comes over whole. The gift is clearly equal to the essence – a very rare case, a miracle, for nearly every book by a poet makes us sigh: 'With *such* potentialities...', or (immeasurably less often): 'Well, at least *something* gets across...' No, God spared Pasternak this, and Pasternak spared us. He is unique and indivisible. His verse is the formula of his essence. The divine case of 'couldn't be done any other way'. Wherever there may be a dominance of 'form' over 'content', or of 'content' over 'form', no essence ever set foot. And you can't copy him: only garments can be copied. You'd have to be born as another him.

Of the demonstrable treasures in Pasternak (rhythms, metres, and so on) others will speak in their turn – and doubtless with no less feeling than I when I speak of the *non*-demonstrable treasures.

That is the job of poetry specialists. My speciality is Life.

\*

*My Sister Life!* The first thing I did, when I'd borne it all from the first blow to the last, was spread my arms out wide, so that the joints all cracked. I was caught in it as in a downpour.

Downpour: the whole sky onto my head, plumb-down, pouring vertically and pouring slantingly – a drench, a draught, a quarrel of rays of light with rays of rain – and you don't count here: once you're caught in it, grow!

A downpour of light.

Pasternak is a major poet, at the moment bigger than any other: most present poets *have been*, some *are*, he alone *will be*. For in reality he isn't yet: a babbling, a chirping, a clashing – he is all Tomorrow! – the choking cry of a baby, and this baby is the World. A choking. A gasping. Pasternak doesn't speak, he hasn't time to finish speaking, he's wholly exploding – as if there weren't room in his chest: a-ah! He doesn't yet know our words; it all seems to come from an island, childhood, the Garden of Eden, and it doesn't make sense – and knocks you over. At three this is common and is called 'a child', at twenty-three it is uncommon and is called 'a poet'. (Oh equality, equality! How many God had to rob, even down to the seventh generation, just to create one Pasternak like this!)

Forgetting himself, beside himself, he'll sometimes wake up suddenly, and thrusting his head through the winter-window (into life, with a small 'l') – but wonder of wonders! instead of the three-year-old's illumined dome it's the crankish cap of the Marburg philosopher – in a sleepy voice, from his garret heights, he'll call down into the yard to the children:

Tell me, my dears, what
Millennium is it out there?

You can be sure he won't hear the answer. Let me return to Pasternak's childlikeness. It isn't that Pasternak is a child (for then he would grow up not into dawns but into a forty-year-old repose, the lot of all earthborn children!), not: Pasternak is an infant, but: the world is an infant within him. Pasternak himself belongs more to the very first days of creation – the first rivers, first dawns, first storms. He is created *before* Adam.

I'm afraid, too, that my helpless effusions may convey only one thing: Pasternak's gaiety. Gaiety. Let me think. Yes, the gaiety of an explosion, an avalanche, a stab, the sheerest discharging of all vital fibres and forces, a kind of white-heat which you might – from a distance – take to be just a white page.

I'm still thinking: what is *not* in Pasternak? (For if everything were in him he'd be life, and then he himself would not be. Only through a 'no' can we fix the existence of a 'yes': something distinct.) I listen for an answer: the spirit of gravity! Gravity is for him only a new form of action, something to be thrown off. You'll more likely see him hurling down an avalanche than sitting somewhere in a snowbound hut watching over its deadly thud. He will never wait for death: far too impatient and eager, he'll throw himself into it, head-first, chest-first, everything first that persists and outstrips. Pasternak cannot be robbed. Beethoven's 'Durch Leiden – Freuden'.[4]

The book is dedicated to Lermontov. (To a brother?) The illumined to the darkened. A natural gravitation: the general pull toward the precipice: precipitate. Pasternak and Lermontov. Related yet thrusting apart, like two wings.

\*

Pasternak is the most penetrable poet, and hence the most penetrating. Everything beats into him. (Evidently, there's justice even in inequality: thanks to you, a unique poet, more than one human dome is delivered from celestial thunders!) A blow – a rebound. And this rebound's thousandfold lightning speed: the thousandmound echo of all his Caucasuses. No time to understand! (Which is why, most often in the first second, but often at the last as well, there is bewilderment: – What? What's going on? – Nothing! It's gone!)

Pasternak is all wide-open – eyes, nostrils, ears, lips, arms. Before him there was nothing. Doors all swing off their hinges: into Life! Nonetheless, more than anyone else he needs to be *opened up*. (A Poetry of Intentions.) Thus you understand Pasternak in spite of Pasternak, by following some latest track, the latest of all. Lightning-like, he is lightning to all experience-burdened skies. (A storm is the sky's only exhalation, as the sky is the storm's only chance of *being*, its sole arena!)

Sometimes he is knocked down: life's pressure through the suddenly flung-open door is stronger than his stubborn brow. Then he falls – in bliss – on his back, and is more effective in his knocked-down state than all jockeys and couriers from Poetry, panting this very moment in full gallop over the barriers.[†]

\*

A flash of illumination: why, he's simply the beloved of the gods! No, a more luminous illumination: not simply, and not the beloved! The *unbeloved*, one of those youths who once heaped Pelion on Ossa.[5]

\*

Pasternak is spendthrift. An outflow of light. An inexhaustible outflow of light. In him is made manifest the law of the year of famine: Waste, and you won't want. So we are not anxious for *him*, but we may reflect, about *ourselves*, being confronted with his essence: 'Who is able to contain this, let him contain it.'

\*

Enough chokings. Now for a sober and sensible attempt. (No need to worry: he will still be there in the clearest light of day!) By the way, a word on the element of light in Pasternak's poetry. Photo-graphy (light-writing), I would call it. A poet of *lightnesses* (as there are, for instance, poets of darknesses). Light. Eternal courage. Light in space, light in movement, gaps (draughts) of light, explosions of light – very banquetings of light. He is flooded and whelmed. Not just with the sun, but with all that radiates – and for Pasternak everything gives off rays.

And so, having worked my way out at last from the dreamy eddies of commentary – out into reality, onto the sober shoal of propositions and quotations!

1. Pasternak and everyday life.
2. Pasternak and day.
3. Pasternak and rain.

† The following two facts turned up at the last moment: (1) *My Sister Life* is *not* his first book; (2) the title of his first book is neither more nor less than *Over the Barriers*. In any event, in *My Sister Life* this barrier has been – taken. M.Ts.

# Pasternak and Everyday Life

*Byt* ['everyday life']. A heavy word. Almost like *byk* ['bull']. I can only bear it when it's followed by 'of nomads'. *Byt* is an oak, and under the oak (around it) a bench, and on the bench a grandfather who was yesterday a grandson, and a grandson who will tomorrow be a grandfather. The oak of everyday, the oaken everyday. Solid, stifling, ineluctable. You almost forget that the oak, as a tree sacred to Zeus, is honoured more often than others by Zeus' favour, lightning. And it's just when we are completely forgetting this that there come to our rescue, at the very last second, like lightning striking our oaken brows – Byron, Heine, Pasternak.

\*

The first thing to strike us in Pasternak's verse, an unbroken chain of first things, is: everyday life. Its abundance, its detail, its – 'prosiness'. Tokens not just of the day, but of the hour!

I fling the book open – 'To the Memory of the Demon'.

> A yard or so from the window,
> Plucking the woollen threads of a burnous,
> He swore by the ice of steep places:
> Sleep on, my girl, but I…return as avalanche!

Further, in the poem 'My Sister Life':

> That in the thunder eyes and lawns are lilac,
> And the horizon breathes moist mignonette,
> Or that in May when you in transit scan
> Timetables on a branch-line to Kamyshin…

(I'm giving the accompanying lines on purpose, to establish the context.)

Further, about a fence:

> Unforgettable the more
> For dust distending it,
> For wind uncasing spore
> To cast abroad on burdocks.

About the wind:

> Wind attempts to raise
> The rose's head, requested
> Thereto by lips, hair, shoes,
> Familiar names and hemlines.

About a house in the country:

> Still the woods are ours, for porch;
> Moon's fire behind the pines, for stove;
> And like an apron hanging out, fresh laundered,
> A thundercloud that mutters, drying out.

About the steppe:

> Mist from all quarters is a sea about us
> As thistle-patches check us, catch at socks...

Just a moment! 'The choice of words – it's all for the sake of repeating the ch...' But ladies and gentlemen, has none of you ever had burrs biting into your socks? Especially in childhood when we're all in short clothes. True, it isn't 'burr' here, but 'thistle-patch'. But isn't 'thistle-patch' better? (For its rapacity, tenacity and wolfishness?)

Further:

> In the gutters
> Like sleeves of damp shirts
> Branches went limp...

From the same poem:

> In the powdery stillness
> Sodden, like an overcoat...

(This poem is 'A Still More Sultry Dawn'. My fingers itch to quote it in full, just as they do to tear to bits all these thoughts on the subject and send *My Sister Life* herself around the bookstalls of the West. Alas, I've not enough hands!)

Further:

The mills have the look of a fishing-village:
Grizzled nets, corvettes...

Then, in the tea-room:

Even in the nights they flow,
Flies off dozens, pairs and portions,
Off the wild convolvulus,
Off the poet's turbid book,
Like delirium from the pen...

Approaching Kiev by train:

Approaching Kiev – sands
And spattered tea
Dried on to hot temples
Burning through all the classes...

(Tea that has already turned into sweat, and dried. A Poetry of Intentions!
'Burning through all the classes' – third-class carriages are hottest of all!
This quatrain contains all the Soviet 'hunt for bread'.)[6]

'At Home':

The turban slips from the sun:
Time for renewing towels
(One soaks in the pit of a pail).

In town – the discoursing of membranes,
Shuffle of flowerbeds and dolls...

Then, on the eyelids of a sleeping woman:

Dear and deathly apron,
And the pulsing temple...
Sleep on, Queen of Sparta,
It is early still, still damp...

(The eyelid: an apron to protect a feast from dust, the magnificent feast
of the eye!) Then, in the poem 'Summer':

The small rain stamped its feet at the doors.
There came up a smell of wine-corks.

So smelled the dust. And such was the smell of the weeds.
And if you look into it closely
That was the smell of all the gentry's screeds
About equality and brotherhood.

(Smell of young wine: of storm! Isn't the whole of the *Serment du Jeu de Paume*[7] in this?)
And now, ladies and gentlemen, the final quotation, which seems to contain the whole solution to Pasternak and everyday life:

When towards the well-head rushes
The whirlwind, anguish, pausing in mid-passage
The storm applauds our household management
– What more do you ask for?

Why nothing! It seems not even God has the right to ask more from a storm!

Now let us think it over. The presence of everyday life seems proved. Now, what shall we do with it? Or rather, what does Pasternak do with it and what does it do with him? First of all, he sees it clearly: he'll grasp it and let it go. Everyday life, to Pasternak, is like the earth to a footstep: a moment's restraint and a pulling away. In his work (check by the quotations) it's almost always in movement: a windmill, a carriage, the vagrant smell of fermenting wine, the discourse of membranes, the shuffling of flower-beds, spattered tea – I'm not having to hunt for examples! Check for yourselves. In his poems even sleep is in movement – a pulsing temple!

Everyday life as inertia, as furniture, as an oak (a dining-room of oak, as advertised, which poets so often repanel in Paul and Catherine rosewood), everyday life as an oak won't be found here at all. His everyday life is in the open air. Not settled, but in the saddle.

Now about the prosiness. There's a lot to say here – it's bursting out! But I'll give way to what's bursting out even more strongly: Pasternak himself:

He sees his neighbours celebrating weddings,
How they get roaring drunk and sleep it off,
How they call common roe – that pickled frogspawn –
Once ritually treated, caviare.

And how life like the pearl of a jest by Watteau
They can contrive to cram into a snuff box
And are a scourge to him, perhaps, because
All the time that they contort and crook,

> Through the lickspittle lies of sniggering comfort
> While, like the drones they are, they creep and crawl...

Pasternak's prosaic quality, besides being a natural clear-sightedness, is Life's holy rebuff to aestheticism – the axe to the snuffbox. Most priceless of all. Where, in the whole length of these 136 pages, will you find a single aestheticising comma? He is as free of the common poetical stock of 'moons' and 'swoons' as he is of the 'oh so distinctive' tooth-picks of aestheticism. This double vulgarity misses him by a hundred-mile loop. He is human – *durch*.[8] Nothing but life, and every means to it the best. And it is not the Watteau snuffbox he stamps on, this infant Titan of everyday life, but the kind of life that will fit into a snuffbox.

Pasternak and Mayakovsky. No, Pasternak is more formidable. His 'Afterword' alone completely eclipses all Mayakovsky's 150 millions.

Look at the end:

> And all that was breathed to the age's ravines,
> All the dark of the botanic vestry,
> Wafts over the typhoid yearning of a mattress,
> Thrusts out, chaos of herbage, spurting.

*This* is – Retribution! Chaos of herbage smothering the rotting mattress of aestheticism!

What's a decree and a bayonet – to the Ganges!

For Pasternak everyday life is a curb, it's no more than an earthly token (a tie) of holding back (holding out).

For the immemorial lure of such souls – undoubtedly – in all their radiance, is: Perdition.

# Pasternak and Day

Not cosmic day which is heralded by dawn, not broad daylight which makes everything clear, but the element of day (light).

There is another day – evil (because blind), effective (because blind), irresponsible (because blind); tribute to our transience, day as tribute – today. Endurable only because yesterday it was tomorrow and tomorrow it will be yesterday: from transience to forever: under eyelids.

The summer day of 1917 is hot, aglare under the tramp of the stumbling front. How did Pasternak meet this avalanche of avalanches – Revolu- tion? There are few definite signs of 1917 in this book; but if we listen with vigilance, take up the faintest hints – some three, or four, or five, such signs.

Let's start. In the poem 'The Model':

> All years that were erewhile
> One year like this outdoes.
>
> All lived it dry, half-starved,
> And in the struggle hardened.
> And none cared that the prodigy
> Of life was one hour long.

Then, in the poem 'Break up':

> It, where the eye was used to yield
> To the small mercies of the droughty steppe,
> Now, muffled in mist, arose,
> Haystack of revolution!

And further on, in the same poem:

> And the air of the steppe is stirred.
> It takes the scent, it drinks the air
> Of soldiers' mutinies and summer lightnings.
> It freezes in its tracks, it is become all ears.
> It lies full length, then hears the summons: Turn!

(Doesn't he mean himself?)

Again, in the poem 'The Militiaman's Whistle' (needless to say, omitting the militiaman):

> ...behind the fence
> The north of villainy grows grey...

Three more lines from the poem 'A Sultry Night':

> In the unparented, insomniac
> Damp and universal vast
> A volley of groans broke loose from standing posts...

I'd interpret the poem to Kerensky,[9] 'Spring Rain' – with these amazing lines:

> In whom was that heart where all the blood in him fast
> Gushed to glory, sucked back out of the cheeks...

– as the magic the word 'enthusiasm' works upon youth, not at all as a political preference.

That's all.

One thing is clear from these conjectures: Pasternak didn't hide from the Revolution in any of the intelligentsia's cellars. (No cellar in the Revolution – only an open square and a field!) He did have an encounter with it. He saw it for the first time – somewhere far off – in a mirage – as a haystack rearing wildly in the wind, he heard it – in the groaning flight of the roads. It gave itself to him (reached him), like everything in his life – through nature.

Pasternak's word about the Revolution, no less than the Revolution's word about itself, is yet to come. In the summer of 1917, he walked in step with it, listening.


## Pasternak and Rain


*Dozhd'* ['rain']. What first springs to mind, in the fellowship of assonances? *Dazhd'* ['grant'] . And with 'grant' – naturally – 'God'.

God grant – what? – Rain! The very name of the Slavonic sun[10] contains a prayer for rain. More, rain is somehow already granted in it. How amicable! How succinct! (Your teachers, Pasternak!) And, turning our brow to the past decade, which of us has written nature?[11] I don't want to stir up names (tear myself away and think about others), but – at a lightning glance – no one, ladies and gentlemen. A lot has been written (above all by Akhmatova) about oneself in nature, eclipsing nature so naturally (when the poet's Akhmatova!); about nature in ourselves (becoming like it, likening it), about happenings in nature, its separate countenances and seasons; but, however amazingly, all wrote *about* it, no one wrote *it* itself: point blank.

But here's Pasternak. And a wondering starts: who is really writing whom?

Clue: penetrability. He lets the leaf, the ray, pierce him so deeply that he is no longer he, but a leaf, a ray. Rebirth. Miracle. From the Lermontov avalanche to the Lebedyan'[12] burdock, everything is present, nothing's left out, nothing missed. But the rain fell in love with Pasternak more passionately than the grasses, dawns and blizzards. (And how it be-rained the poet – the whole book swims!) And this isn't the sparse little rain of autumn! Not drizzling, but driving; not pedestrian – equestrian!
We'll begin.

My sister, life! Today in the flooding over
Shattered in spring rain on us all...

Further, 'The Weeping Garden' (astounding from the first line to the last; I'm biting my fingers, being forced to pull it to pieces):

Appalling! it drips and listens – is it
Alone in the world or (now it presses
Lace-like, a twig upon the window-pane)
Does it have witnesses?...

...No sound. No hint of espionage,
Assured all's empty, it takes up
Its old affairs, it sheets athwart
The roof, brims over gutters, and across.

(I stress: it's the loneliness of the rain, not that of the man being rained on!)

Next, 'The Mirror':

Thus after rain the slugs crawl journeying
Like eyes of garden effigies.
Water lisps in the ear...

And here is something wholly enchanting:

Drops weigh as collar-studs, the garden
Dazzles like a stretch of waters,
All besplotched and all bespattered
With a million bluish tears...

Further, in the poem 'Rain':

> Come spin, as mulberry worm,
> Beat at the window pane,
> Come swathe, come swaddle yet,
> Thicken the murk again...
>
> ...And now come run, as if
> A hundred guitars made moan,
> To know the lime-washed, dim
> Saint-Gotthard, garden-adorned.

Further (my fingers will be gnawed to bits!):

> From calyx onto calyx sliding
> It has slipped athwart a pair of them – in both
> Like an immense drop formed of agate
> It is hung up, and dazzles there, and trembles.
>
> Let the wind, that breathes past meadowsweet,
> Flatten it out, that drop, and worry it,
> It's whole, and does not break apart but, twinned,
> The couple that it is still drink and kiss.

Next, the opening of the poem 'Spring Rain':

> It laughed at the bird-cherry, sobbing, wetted
> Lacquer of landaus, tremor of the trees...

Further ('Earth's Sicknesses'):

> And here's the downpour. Brilliance of hydrophobia,
> Vortex, flecks of a rabid saliva...

A quatrain from the poem 'Our Storm':

> Still at the waterbutts they drink the storm
> From the sweet bonnets of profusion.
> The clover is as tossed and crimson
> As claret-coloured splotches of house painters.

A few pages later:

> The rain will pierce the wing with pellets...

Further (opening of the poem 'Sultry Night', one of the most ineffable in
the book):

> A spattering came, but one that did not bend
> Even the grasses in the thunder's sack.
> Only the dust swallowed the rain in pellets,
> Iron in powder, speck on quiet speck.
>
> The village hoped for no alleviation,
> The poppy-head was deep as fainting is...

And – let's just list them:

> Hard behind in an unseeing scurry
> Some slant drops fled...
>
> ...A thin rain wrapped
> The cornfield in a quiet treading-across...
>
> Spatter of rain. Light-footedly
> Clouds moved over a dusty market square...
>
> Rain rushed down, a solid fence...
>
> With madder and with lemon
> Leafage is asperged...
>
> ...rain in the brain-cells
> Roared, not echoing back as thought...

(That's why it is *rain* (life!), and not thoughts on the subject!) And on the
last page of the book:

> ... in the rain each leaf
> Tears loose for the steppe...

Ladies and gentlemen, now you know about Pasternak and rain. The same
thing happens with dew, leaves, dawn, earth, grass... By the way, note the
striking absence of the animal kingdom in Pasternak's nature – not a tusk,
not a horn. Only some scales slide by. Even birds are rare. As if for him
the creation of the world stopped on the fourth day – yet to be grasped,
yet to be thought through.
    But let's return to the grass; or rather, let us stride after the poet

...into the dark, past the wicker-fence,
Into the steppe and the smell of sleepy drugs...

(mint, camomile, sage).

Sage? Yes, ladies and gentlemen, sage. The poet, like God, or a child, or a beggar, doesn't disdain anything. And isn't this *their* horror – God's, the child's, the beggar's?

...crossing the road and passing behind the fence
Is not to be done but you tread the frame of the world...

Responsibility for every step, a trembling warning: 'Don't disturb!', and what vast – inescapable – awareness of power! If the poet hadn't already said this of God, I'd say it of the poet himself: he's the one 'to whom nothing is bauble...' Tokens of the earth, his poem of genius 'The Great God of Details':

You ask, who stablishes
That August be a power?
To whom nothing is bauble,
Who goes about to staple
Light leaves to the maple,
And since Ecclesiastes
Has never left his station,
Working the alabaster?

You ask, who stablishes
That asters taste, and peonies,
Agonies, come September?
That the meagre leaf of broom
From grey of caryatids
Come down upon dank flags of
Infirmaries of the fall?
You ask, who stablishes?

The omnipotent God of details,
The omnipotent God of love,
Of Hedwigas, Yagailos...

No questions in Pasternak, only answers. 'If I've given this answer, then somebody somewhere must have asked the question; maybe I did in my sleep last night, maybe I'll ask it in my sleep tomorrow.' The whole book is an affirmation, for everyone and everything: I am! Yet how little directly about himself. Beside himself...

Pasternak and thought. Does he think? No. Is thought there? Yes. But beyond the gesture of his will. Thought is what works in him, digs out subterranean burrows till suddenly – in an explosion of light – it bursts to the outside. Revelation. Illumination. (From within.)

But we shall die with all the suffocation
Of these investigations in our breast...

Perhaps in this couplet is the chief tragedy of all Pasternak's kind: the impossibility of spending himself – income tragically exceeds expenditure.

Gardens and garden-ponds and palisades,
And, seething in white lamentations,
The world's whole frame, are but the types of passion,
The kinds of it man's heart accumulates.

And more helplessly and simply:

Where shall I put this happiness of mine?
In verses? In a rigorous eight-line stanza?

(And still they say 'the poor in spirit!')

It seems this moment is the time
For every coiled-down spring to fly apart.

Where? In what places? Or in what
Wildly envisaged region?
The most I know is, in the drought, in thunder,
July, a storm impending – this I know...

(What else but an illumination?)

And the last:

How drowsy living is,
And openings-up, how sleepless!

Pasternak, when do you sleep?
I'm stopping. In despair. I've said nothing. Nothing – about nothing – for before me is Life, and I haven't the words.

And only the wind can bind
What breaks into life and breaks in the prism
And is glad to play in tears.

This is not a review: it's an attempt to get out, so as not to choke. The only one of my contemporaries for whom my lungs have not sufficed.

One doesn't write of contemporaries like this. I repent. It's solely the zeal of the Trade. Not to surrender to the first glib pen, in some fifty years, this my heartfelt hymn of praise. Ladies and gentlemen, this book is for everyone. And everyone ought to know it. This book is for the soul what Mayakovsky is for the body: a release in action. Not merely healing – like those slumbrous grasses of his – but wonder-working. Read it trustingly, without resistance and with utter meekness: it will either sweep you away or it will save you! A simple miracle of trust: go as a tree, a dog, a child, into the rain!

And no one will want to shoot himself, and no one will want to shoot at others...

Suddenly there was a sense
Of people being discharged from a thousand hospitals!

# THE POET ON THE CRITIC

Souvienne vous de celuy à qui comme on
demandoit à quoi faire il se peinoit si fort en
un art qui ne pouvoit venir à la connoissance
de guère des gens –

'J'en ay assez de peu,' répondit-il. 'J'en ay
assez d'un. J'en ay assez de pas un.'[1]

Montaigne

Criticism: absolute pitch in relation to the
future.

M. Ts.

## I. *He cannot be a critic...*

The first duty of a poetry critic is not to write bad poems himself. At least,
not to print them.

How am I to trust the voice of, let's suppose, N, if N cannot see the
mediocrity of his own poems? The first virtue of a critic is the ability to
see. N, since he not only writes but publishes, is blind! It's possible to be
blind to one's own work while able to see that of others. There have been
examples of this. Take the mediocre poetry of that colossal critic, Sainte-
Beuve. But, for one thing, Sainte-Beuve stopped writing; that is, he acted
towards himself precisely as a major critic would: judged and condemned.
For another, even if he'd gone on writing, Sainte-Beuve the poor poet
would have been concealed by Sainte-Beuve the good critic, the leader
and prophet of a whole generation. In a great man, poems are merely a
weakness. To be seen as a weakness and an exception. What won't we
forgive the great!

39

But to return to certainties. Sainte-Beuve, with a lot of creative activity behind him, stopped writing poems – that is, he rejected the poet in himself. N, with no kind of activity behind him, does not stop – he persists in considering himself a poet. A strong man with a right to weakness scorns this right. A weak man with no such right comes to grief at this very point.

Judge, punish yourself!

The sentence the colossal critic Sainte-Beuve passed on himself as poet assures me he will not call the bad in me good (as well as his authority, our evaluations coincide: what is bad to him is bad to me). The judgment Sainte-Beuve the critic passed on Sainte-Beuve the poet means that, from now on, the critic is infallible and unindictable.

But the encouragement the mediocre critic N gives to the mediocre poet in himself assures me he will call the good in me bad (as well as distrust of his voice, our evaluations don't coincide: if *that* is good, then mine is certainly bad). Make Pushkin my model and I daresay I'll keep quiet, I'll certainly give it some thought. But don't make N the model and I shan't miss him, I'll laugh. (What else are poems by a poetry critic, who's been made wise by everyone else's mistakes, if not models? His aberrations? Any person who publishes thereby declares: 'This is good.' A critic who publishes thereby declares: 'This is a model.' Therefore, the only poet who deserves no leniency is a critic, just as the only accused who deserves no leniency is a judge. *I judge only judges.*)

N-the-poet's self-delusion is confirmation that N-the-critic is fallible and indictable. By failing to condemn himself he has become the accused, and turned us, the accused, into judges. I shall not judge N the merely bad poet. Criticism exists for this. But N the judge who is himself guilty of what he accuses me of – I shall judge. A guilty judge! Quick revision of all his cases!

So, unless we are considering a major activity with a major person behind it, the rule is: bad poems are unforgivable in a poetry critic. He's a bad critic, but maybe his poems are good? No, the poems are bad too. (N being the critic.) They're bad poems, but maybe the criticism is good? No, the criticism is bad too. N-the-poet undermines our trust in N-the-critic, and N-the-critic undermines our trust in the N-the-poet. Whichever way you approach it...

I'll support this with a real-life example. G. Adamovich accuses me of neglecting grammar-school syntax, and in the same review, a few lines earlier or later, he resorts to the following turn of phrase: '...in a dry, impudently-breaking[2] voice'.

The first thing I felt was – something's wrong! A breaking voice is involuntary, not deliberate. While impudence is an act of will. The hyphen linking 'impudently' [*derzko*] and 'breaking' [*sryvayushchimsya*] makes 'impudently' a defining attribute of 'breaking' and thus provokes the question: breaking in what way? rather than: breaking from what cause? Can a voice break impudently? No. From impudence, yes. Let's substitute 'insolently' [*naglo*] and repeat the experiment. It's the same answer: from insolence, yes; insolently, no. Because both 'insolently' and impudently' mean something intentional and active, while a breaking voice is involuntary and passive. (A breaking voice; a sinking heart: similar example.) It seems, then, that from impudence I deliberately made my voice break. Conclusion: absence of grammar-school syntax and, still more serious, absence of logic. Impressionism – whose roots, by the way, I understand perfectly well, though I don't commit this sort of sin. G. Adamovich wanted to give an impression of both impudence and a breaking voice at the same time, to speed up and strengthen the impression. He snatched at a hyphen without thinking. He misused the hyphen. Now, to finish this lesson:

Angrily-breaking, yes. Manifestly-breaking, yes. Angrily, manifestly, languidly, noticeably, maliciously[†], nervously, piteously, ridiculously... Anything that doesn't imply forethought or activity will do, anything that doesn't conflict with the passivity of a breaking voice.

'Impudent, breaking' – yes; 'breaking from impudence' – yes; 'impudently-breaking' – no.

Physician, heal thyself!

\*

Series of magic alterations
In a beloved face...[3]

No one has the right to judge a poet who has not read every line that poet has written. Creation takes place gradually and successively. What I was in 1915 explains what I am in 1925. Chronology is the key to understanding.

– Why are your poems so different from one another?
– Because the years are different.

---

[†]'Malevolently' won't do, because it contains purpose.

The ignorant reader takes for a manner of writing something incomparably more simple and more complex: time. To expect identical poems from a poet in 1915 and 1925 is like expecting identical facial features in 1915 and 1925. 'Why have you altered so much in ten years?' Nobody asks this, the matter is so obvious. They won't ask, they'll just look, and after looking they themselves will say: 'Time has passed.' It's exactly the same with poems. The parallel is so close I'll continue it. Time, as we all know, does not make us prettier, unless in childhood. And no one who knew me at twenty will say to me now I'm thirty: 'How much prettier you've become.' At thirty I've become more defined, more significant, more original – more beautiful, perhaps. But not prettier. It is the same with poems as with features. Poems do not get prettier with time. The freshness, spontaneity, accessibility, *beauté du diable*, of poetry's face give way to – features. 'You used to write better' – a remark I hear so often! – only means the reader prefers my *beauté du diable* to my essence. Prettiness – to beauty.

Prettiness [*krasivost'*] is an external criterion, beauty [*prekrasnost'*] an internal one. A pretty woman – a beautiful woman; a pretty landscape – beautiful music. The difference is that a landscape may be beautiful as well as pretty (an intensification, elevation, of the external to the internal), while music can be beautiful but not pretty (an enervation, reduction, of the internal to the external). What's more, the moment a phenomenon leaves the realm of the visible and the material, the word 'pretty' can no longer be applied to it. A pretty landscape by Leonardo, for example. One wouldn't say this.

'Pretty music', 'pretty poems' – a measure of musical and poetic illiteracy. Bad common parlance.

So, chronology is the key to understanding. Two examples: law and love. Every investigator and every lover moves backward from the present moment to the source, the first day. The investigator follows the track backwards. There is no act in isolation, there is a coherence of acts: the first one and all subsequent ones. The present moment is the sum of all preceding moments and the source of all future moments. Whoever has not read all I have written, from *Evening Album* (childhood) to *The Ratcatcher* (present day) has not the right to judge.

A critic: an investigator and a lover.

I do not trust the also-critics: not quite critics and not quite poets. The thing has failed, it's fallen through, and, though one would like to stay in this sphere, to stay on is to be stunted, not taught but caught by one's own (unsuccessful) attempt. If I couldn't do it, then no one can do it; if there's no inspiration for me, there's no such thing as inspiration. (If there were, I'd be the first.) 'I know how it's done'... You know how it is done, but you don't know how it comes out. Which means, after all, that you don't know how it is done. Poetry is a craft, the secret is technique, success depends on greater or lesser *Fingerfertigkeit* (dexterity). Hence the conclusion: no such thing as *talent*. (If there were, I'd be the first!) Failures of this sort usually turn into critics who are theorists of poetic technique, technical critics – meticulous ones at best. But when technique is an aim in itself, it is itself at worst.

Someone unable to be a pianist (a strained sinew) becomes a composer; unable to do the lesser, he does the greater. A delightful exception to the sad rule: unable to do the greater (be a creator), one becomes the lesser (a 'fellow-traveller').

It's the same as if someone who despaired of finding the gold of the Rhein were to declare that there is no gold in the Rhein and to take up alchemy. Add this to this and you'll get gold. But where is your *what*, since you know – how? Alchemist, where then is your gold?

We seek the gold of the Rhein and *we believe in it*. And finally – this is where we differ from the alchemists – we shall find it.[†]

Stupidity is as various and multiform as intelligence, and it contains – as does intelligence – all contraries. And you'll recognise it, like intelligence, by its tone. For instance, the assertion: 'no inspiration, only craftsmanship' ('the formal method', which is a modified Bazarovism)[4] calls up an instant response from the same camp (stupidity): 'no craftsmanship, only inspiration' ('pure poetry', 'divine spark', 'true music' – all the philistine commonplaces). A poet hasn't the slightest inclination to prefer the first assertion to the second or the second to the first. A familiar falsehood, in a foreign tongue.


## II. *He must not be a critic...*

> We mustn't presume
> To have an opinion.[6]

Ladies and gentlemen, let's have justice, or if we can't – at least some commonsense!

[†] I'm deliberately taking the conjectural gold of the Rhein, which only poets believe in (Rheingold, Dichtergold).[5] If I took the gold of Peru, the example would be more convincing. This way it is more honest.

To have an opinion of a thing, you must live in that thing and love it.

Take the crudest, most obvious example. You buy yourself a pair of boots. What do you know about them? That they suit you or they don't, that you like them or you don't. What else? That they were bought in a certain shop, the best one, say. Your relation to them, and the trade mark. (In this case the trade mark is the author's name.) And nothing else. Can you judge their durability? Wearability? Their quality? No. Why? Because you're not the bootmaker and you're not the tanner.

A judgment of the quality, the essence, everything that is not the visible object, can only be made by someone who lives and works in that sphere. The relation to them is yours, the evaluation is not.

It's the same with art, ladies and gentlemen, exactly the same. Here is my poem. You either like it or you don't, it comes across to you or it doesn't, you find it 'pretty' [krasivyi] or not pretty. But whether it is good or bad as a poem only an expert can say, or one who loves it – or the master craftsman. In judging a world you do not live in, you are simply exceeding your rights.

Why is it that I, a poet, don't offer advice to a bank manager or a politician when I talk to them – not even *post factum*, after the bank has failed or the state has collapsed? Because I neither know nor love either the bank or the state. The most I'll do, when talking to a banker or a politician, is ask questions. 'Why did you act in that way in that case?' I ask questions, which means I wish to hear an opinion about something unfamiliar to me, and, if possible, adopt it. Not having or presuming to have an opinion of my own, I wish to hear someone else's – I am learning.

Why is it that you bankers and politicians, in your turn, don't give advice to a shoemaker when you talk to him? Because any shoemaker will laugh at you, either up his sleeve or to your face. 'Not your business, sir.' And he'll be right.

So why is it that you same bankers and politicians, when talking to me, a poet, do give me advice: 'Write like this', 'Don't write like that'; and why is it – this is the most astonishing part! – that I, a poet, have never once yet laughed in the face of any one of you, like that hypothetical shoemaker: 'Not your business, sir.'

There is a subtle nuance here. When the shoemaker laughs, he isn't afraid of offending – for the sir's business is loftier than his. His laughter only points to an incongruity. But if the poet laughs he will inevitably offend – for, in philistine terms, 'poet' is higher than 'banker'. In this case our laughter does not just show the other his place, it shows him a lower place. 'The sky' shows something to 'the earth'. This is how the philistine thinks, how he sorts things out. And in this way he unwittingly deprives us of our last protection. There's nothing insulting in not understanding boots, but it is highly insulting not to understand poetry. Our self-defence insults the other person. And a very great deal of water has got to flow, offence accumulate, before the poet will conquer his false shame and resolve to say in the face of the lawyer, the politician, the banker: 'You are not my judge.'

It is not a matter of higher and lower, it's solely a matter of your ignorance in my sphere, like mine in yours. After all, I'll say those very words – I do say them – to a painter, a sculptor, a musician. Is it because I consider these people lower? No. Nor do I consider you lower. I say the same to you, a banker, as to Igor Stravinsky himself if he doesn't understand poetry: 'You are not my judge.'

Because – to each his own.

All I have said so far immediately collapses when one thing is present: crossing the threshold of the profession. Thus, more than to critics and poets I used to listen to the late F. F. Kokoshkin,[7] who loved and understood poetry certainly no less than I do. (A public figure.) Thus, more than what critics and poets say, I value what A. A. Podgaetskii-Chabrov[8] says (a man of the theatre).

Read and love my things as if they were your own. Then you are my judges.

Returning to boots and poems. Which boots are bad? The ones that are going to fall to pieces (bootmaker). The ones that have fallen to pieces (purchaser). Which work of art is bad? The one that won't survive (critic). The one that hasn't survived (public). Neither the cobbler nor the critic – masters of their trade – need to see it tested. They know in advance. But the purchaser, whether of a pair of boots or of a slim volume of verse, needs a long time with it, the testing of time. The whole difference is in the length of this testing. A bad boot will make itself known in a month, a bad work of art often takes a century. Either the 'bad' (which was not understood, which lacked a prophet) turns out to be excellent, or the 'excellent' (which had not found a judge) turns out to be bad. Here we come up against the quality of the material of boots and of poems, and all its consequences, the *calculability* of matter and the *incalculability* of spirit. Any average shoemaker will take one glance at the boot and say 'good', or 'not good'. He doesn't need a special flair for this. But if a critic is to define, now, *once and for always*, whether a work is good or not, he needs not only all the data of information, but a flair as well, the gift of a seer. A shoe's material – leather – is calculable and finite. A work of art's material (not sound, not word, not stone, not canvas, but spirit) is incalculable and infinite. There are no shoes once for always. Every lost line of Sappho is once for always. This is why (calculability of material) boots held by the bootmaker are in better hands than are poems in the hand of the critic. There are no misunderstood boots, but how many misunderstood poems!

However, both boot and poem, at their moment of creation, bear in themselves an absolute judgment on themselves – that is to say, from the very beginning they are either of good quality or they are not. Good quality is the same for both – durability.

To coincide with this inner judgment of the work upon itself, to get ahead – hear ahead – of one's contemporaries by a hundred or by three hundred years: this is the critic's task, which he can accomplish only if he has the *gift*.

In criticism, whoever is not a prophet is an artisan. With a right to work, but not a right to judge.

Critic: to see beyond three hundred years, beyond the thrice-ninth[9] land.

All I have said applies to the reader as well. Critic: an absolute reader who has taken up the pen.

## III. *Who I listen to…*

Among non-professionals (which doesn't mean I listen to professionals), the people I listen to are: all major poets and all major persons, and, better still, the two in one.

A major poet's criticism is in the main a criticism of passion: of kinship and non-kinship. This is why it is a relation, not an evaluation, this is why it isn't criticism, perhaps this is why I listen to it. Even if what his words produce isn't me, at least he himself is visible. A kind of confession, like the dreams we dream of others: you acting, but me prompting! The right to assert, the right to deny – who disputes these? I'm only against the right to judge.

An ideal example of such loving self-sufficiency is Balmont's delightful book *Mountain Heights*, a collecting-glass of all his yea-sayings. Why do

I trust Balmont? Because he is a major poet. And because he speaks of what he loves. But can't Balmont be mistaken? He can, and recently he was very badly mistaken: in X. But whether or not X corresponds to Balmont's vision of him, in his evaluation of X, Balmont corresponds to Balmont; in other words the major poet Balmont is conveyed full-size. He looked at X and saw himself. We bypass X and see Balmont. And to look at Balmont and see Balmont is – worthwhile. Consequently, even in the case of an error, a poet's judgment of a poet (in this case, of a prose-writer) is a good thing.

Besides, is it possible to be mistaken in one's attitude, one's relation to something? For, all Balmont's evaluating of X is a manifest relating to him. When he hears or sees this or that in him, he experiences this and that. What can be disputed here? It is so uniquely personal it can't even be taken into account.

To evaluate is to define a thing in the world, to relate to it is to define it in one's own heart. Relating is not just not judging, it is – beyond judgment.

Who will argue with a husband who admires his obviously ugly wife? Everything is permitted to an attitude, a relation,[10] bar one thing: to call itself an evaluation. If that same husband proclaims that same ugly wife to be the most beautiful woman in the world, or even in his district, everyone will dispute this and deny it. A relation, the most extreme and no matter what it is *to*, is permitted not only to a major poet, but to absolutely anyone – on one condition: not to go beyond the limit of the personal. '*I* consider it such and such, it pleases *me* '; provided he says 'I' and 'me' I will let even a shoemaker negate my poems. Because 'I' and 'me' bear no responsibility. But let that same shoemaker drop the 'I' and the 'me' and affirm that my work is altogether worthless – then what? – then, as always, I shall smile.

Can we conclude from the example of Balmont and X that a poet is no judge? Of course not. If, by virtue of his nature, a lyric poet replaces the pull of judgment with the luxury of relation (the pull of impartiality with the luxury of preference) this still doesn't mean that (1) all poets are lyric poets, or (2) a lyric poet can't be a judge. He just doesn't want to be one, he wants (unlike the philistine) to love, not judge. Two different things: unwilling and unable.

Willing and able: the whole critical-bibliographical activity of the lyric poet Khodasevich.

When I hear tell of some special, unique, 'poetic structure of the soul', I consider it untrue, or, if true, then not only of poets. A poet is a thousandfold human being, and individual poets are no less various than are human individuals in general. 'In his soul he's a poet' (a phrase often heard in common parlance) is no more a definition than 'in his soul he is a human being'. For one thing, a poet is someone who goes beyond the soul's bounds. A poet is *out* of his soul, not *in* it – his very soul *is* the being out! For another, he goes beyond the soul's bounds – in words. Thirdly ('in his soul he's a poet'), *which* poet? Homer *or* Ronsard? Derzhavin *or* Pasternak? It's a difference not of epochs, but of essences: Goethe *or* Schiller, Pushkin *or* Lermontov, and to cap it, Mayakovsky *or* Pasternak!

Equality in gift of soul and gift of language – that's what a poet is. So there are no poets who don't write and no poets who don't feel. If you feel but don't write, you're not a poet (where are the words?). If you write but don't feel, you're not a poet (where is the soul?). Where is the essence? Where is the form? Same thing. Indivisibility of essence and form – that is a poet. Naturally I prefer someone who feels but doesn't write, to someone who writes but doesn't feel. The first may be a poet tomorrow. Or tomorrow's saint. Or a hero. The second (the verse-writer) is nothing at all. And his name is legion.

Now that we have established the poet-in-general, the uttermost essential sign of belonging to poetry, we shall affirm that the statement 'Essence is form and form is essence' is where the similarity between poets ends. Poets are as different from one another as planets are.

An indispensable note. In the lyric poet's judgment (which is a relation), over-estimation clearly prevails. (Look through the opinions French and German Romantics had of one another.) In the epic poet's judgment (which is an evaluation), underestimation. Example of the supra-personal Goethe who undervalued Hölderlin, undervalued Heine, undervalued Kleist. (Instructive – the undervalued are his contemporaries! And, among contemporaries, they're his compatriots! The same Goethe who *did* value the young Byron and *over*-valued Walter Scott.) The example seems to shatter my declaration of a poet's right to judge a poet. Only seems to, however. The right to judge is not a right to punish. More precisely: sentencing is not punishing. Or: punishment is not yet death. No one – not even Goethe – and no one's word – not even the eighty-year-old Goethe's – is given the right to slay Heine: 'I am!' Goethe undervalued him; Heine abides. But (a rejoinder) had Heine been weaker, he might, upon Goethe's unflattering opinion, have put an end to himself – as person or as poet. But had Heine been weaker he would not have been Heine. No, Heine is life and is *unslayable*. Goethe's opinion of Heine is only a further spur to work. ('You've missed something – you'll see!') And for us, a hundred years later, it is a spur to thought. Goethe – and such a blunder! What caused it? We start reflecting. First on Goethe and Heine, an immemorial difference; then on ages: eighty and thirty; on age itself, whether there is such a thing and what it is; on the Olympian and the daemonic, on attraction and repulsion, on very many things...

Thus, even in the cruel case of a poet undervaluing a poet, a poet's judgment of a poet is a good thing.

All this is about poets. Who else do I listen to?

I listen to any major voice, whosesoever it may be. If an old rabbi, made wise by blood and age and prophets, talks to me about my poems, I listen. Does he like poetry? I don't know. Perhaps he has never read any. But he loves (knows) everything poems come *out of*, the source of life and being. He is wise, and his wisdom is enough for me, for my lines.

I listen to the rabbi, I listen to Romain Rolland, I listen to a seven-year-old child – and to everything representing wisdom and nature. Their approach is cosmic, and if the cosmos is in my poems, they will hear it and respond to it.

I don't know whether Romain Rolland loves poetry – I'll take the extreme case: that he doesn't. But in poems, besides verse (the verse-making element), there are *all* the elements. Certainly Rolland loves those. He isn't and can't be disturbed by the verse-making element in me, and I'm not and can't be disturbed by the absence of it in him.

'I'll speak of the essence...' That is all I need.

In talking of a seven-year-old child, I also mean the folk, the un-corrupted primary hearing of the savage.

Who else do I listen to, besides the voice of nature and wisdom? The voice of all craftsmen and master-craftsmen.

When I recite a poem about the sea, and a sailor who knows nothing about poetry corrects me, I am grateful. Same with a forester, a black-smith, a stonemason. Any offering from the outside world is a blessing, for in that world I am nothing. And I need it hourly. Imponderables may not be spoken of imponderably. My aim is to affirm, to give a thing weight. And for my 'imponderable' (the soul, for instance) to have weight, something is needed from this world's vocabulary and usage, some meas-ure of weight already known to the world and affirmed there. The soul. The sea. If my sea simile is incorrect the whole poem will founder. (Only details convince: a particular time of day at the sea, a particular hue and habit of the sea. In love, you won't get by with 'I love'.) For a poet the most fearful, inveterate (and honoured!) enemy is the visible. An enemy he defeats only by means of knowledge. Enslaving the visible for service to the invisible – this is the life of the poet. Enemy, I take you as my slave, with all your treasures. And what straining of external seeing is required, to translate the invisible into the visible. (The whole creative process!) How well one has to know the visible! More simply still: the poet is one who has to know everything down to its detail. Doesn't he know everything already? What he knows is something else. Though he knows the invisible, he doesn't know the visible, yet he incessantly needs it for symbols. 'Alles Vergängliche ist nur ein Gleichniss'.[11] Yes, but I have to know this *Vergängliches*, otherwise my likeness will be false. The visible is cement, the feet a work stands on. French: 'Ça ne tient pas debout.'[12]

Théophile Gautier's formula (compare it with Goethe's!), which has been and is being so much misused – 'Je suis de ceux pour qui le monde visible existe'[13]– stops short of the main thing; exists *as a means*, not an end! To a poet it's nonsense to say the world has value in itself. In the philosopher such value provokes a question, in the poet – an answer. (Don't believe in a poet's questions! All his wherefores are therefores, all his whys mean 'this is why!') But in arguing (likening), a poet must be careful. If I compare, say, the soul to the sea or the mind to a chessboard, I have got to know both ocean and chess, every hour of the ocean and every move on the board. Life isn't long enough to study everything. So experts in their own field, master-craftsmen, come to my help.

A poem is convincing only when we check it by a mathematical (or musical, which is the same thing) formula. The checking will not be done by me.

This is why I take my poems about the sea to a sailor, and not to a poetry-lover. What will I get from the former? A backbone to my soul. What from the latter? At best, a weakened echo of that soul, of myself. In everything that isn't the soul, I need someone other.

So, from professions and crafts to sciences. From the known world to the knowable world. So, from the sailor, the forester, the blacksmith, the locksmith and the baker – to the historian, the geologist, the physicist, the geometer; widening and widening the circle.

No poet knows from birth the stratifications of the soil or historical dates. What do I know from birth? The soul of my heroes. Clothing, customs, houses, gestures, speech – that is, everything which knowledge gives – I take from the experts, from historian and archaeologist.

In a poem about Joan of Arc, for example:

The charges are theirs.
The pyre is mine.

# IV. *Whom I obey*

> J'entends des voix, disait-elle,
> qui me commandent...[14]

I obey something which sounds in me; constantly, but not consistently –
sometimes it points, sometimes commands. When it points I argue, when
it commands I submit.

That which commands is the primary, unchangeable, inexchangeable
poem, *essence appearing as verse*. (Most often the final couplet, to which
all the rest then grows on.) That which points is an aural path to the poem:
I hear a tune, I don't hear the words. I seek the words.

More left – more right, higher – lower, faster – slower, spin out, snap
off – these are the precise pointings of my hearing, or of something *to* my
hearing. All my writing is careful listening. Hence, in order to write more:
continual re-readings. Without re-reading at least twenty lines, I shan't
write a single one. It is as if the whole piece is given to me from the very
beginning – a kind of melodic or rhythmic picture of it; as if the work
being written at this moment (I never know if it will be finished) is already
written somewhere, very exactly and completely. And I am only restoring
it. Hence this constant alertness: am I getting it right? am I not diverging?
am I not allowing myself – self-will?

To hear correctly is my concern. I have no other.

# V. *Who I write for*

Not for the millions, not for a particular person, not for myself. I write for
the work itself. The work writes itself through me. Have I time for others,
or for myself?

Two stages must be distinguished here: the creative and the post-
creative. The first has no 'for what?', it's all a 'how'. The second I'd call
the practical, the applied. The work is written: what will become of it?
Who is it for? To whom shall I sell it? Oh I don't hide the fact that, once
the work is completed, this latter question is utterly important to me. Thus
the work is twice *given*, spiritually and practically; who will take it?

A few words about money and fame. To write for money is base, to write for fame is valiant. Once again, common parlance and common thinking are mistaken. To write for anything at all except the work itself is to doom the work to a single day's lifetime. The only things written like that, and perhaps they have to be, are editorials. Whether it's fame, or money, or the triumph of some idea or other, every outside purpose is the work's ruin. The work, while it is being written, is its own purpose.

Why do I write? I write because I can't not write. The answer to the question about purpose is an answer in terms of cause, and there cannot be any other.

In 1917-1922 I turned out to have written a whole book[15] of so-called civic (Volunteer)[16] poems. Was I writing a book? No. The book happened. For the Whites' idea to triumph? No. But the Whites' idea does triumph in them. I was inspired by the idea of the Volunteer movement, but forgot about it from the very first line – remembered nothing but the line – and met up with it only when putting the last full-stop: met up, that is, with the living Volunteer movement embodied by me without my will. The pledge of the effectiveness of so-called civic verse lies precisely in the absence of the civic factor in the process of writing, in the sole presence of the purely poetry-making factor. What is true of the ideological is true of the practical. When the poems are written I can recite them from a stage and gain either fame or death. But if I think of this when approaching them, I'll not write them, or else I'll write them in such a way that they'll deserve neither fame nor death.

Pre-completion and post-completion. Pushkin spoke of this in his lines about inspiration and the manuscript, and it is something the simple-minded will never grasp.

Fame and money. Fame – how broad, spacious, worthy, graceful. What grandeur. What peace.

Money – how petty, wretched, infamous, vain. What triviality. What paltriness.

So what is it I want when, having finished the work, I place it in someone else's hands?

Money, my friends, and as much as possible.

Money is the possibility of writing more. Money is tomorrow's poems. Money is the power to pay off publishers, editors, landladies, shop-keepers, patrons – it is my freedom and my writing-desk. Money, besides being my writing desk, is also the *landscape* of my poems, the Greece I wanted so much when I was writing my *Theseus* and the Palestine I shall want so much when I'm writing my *Saul*; it's boats and trains to all countries, to all seas and beyond all seas!

Money is my possibility of writing not merely more, but *better*, of not taking advances, not hurrying events, not plugging gaps in the poetry with random words, not sitting there with X or Y in the hope that he'll publish me or 'fix something up'; it's my choice, my power to select.

Finally – a third and very vital point – money is my possibility of writing *less*. Not three pages a day, but thirty lines.†

My money, reader, is – above all – your gain!

Fame? 'Etre salué d'un tas de gens que vous ne connaissez pas' [18] (said by the late Scriabin – I don't know if they're his own words or borrowed). For everyday living – an added burden. Fame is a consequence, not a goal. All the great fame-lovers have been not fame-lovers but power-lovers. If Napoleon had been a fame-lover he would not have pined away on Saint Helena, that most perfect of pedestals. What Napoleon missed on Saint Helena was not fame, but power. Hence his torments and his telescope. Fame is passive, love of power is active. Fame is recumbent: 'resting on one's laurels'. Love of power is equestrian and wins those laurels as well. 'For the glory of France and his own power' – this is Napoleon's motto, in the purity of his heart. That the world should obey France, and France – me. The name of Napoleon's *gloire* is *pouvoir*. Being primarily a man of action he gave no thought to his personal glory (the sheerest literature). To burn himself at both ends for the bawl of the crowds and the babble of the poets – he despised both crowds and poets too much for that. Napoleon's goal was power, the result of obtaining power is glory.

In a poet I admit fame as publicity – for financial purposes. Thus, squeamish of publicity myself, I do applaud the scale, immense as always, on which Mayakovsky practised it. When Mayakovsky has no money he organises the next sensation ('a purge of poets, a massacre of poetesses', the Americas etc.). People come to see the scandal, bringing money. Mayakovsky, a major poet, cares nothing for praise or abuse. He knows

---

† A point that relates to me least of all: (1) even if I am 'hurrying to live and in haste to feel',[17] at least I'm not in a hurry to print: thus from 1912 to 1922 I did not publish a single book; (2) haste of the soul does not necessarily mean haste of the pen: my *Swain*, allegedly written 'at one sitting', was written day after day continuously, for three months; *The Ratcatcher* (six chapters) – for half a year; (3) under every line: *'all I can do in the limits of the present hour'*.

Let my rough drafts speak of the 'easiness' of my writing.

his own value. But he cares a lot about money. And his self-advertisement, in its very grossness, is much purer than the parrots, marmosets and harem of Lord Byron, who, as is well-known, did not lack money.

An indispensable note: neither Byron nor Mayakovsky use their lyre for the sake of fame, both use their personal life, that piece of refuse. Does Byron desire fame? He starts up a menagerie, moves into Raphael's house, *perhaps* – goes to Greece. Does Mayakovsky desire fame? He puts on a yellow blouse and takes a plain fence as his background.

The scandalous personal lives of a good half of the poets are only their way of purifying that *other* life, to keep *it* pure.

A littered life, a clean† notebook. A noisy life, a quiet notebook. (The ocean, even in a storm, gives an impression of quietness. The ocean, even when peaceful, gives an impression of work. The first is the contemplator *in action*. The second – the worker *at rest*. In every force there is continuous co-presence of quietness and work. The peace that comes upon us from every force is our peace on its account. Such is the ocean. Such is the forest. Such is the poet. Every poet is a *pacific* ocean.)

Thus, before your very eyes, the commonplace is overturned: in poems everything is permitted. No, it's precisely in poems that nothing is permitted. In private life – everything.

The parasitism of fame. Thus, in the plant kingdom: might is the oak, fame is the ivy. In the animal kingdom: fame is a courtesan, resting on the fighter's laurels. A free supplement, even if enjoyable.

Fame is a kind of Dionysus ear turned towards the world, a Homeric 'Qu'en dira-t-on?'[19] The looking backward, listening backward (mishearing) of a maniac. (A mixture of manias: megalomania and paranoia.)

Two examples of unalloyed love of fame: Nero and Herostratus. Both *maniacs*.

Juxtaposition with the poet. Herostratus, to glorify his name, burns down a temple. The poet, to glorify a temple, burns down himself.

The highest fame (epos) – that is, the highest force – is nameless.

There's an utterance by Goethe: 'No need to write a single line that doesn't reckon on millions of readers.' Yes, but there's no need to *hurry* those millions, or to time them for this particular decade or century.

'No need ...' Yet it seems there was need. More like a prescription for others than for himself. The shining example of *Faust*, again, incomprehensible to contemporaries and being deciphered now for a hundred years. 'Ich, der in Jahrtausenden lebe'[20] (Goethe, Eckermann).

What is beautiful about fame? The word.

† For 'clean' read 'black'. The notebook's cleanness is its blackness.

# VI. *Varieties of critics*

Let's turn to the professional critic. Three types can be distinguished here.

The first – very frequent – is the critic-*constateur* (certifier), the critic-who-bides-his-time, certifying a work only when it is established, the critic of ten years' standing. If a true critic is a prophet, then this one is a prophet-backwards. The critic-*post-factum*, honest and often met – it's the whole throng of *honest* readers (there is another sort). This critic discovers no Americas, recognises in no child the future master, stakes on no horse that hasn't run (a novice), eschews the current of the contemporary and never *widely* misses the mark.

The cultured reader.

But there's another reader – the uncultured. The mass reader, the hearsay reader, so long *post factum* that he sees Nadson as a contemporary in 1925 and sixty-year-old Balmont as a youth of promise. The distinctive feature of this reader is his indiscriminacy, an absence of *Orientirungssinn*.[21] With the word 'modernism' he puts Balmont, Vertinsky and Pasternak all in one bag without distinguishing development or value or the place which the poet has created and occupied, and all this he covers with a word he does not understand: 'decadents'. (I would derive 'decadent' from decade, a ten-year period. To every decade its own 'decadents'. However, there would then be 'decaders' or 'decadists'.) This reader calls everything after Nadson 'decadent', and contrasts everything after Nadson with Pushkin. Why not contrast Nadson with Pushkin? Because he knows and likes Nadson. And why Pushkin? Evidently because there is a monument to Pushkin on the Tverskoi Boulevard. For, I maintain, he does not know Pushkin. Here too the reader-by-hearsay is true to himself.

But – the anthologies, the low marks in school, the exams, the busts, the masks. *Pushkin's Duel* in the shop windows, and *Death of Pushkin* on the posters, the Pushkin cypress in Gurzuf[22] and Pushkin's 'Mikhailovskoe'[23] (where's that exactly?), the role of Hermann and the role of Lensky[24] (the philistine really knows Pushkin *by ear*!), the one-volume Sytin-Pushkin[25] with Pushkin-the-child propping up his cheek-bone and five hundred drawings in the text (visual method of teaching poetry, poems *with your own eyes*: the philistine really knows Pushkin *by sight*!) and let's not forget, the Repin,[26] in the drawing-room (or even in the dining-room!), the skirt of an overcoat dragged across snow! – all this is antiquity, greatly respected, abounding in jubilees – and finally the Tverskoi Boulevard with its false-Pushkin couplet:[27]

> *And long shall I be dear to the people*
> Because I roused good feelings with my lyre
> *Because I was useful with the living charm of my verses.*[†]

By hearsay (tenor and baritone), by see-say (the Sytin edition mentioned), by librettos and by anthologies – and more by librettos than by anthologies!): this is the Russian philistine's knowledge of Pushkin. While over against all that stand: Pushkin and the Russian language.

– What do you like in Pushkin? – Everything. – And most of all? – *Evgenii Onegin*. – And which of the poems? – A pause. – Sometimes, remembering the anthologies: 'Winter: solemnly the peasant...' Sometimes, association by proximity: 'The Sail'.[28]

(The philistine in front of the monument to Goethe: 'Wer kennt Dich nicht, O grosser Goethe! Fest gemauert in der Erden!'[29]...Schiller, *The Bell*.)

Of the prose, it's invariably *The Captain's Daughter*. He has never read Pushkin's *Pugachov*.[30]

Altogether, for such a reader Pushkin is like someone having a permanent jubilee, someone who did nothing but die (duel, death, last words to the tsar, farewell to his wife, etc.).

This reader's name is mob. Pushkin spoke of him, hating him, when he said 'The Poet and the Mob'.[31] Mob, darkness, dark forces, underminers of thrones incomparably more precious than those of tsars. This reader is the enemy, and his sin is: slander of the Holy Spirit.

What does this sin consist in? The sin is not in the darkness but in lack of desire for the light, not in the failure to understand but in resistance to understanding, in deliberate blindness and malicious biassedness. In ill will towards the good. I include among the mob-readers all those who heard of Gumilyov for the first time the day he was shot and who now shamelessly proclaim him the most important poet of our age. I include among them: all those who hate Mayakovsky for belonging to the party

---

[†] An uneffaced, ineffaceable disgrace. This is what the Bolsheviks should have done first of all! And done away with! But still the false lines flaunt themselves. A tsar's lie which has now become a people's lie.

of the Communists (I don't even know whether he is a party member – an Anarchist, yes); all those who always add to Pasternak's name: 'son of the artist?'; all those who know that Balmont gets drunk and that Blok 'went over to the Bolsheviks'. (An amazing knowledge of the personal lives of poets! Balmont drinks, has many wives and many blisses; Esenin drinks too, marries first an old woman, then the granddaughter of an old man, then hangs himself; Belyi divorces his wife (Asya) and also drinks; Akhmatova falls in love with Blok, divorces Gumilyov and marries – a whole series of variants. I won't dispute, by the way, the Blok-Akhmatova idyl; the reader sees more clearly! Blok doesn't live with his wife, and Mayakovsky lives with someone else's. Vyacheslav...such and such... Sologub...this and that. And so-and-so – you know...?) Before they've coped with the title, they've become biographers.

Not only does this reader not respect – he doesn't read. And, without reading, not only has he a relation to the work – he judges it. To him and him alone is Pushkin's word addressed: 'And don't contend with the stupid!' Don't contend, but throw him out of the door the moment he starts giving his opinion.

There's also the mob as critic. With slight amendment of the degree of illiteracy, the same is true of the mob as critic as of the mob as reader. The mob as critic is the mob as reader, but not only does he not read – he does write!

On two types of critic who display the contemporary age. The first, the dilettante – in the emigration; the second, the information-giver – in Soviet Russia.

Who doesn't write criticism in the emigration? 'Give an appreciation', 'write a review'. (Give your response – does it mean: respond? Alas! Those who give their response are often responseless, they give what is not given, give nothing.) Lawyers write, young people without a profession write, non-young people of irrelevant professions write, everyone writes, the public writes. Thus to the question: who writes criticism in the emigration? the answer is: who *doesn't*?

The article has wilted, the 'Note' is blossoming. The quotation has wilted, the bare assertion is in full bloom. I read, say, of a completely new author whom I've never read, that he is 'a poseur'. Where's the guarantee? The name at the end of the column. But I have never heard that name! Or I've heard it in some other sphere. Where is the material justifying 'poseur' or 'prophet' – a quotation? Not there. I'm supposed to take his word for it.

The dilettante-critic is the scum on the surface of a dubious cauldron (the public). What is cooking in it? The water is dark. The scum is dark too.

What I've said above is about anonymous criticism, criticism which has not yet put forward a single name. ('Name' does not mean favouritism, but talent.) Nor is there much joy from named criticism, sometimes even from famous-named.

The deplorable article by academician Bunin, 'Russia and Inonia', with its slander of Blok and Esenin and with obviously arranged quotations (better none than this sort!) designed to show the atheism and hooliganism of all contemporary poetry. (Bunin forgot his own 'Village' – a delightful work, but overflowing with obscenities and foul language.) The babbling rose-water of all Aikhenvald's articles. The affected bewilderment of the major poet, Z. Gippius, with regard to the syntax of no less a poet, B. Pasternak (not absence of goodwill, but presence of ill). Articles that are actually indecent include those by A. Yablonovsky on Remizov, by A. Yablonovsky on my 'Germany', and by A. Chorny on Remizov. I've no doubt that I have not listed them all.[†]

A vivid and joyful exception: Prince D. Svyatopolk-Mirsky's judgments on poets without reference to their political labels (*that's* where darkness comes from!). Among the journals – all the bibliographical section of *The Will of Russia* and *One's Own Paths*.

Now on a particular case, an enigma to me. A critic (the most read, liked and recognised) says of the Czechoslovak collection *The Ark*:

> ...We'd do better to note the most interesting pages in the volume. Unfortunately, this means passing over M. Ts's 'Poem of the End', a poem which at any rate the writer of these lines has just not understood; it would seem though that anyone else reading it will also not so much read as decipher, and even if he turns out luckier and better at guessing than we are, he will buy his good luck at the price of considerable mental effort.

The first thing that struck me in this review was its meekness. The critic isn't judging but merely describing his relation to the work. 'I have not understood' – is that a judgment? It's a confession. Of what? Of his own inadequacy. 'Incomprehensible' is one thing, 'I have not understood' is another. To read and not approve is one thing. To read and not under-

---

† 'Remizov and *émigré* criticism'. An article which has yet to be written. If not by me, then by someone else. If not now, then in a hundred years. Note from the editors of *The Benevolent*: opinions about writers are not produced to order. But if we admit that the tone of A.A. Yablonovsky's article on Remizov is not exceptional in its cynicism, then where and in what lies our difference from the purveyors of Marxist ideology?

stand is another. The reply to the first is: 'Why?' The reply to the second is: 'Really?' The first is a critic. The second is a voice from the public. Someone has read and not understood, but he admits the possibility – for some other reader – of better skill at guessing and better luck. True, this luck will be bought at the price of 'considerable mental effort'… A telling proviso. The labour of obtaining it is not – in my opinion – 'worthwhile'. This is no longer meekness but, if not ill will, at least the patent absence of goodwill. A reader may speak like this, but a critic may not. 'I don't understand' is a refusal of rights; 'and I'm not trying to' is a refusal of obligations. The first is meekness, the second is inertia. Stumbling upon a difficulty, the critic simply evades the work. 'Not so much read as decipher' – well, what is reading if not deciphering, interpreting, drawing out something secret, something behind the lines, beyond the limits of words. (Not to mention the 'difficulties' of syntax!) Reading is – above all – co-creating. If the reader lacks imagination, not a book will withstand. Imagination and goodwill towards the work.

I have often had to hear such opinions from people working in the other arts: 'It's too hard. You want to relax, but you find you're expected to search out a meaning, do some thinking'…Relax from what? From *labour* at their own art. That means that you recognise labour in your own art. You just don't want the same in mine. Well, perhaps, in your way, you are right. You do your thing, and I'll do mine. In such cases, incidentally, they were always defeated by a rejoinder that went: 'And suppose I ask you, a serious musician, for a waltz instead of your difficult sonata – what will you say? After all, I'm tired from my work too, and I too want to relax.' (Sheer pedagogic method!)

The person would understand, and even if he didn't read my poems he would at least respect my labour and not ask me for 'light music'. But that's the musician, the worker in sounds. What is to be said of a critic, no less a worker in words, who does not want to expend mental effort, so leaves it to *others to understand*? Of a worker in words asking a worker in words, me, for 'light verse'.

There is a formula for this – an ancient one. The critic under consideration can put his signature to it with an easy conscience:

Poetry is agreeable to you,
Pleasant, sweet and useful,
Like tasty lemonade in summer.[32]

Lemonade is precisely what this critic is requesting from me (and from poetry altogether). To support what I'm saying I will quote one more

sentence, this time about another writer: if so and so were to do such and
such 'he would not end up exhausted himself nor would he weary his
reader: on the contrary, he would gladden him by putting in some
*attractive interweavings of language*' (my italics).

To gladden the reader with attractive interweavings of language is not
the purpose of creative work. My purpose, when I sit down to a work, is
not to gladden anybody, either myself or any other, but to make the work
as perfect as possible. Gladness afterwards, when it's done. A com-
mander opening battle does not think of laurels or roses or crowds, only
of the battle, and less of victory than of this or that position he has got to
take. Gladness afterwards – and a lot of it. But a lot of tiredness too. This
tiredness of mine when the work is finished is something I honour. It
means that there was something to overcome and that the work did not
come to me without cost. It means it was worthwhile waging the battle.
That same tiredness I honour in a reader. If he is tired from my work, it
means he has read well, and read something good. The reader's tiredness
is not devastating, but creative. Co-creative. It does honour to both the
reader and me.

We shall return to the *émigré* amateur-critic (this one is not an ama-
teur) with a striking example. For the moment let us turn to another type
of critic who has become established in Soviet Russia and is, naturally
enough, the *émigré* critic's opposite – this is the informatory critic. This
critic I'd call 'the singer of wrong choice'.

When, in response to the thing I offer, in which form has been
vanquished, removed by means of rough drafts, I hear: 'There are ten 'a'
sounds, eighteen 'o's, assonances...' (I don't know the professional
terms), I realise that all my rough drafts have been in vain, that's to say
they've come to the surface again, and what was created is again
destroyed. Dissection, but not of a corpse – of a live body. Murder.

'In order to achieve such and such an effect, Mme Ts. had to do this
and this...' First: how often they miss the mark! Second: who needs this
'had to', once the thing is *done*? The reader? As an attentive and inquiring
reader I can answer: no. The writer? But if I've done it and, let's say, done
it well, why do I need to hear from someone else's lips what I already know
from my experience of the labour? It's at best a repetition, a confirmation.
Going over a problem that is already solved beyond dispute. A formality.
Young poets, perhaps? A recipe for getting certain effects? But just name
me one important poet who ever wrote by someone else's (always
unique!) recipes. (In creative work there is no one who is not unique.)
Moreover, 'what's good for a Russian is death to a German'. For a poet,
theory always comes *post factum*, a conclusion from his own experience

of the labour, following his tracks in reverse. I did it. How did I do it? By carefully checking through the rough drafts, calculating vowels and consonants, studying the stresses (I repeat, I'm not familiar with these matters), the poet reaches a certain conclusion which he then works at and presents in the form of some theory or other. But, I repeat, the basis of every new theory is one's own experience. Theory, in this case, is verification, *the intelligence of the ear*, merely a becoming-conscious of one's hearing. Theory as a free supplement to practice. Can such theory be of use to others? It can, as a check. The path of (Belyi's) hearing corroborated by Belyi's own ready-made conclusion. What is left out is only the labour of becoming conscious. All the rest is the same. In brief: to write a fair [white] copy not according to Belyi [White]. To write a fair copy and, if need be (?), confirm it by Belyi. But that is all I am able to say in approval of schools of verse-composition and the method of formal analysis in its application to market journalism. Either the work of a scholar and for scholars (theory of verse), or a live word – about something alive – to a live person (criticism).

The informatory critic who looks at a work from the formal point of view, evading the 'what' and seeing only the 'how', the critic who sees in a narrative poem neither hero nor author (and says 'made' instead of 'created'), who gets out of everything with the word 'technique', is, if not harmful, certainly useless. Because: ready-made formulas of poetics are not needed by major poets, and non-major poets are not needed by *us*. I'll say more: to engender lesser poets is sinful and harmful. To produce mere craftsmen of poetry is to produce deaf musicians. By proclaiming poetry as a craft, you draw into it circles which were not created for it, all those to whom it is not given. 'If it's a craft – why not me?' The reader becomes a writer, and the real reader, overwhelmed by countless names and trends (the smaller the value, the brighter the signboard), despairs and stops reading altogether.

Poetic schools (a sign of the age!) are a vulgarisation of poetry, and I'd compare formal criticism to 'Advice to Young Housewives'. 'Advice to Young Housewives' is 'Advice to Young Poets'. Art is a kitchen. All you need is skill! However, to complete the parallel, in both there is the cruel law of inequality. Just as a poor person cannot break twelve dozen egg-yolks into a pail of cream and pour a quarter of Jamaican rum over the mixture, so a poor person in poetry cannot magic up out of himself the material he is poor in – talent. What remains is empty gestures over empty saucepans.

The only book of information is your own ear, and, if it's really needed (?), Savodnik's theory of literature: drama, tragedy, epic poem, satire, etc.

There is only one teacher: your own labour.

And only one judge: the future.


## VII. *Author and Work*

Often, when I read some review of myself and learn from it that 'the formal problem has been brilliantly solved', I start thinking: did I have a formal problem? 'Madame Ts. wanted to convey a folk tale, introducing such and such elements into it', and so on.

Did I (stress on the I) want to do that? No. Did I want to do *that*? No, definitely not. I read the tale *Vampire* in Afanasyev and began wondering why Marusya, who was afraid of the vampire, so stubbornly refused to confess what she had seen, though she knew that to name it meant to be rescued. Why no, instead of yes? Fear? But fear doesn't only make people hide in bed, it also makes them throw themselves out of the window. No, not fear. Or if fear, then something else as well. Fear and what? When I'm told: do this and you're free, and I don't do this, it means I don't greatly want freedom, it means that to me non-freedom is more desirable. And what is desirable non-freedom among human beings? Love. Marusya loved the vampire, and that's why she did not name him, why she lost, one after the other, her mother – her brother – her life. Passion and crime, passion and sacrifice...

That was *my* problem, when I started work on *The Swain*. To open up the essence of the tale which had been given in skeletal form. To unmagic the thing. Not in the least to create a 'new form' or a 'folk form'. The thing was written, I worked at it, listening to every word (not weighing them up – hearing them out!). That there is labour in it is evidenced by: (1) its imperceptibility to the reader, (2) the rough drafts. But all this is the work's process, its coming into being, not a plan for it.

How could I, a poet, that is a person of the essence of things, be seduced by form? If I'm seduced by the essence, the form will come by itself. And it does come. And I don't doubt that it will come. The form required by a particular essence and overheard by me, syllable after syllable. I mould a shape, then fill it up...? But it isn't a plaster cast! No, I am seduced by the essence and then I embody it. That's what a poet is. And I shall embody it (here comes the question of form) as *essentially* as possible. *Essence* is form – a child *cannot* be born other than he is! The gradual appearance of features – such is the growth of a human being and the growth of a work of art. So, to approach it 'formally', i.e. to tell back to me (often highly incorrectly) my own rough drafts, is an absurdity. Once there's a fair copy, the rough draft (the form) is vanquished.

Instead of telling me what I wanted to convey in a given work, it would be better to show me what *you* have managed to *take* from it.

In the folk tale, the folk have interpreted the dream of the elemental; in his narrative poem, the poet has interpreted the dream of the folk; the critic (*in a new poem!*) has interpreted the dream of the poet.

Critic: the last stage in the interpretation of dreams. The one before the last.


# VIII. *What a critic should be*


God of paths and crossroads, a two-faced god, looking backwards and forwards.

The critic: Sybil over the cradle:

Old Derzhavin noticed us
And blessed us as he went down into the grave.

# HISTORY OF A DEDICATION
## THE TOWN OF ALEXANDROV IN THE PROVINCE OF VLADIMIR

Alexandrov. The year 1916. Summer.

The town of Alexandrov in the province of Vladimir, which is also the Alexandrov settlement where Ivan the Terrible killed his son.

Red ravines, green hillsides with red calves on them. A small town covered in bird-cherry trees, wattle fences, military overcoats. 1916. The people are going to war.

*

The town of Alexandrov in the province of Vladimir, my province, Ilya Muromets' province. From there, the village of Talitsa, near the town of Shuya, comes our Tsvetaev line. A line of priests. From there the Alexander III Museum on the Volkhonka (Mal'tsev's money, my father's project and his fourteen years of unpaid labour); from there my epics, two thousand lines each, and their rough drafts, twenty thousand; from there my son's head which won't fit into any headgear. We're all large-headed. *Our* feature.

From there comes something better, something more, than poems (the poems are from my mother, like my other misfortunes): the *will* to them, to them and to everything else – from a four-line poem to a four-*pood*[1] sack that has to be lifted – more than that! – transported.

From there – my heart, not allegory but anatomy, the organ, the sheer muscle, the heart that carries me uphill at a gallop for two versts without stopping, and more if necessary; the same heart that sinks and knocks me down at the first swerve of a car. Not a poet's heart, a pedestrian's. A walker's heart, which doesn't faint from escalators and lifts only because it outgallops them. The walking heart of all my forest ancestors, from my grandfather, Rev. Vladimir Tsvetaev, to my foreforefather Ilya.

From there – my feet, but on this we have an eye-witness report. *Vendée*, the fishmarket, I'm going home, two fisherwomen – 'Comme elle court, mais comme elle court, cette dame!' – 'Laisse-la donc courir, elle finira bien par s'arrêter!'

When my heart stops.

From there (the village of Talitsa in the province of Vladimir where I've never been), from there comes – everything.

The town of Alexandrov in the province of Vladimir. A little house on the outskirts facing – porching – the ravine. A little wooden house, a witch's house. In winter, it's all stove (with oven-forks and roosts!); in summer, it's all wilderness: of greenery seething in at the windows.

A balcony (so reminiscent of a wattle-fence!), and on the balcony, upon a pink tablecloth – a little cloth – a huge dish of strawberries and a copybook with two elbows. Strawberries, copybook, elbows – are mine.

1916. Summer. I'm writing poems to Blok and reading Akhmatova for the first time.

In front of the house, beyond the dishevelled garden, a small square. On it soldiers are learning to shoot.

Here are some lines from that summer:

White sun and low low clouds,
Down kitchen-gardens, past a white wall – a graveyard,
And on the sand, rows of straw dummies
Beneath horizontal bars at a man's height.

And, leaning over the stakes of the fence,
I see: roads, trees, soldiers – all pell-mell.
At the wicket-gate an old woman chews a black
Slice of bread sprinkled with large-grained salt.

How did these grey huts anger you, oh Lord!
Why must so many have bullets through their chests?
A train passed with a howl, the soldiers howled,
The receding road sent out clouds of dust.

To die! No, better never to be born
Than this piteous, plaintive, penal-colony howl.
This singing of black-browed beauties. – Ah, how
Soldiers sing nowadays! Oh my Lord God!

In this way, with the same feeling, another woman, a year and a half later, from the height of her own heart and a children's ice-hill, saw the people off to war.

*

We waved to them with handkerchiefs and they to us with caps. The howl of song struck us in the face with the engine smoke, long after the last carriage was hidden from sight.

I remember, less than a year later (March 1917), in that same Alexandrov, a batman said to me: 'I've read your book, lady. It's full of avenues and love. You ought to write down how we live. Soldiers and peasants.'

– But I'm not a soldier and I'm not a peasant. I write about what I know; *you* should write about what you know. It's your life, *you* write about it.

The batman Pavel – young but sharp. ('Full of avenues and love' – isn't that the whole social reproach of the Soviets?) But what I said then was stupid – Nekrasov was no peasant, yet his 'Korobushka' is sung to this day. I simply snapped back – bit back – at the threat of a command. By the way, very briefly: the social demand. Social is no disaster, and demand is no disaster. *What makes the social demand a disaster is that it is always a command.*

It was also in Alexandrov that I heard the news of the murder of Rasputin.[2]

Not: a word or two about Rasputin, but: Rasputin in a word or two. There is a poem by Gumilyov, 'The Peasant', which the tsarist censorship in its time scrutinised and passed, and which contains this quatrain:

Into our proud capital
He walks – God save us!
He enchants the Tsaritsa
Of all boundless Rus'...

Here, in a word or two, in four lines, is everything about Rasputin, the Tsaritsa, the whole swarm of them. What is in this quatrain? Love? No. Hatred? No. Judgment? No. Justification? No. Fate. The footstep of fate. Read it, read it attentively. Every word is worth its weight in blood.

'Into our proud capital'[3] (*two* glorious, *one* proud: the one that isn't Petersburg cannot arise); 'he walks' (the foot-walking, wood-demon, fate of Russia!); 'God save us' (knowing he *won't*!); 'he enchants the Tsaritsa' (with a rustic version[4] of the word 'enchants'); 'of boundless[5] Rus' – I don't know about others, but this 'boundless' (with all the dawns ringing in it) pierces me like a knife.

One thing more: this capital letter for 'Tsaritsa'. No, not servility! (To write someone else with a large letter doesn't mean to be small oneself.) It's called for by the greatness of the land; here the land bestows the title, the large initial, through the force of things and distances. Four lines – and everything is given: fate and magic and retribution.

Explain poems? Dissolve (kill) the formula, imagine our own plain words to be stronger than the singing word – *than which no power is stronger*; describe – song! (As we had to in school: Lermontov's 'Angel' 'in your own words', and they must *be* your own, not a single one of Lermontov's – and what came of it? Lord above! What absolute nothing came of it except for this certainty that *it can't be put in other words*. What did the poet mean to say in these lines? *Precisely what he said.*)

I'm not elucidating, I'm celebrating; not proving, but pointing: pointing with my index finger at that page headed 'Peasant', a verse-*creation* unnoticed by readers and the press for the same reason as it was unnoticed in its time by the censor. And if there's fate in verses, then fate is in these; if there's magic, it's in these; if there's history, so much insisted on nowadays in Soviet literature both 'from above' (the government) and 'from the side' (fellow-travellers), then it's in these verses. For Gumilyov's Fate, that day and hour, was entering as well – in boots or in felt-shoes (red Siberian feltboots), on foot, unheard, over dust or snow.

Were it headed 'Rasputin' everyone would know it (by heart), but as 'The Peasant' – well, it's just one more peasant. I've noticed, by the way, that the best poets (especially the Germans, who are the *best poets of all*), when they put an epigraph, often don't state where it comes from, or when they portray someone, often don't state *who*, so that, as well as conveying the immemorial secrecy of love and letting the thing speak for itself, they give the best reader this incomparable delight (I know it from experience!) of uncovering what's been covered up.

Dear Gumilyov, who, with your theories of poetic composition, gave birth to a series of decomposing poem-writers, and, with your poems about the tropics, to a series of trope-followers –

Dear Gumilyov, whose immortal parrots repeat with maniacal (that is, unintelligent, that is, in fact, parrotical) invariability your – twenty years ago! – young-*maître* maxims, scattered without trace under the wheels of your own 'Tram'...

Dear Gumilyov, whether or not there is another world, hear, in the name of all Poetry, my gratitude for this double lesson: to poets – on how to write poems; to historians – on how to write history.

The sense of History is only the sense of Fate.

Gumilyov was no *maître*, but a master: a god-inspired master-craftsman, already an *anonymous* one in those lines of his, cut down in the very morning of his mastership, his apprenticeship, which he had reached the full height of in his 'Bonfire' and in the surrounding bonfire of Russia – so marvellously, so arboreously.

The town Alexandrov. 1916. Summer. Aslant to the house, downhill, a cemetery. The favourite walk of the children, three-year-olds, Alya and Andryusha. The point of attraction: a ruined burial-vault with icons peering out from the earth. – I want to go to the pit where the dear Lord lives!

Favourite of the children and non-favourite of – Osip Mandelstam. It was because of this vault that he left Alexandrov so soon. (He wanted 'the whole of life'!)

– Why have you brought me here? I'm frightened.

Mandelstam is my guest, but I'm a guest myself. Of my sister who has gone to Moscow; I'm minding her son. My sister's husband is at work all day; the family is: me, Alya, Andryusha, the nurse Nadya, and Osip Mandelstam.

Mandelstam, after the first raptures, feels out of place in Alexandrov. A Petersburger and a Crimean, he is not used to my hillsides. Too many cows (passing by, mooing by, twice a day), too many crosses (standing too eternally). A cow might butt you to death. A corpse might rise. And go rabid. And appear in dreams. In the cemetery I'm – in his words – 'somehow absentminded'. I forget about him, Mandelstam, and I think about the dead, I read the inscriptions (instead of poems!), I work out the ages of the ones who are lying there and the ones who are growing above them – in short, I look either up or down, but definitely *away*. I get distracted.

– It's nice lying there! – Not nice at all: you'll lie there and people will walk over you. – And didn't they in life? –That's a metaphor! I mean feet, and boots, even. – But it won't be over *you*! You'll be...a soul. – That's just what I'm afraid of! We can't tell which is more terrifying, a bare soul or a decomposing body. – What do you want, then? To live for ever? Without even the hope of an end? – Oh, I don't know! I only know I'm frightened and I want to go home.

Poor dead people! Nobody thinks of you! They think of how they themselves could lie here and will indeed lie somewhere. *Of themselves lying here.* Not enough that your life's been taken by God – your death is taken too, by people, by Mandelstam with his 'frightened', and me with my 'nice'! Not enough that God has taken away the whole earth – we're taking your last seven feet of it.

Some come to the cemetery to learn, others come to be afraid, and yet others (like me) – for consolation. Everyone comes – to measure up. The whole earth, with all its hills and houses, isn't enough for us, we need your hill and your house as well. For the habit, the lesson, the fear, the salvation. We all come – to measure up. Then we're innocently surprised when, at the turn in the path or corridor...

If there's anything to be surprised at, it's how rarely you visit, how modestly and how shamefacedly... Were I in your place...

A quiet answer: 'Were we in yours...'

*

I remember the words of another poet who was also from the East and had also seen Moscow for the first time with me – in the graveyard of the Novo-Devichii Monastery,[6] under its divine vault: 'It's worth dying, to be buried here.'

Home, tea, welcoming squeals from Alya and Andryusha. A nun has come, with shirts. Mandelstam, whispering: – Why is she so black? – I, whispering too: – Because *they* are so white!

Whenever I see a nun (or monk or priest or any religious person), I feel ashamed. Of poems, unkempt hair, cigarette ends, my engagement ring – of myself. Of my own baseness (worldliness). And it's I, not the monk, who lower my eyes.

Mandelstam's eyes are always lowered: timidity? greatness? heavy eyelids? heavy centuries? His eyes are lowered, but his head is thrown back. Considering the length of his neck, it's the head stance of a camel. Three-year-old Andryusha, to him: – Uncle Osya, who twisted your head like that? – And the hostess of the house I first took him to, to me: – Poor young man! So young – and already blind?

But he takes a sidelong look at the nun (fear has large eyes!) and, using a moment when she's leaning over the smooth surface of a shirt, he even opens his eyes very wide. Mandelstam's wide-open eyes are stars, with the curly lashes reaching the brows.

– Is she going soon? Look, really, it's making me uneasy. I can absolutely definitely smell incense. – Mandelstam, you just think you can! – What about the ruined vault with bones in it? Do I just think I see it?

When all I want is a cup of tea!

The nun, standing over the shirt as over a dead body: – I'll do this one with a band[7] round the neck. – Mandelstam, behind the nun's back, in a hissing whisper: – Won't you be afraid to wear these shirts? – Just you wait, my friend! I'll die and appear to you in this very shirt. Lucky it's a night-shirt!

At tea Mandelstam thawed out.

– Maybe it isn't so frightening after all? Maybe if I go there every day, I'll get used to it? But better not go tomorrow...

Next day, inevitably, we went again.

\*

And once a calf pursued us. On the hillside. A red steer.

We were out for a walk, the children, Mandelstam, I. I was leading Alya and Andryusha along, Mandelstam was walking by himself. At first everything was fine, we lay on the grass, digging out clay. Burrows. Digging through to each other, and whenever the hands met we laughed – actually he alone laughed, I was playing, as always, for his sake.

The sun was consuming my lightness, his brownness. – Sun, the only hair-dye I recognise! Taking advantage of the grown-ups' game, the children were pulling the cloth-mushrooms off their heads and making a breeze with them. Andryusha kept flapping into Alya's face. Alya was quietly whining. Then Andryusha, wanting to make amends, would smear her blue-eyed tears down her cheeks with his clayey hands. Yanking their caps onto their heads, I would make them sit down apart from each other. Mandelstam would be frenziedly digging the next tunnel, indignant that I wasn't playing. The sun was burning.

– Ho-ome!

It must be said that Mandelstam, whether at the cemetery or on a walk or at the fair, wherever he was, always wanted to go home. And always before the other person (I) did. And when home – invariably – he wanted to go out. I think – humour aside – that whenever he was not writing (and he was always not-writing, namely, one poem in three months), he was pining. Without poems Mandelstam didn't feel right sitting – or walking – or living – in this world.

So, home. All of a sudden – a sound of galloping. I look round – a young bull. Red. A tail like lightning, a white star on the forehead. Coming at us.

Fear of bulls is an ancient fear. I am madly afraid of bulls and cows (without distinction) for the arrested gentleness of their eyes. Also, though, for their horns. 'It will suddenly catch you up on its horns!'[8] – who hasn't been sung to sleep with these words? And all the stories about the boy – or the peasant – or someone's grandfather – who was suddenly caught on the horns of a bull. The Russian cradle rocks beneath a *bull's* horn!

But I've *two* cradles on my hands at this moment! The children aren't in the least afraid, they take it as a game, flying along on my outstretched hands as though on giant-stride ropes, not over the earth but above it. The galloping increases, comes nearer, catches up. I can't bear it, I look round. It's Mandelstam galloping. The steer was left behind long ago. Perhaps it didn't pursue us at all?

I now know that the whole of my Red Steer[9] is from there, from that chase. It slept in me from May 1916 and rose again, Paris 1929, in a Volunteer's deathbed-delirium. I know that his steer was actually mine – ours – the Alexandrov one. And the laugh he laughed at the steer, as he died, was the very laughter of Alya and Andryusha: the pure joy of the run, the game, the bull.

Laughing, he didn't know it was death. And it was not as a thirty-year-old fragment of a non-existent army, citizen of a non-existent state, not on the alien soil of the capital of the world: no! but on his own soil, mine! – with all the protection of mother and native land – laughing! – three years old – and running – that he died.

– Madam! Why is our Osip Emelyich so peculiar? Today when I'm giving Andryusha his porridge he says to me: 'He's lucky, Nadya, that Andryusha of yours, his porridge always ready for him, and the holes in his socks all darned. As for me,' he says, 'nobody feeds me porridge, nobody', he says, 'darns my socks.' And then he sighed, such a dee-eep sigh, the poor orphan.

That was Nadya, Andryusha's nanny, also a native of Vladimir. A book could be written about this Nadya, but, for the time being: she came to me from my sister who'd gone away without taking her, and left me only in 1920, forced to leave, spitting blood from hunger (devotion) and stealing from me (tradition); called my sister 'Asya' and me 'Marina' when we weren't there; was proud of us, could never have served anyone else. A tamed she-wolf. Men, irrespective of class, she regarded with haughty pity, to her they were all 'poor wretches'.

Eighteen years old, a wolfish grin, brows at an angle, eyes like coals.[10] She loved my sister – who for that reason couldn't stand her – with such passionate jealousy that she used to invent all sorts of illnesses for

Andryusha on purpose to keep her at home. – Nadya, I'm going now. I'll be back late. – Yes, madam, but what shall I give Andryusha if the thermometer *goes up* again? – *What do you mean, goes up? Why?* – Didn't I tell you he kept complaining of a headache on our walk...and so on. Naturally Asya stays, Nadya triumphs. And it wasn't that noble jealousy nannies often show for the child's welfare ('What a lady, neglecting her child' and so on), but a woman's most base, ignoble, criminal jealousy towards someone she loves. A frenzy that finally leads to crime. Whether lying or not (she did lie, constantly, uselessly, frenziedly), when she left me (makes no difference, nothing to lose! there's no third sister!), she confessed she had often fed Andryusha crushed glass (!), and in the Crimea, in the epidemic, deliberately gave him unboiled water to drink so that he'd fall ill and thus *bind* Asya. To me, she always called Asya 'our lady' and used her to tell me home truths: 'and in our lady's house' such and such is done in such and such a way; occasionally, though, in a burst of emotion: – Madam! I've noticed something: for the washing, you take everything off yourself! Just like our lady. – She had come to me, to the manifest cold and hunger, despite all my warnings (no firewood, no bread, no...no...), exclusively out of love for my sister. Thus do widowers, without love – loving *her* – marry the dead woman's sister. Then all their life long – till they're driven into the grave – they take it out on the one who is *not* her.

To conclude, a small picture. That same Alexandrov. I'm sitting on the sand after a swim. Next to me, a huge dog, improbably hairy. Nadya: – Madam, it's peculiar looking at you: one's got too much on, it looks like, and the other's got too little!

Talent is that for which nothing should be forgiven, and for which we forgive everything.

– And I say to him: Osip Emelyich, you ought to get married. Any young lady would marry you. Shall I find you one? A priest's daughter.

I: – Nadya, do you seriously think any young lady...?

– Of course not, Madam, I just say it to comfort him, I feel so sorry for him. Not just *any* young lady wouldn't – *no* young lady would, or maybe one with a withered arm. He's that peculiar!

– What sort of person is that Nadya of yours? (this is Mandelstam) A nanny, with the eyes of a wolf. I wouldn't trust her with a child for anything, nor even with a kitten! When she's doing the washing she bursts out laughing, all alone in the empty kitchen. I asked her for some tea, you'd gone out with Alya, and she said there was none left. – Buy some! 'I can't leave Andryusha.' – Leave him with me. – 'With you-ou!' – And that insulting guffaw. Her eyes are slits, her teeth are enormous! A wolf!

– So, Madam, I pour him a glass of hot water and I take it to him. And he says to me so pi-iteously: 'Nadya! Isn't there any chocolate?' – No, I say, but there's jam. Then how he starts groaning: 'Jam, jam, I eat jam all day long, I don't want your jam! What a house! With no chocolate!' – Well, Osip Emelyich, there is a small bar, but it's Andryusha's – 'Andryusha's! Andryusha's! The biscuits are Andryusha's, the chocolate is Andryusha's, yesterday I wanted to sit in the armchair but that's Andryusha's too!... Break a bit off.' – I shan't break a bit off, I'll bring you some nice jam. – So he drank his hot water with jam.

*

His departure was unexpected: not so much for me, with my four-months' – February to June – experience of Mandelstam comings and goings (raids and *flights*), as for him with his childish longing for home, which he always ran away from. If a person says 'for ever' to a place or to another mortal, it only means that for the moment he's happy here – or with me, for example. This is the only way we should listen to vows. This is the only way we should require them to be kept. In brief, one – fine, as it happened – morning, he came down to breakfast – ready.

In lordly tone, as he broke his bread-roll: – And when does the train leave from here? – Train? From here? Where to? – To the Crimea. It must be today. – Why? – I...I...can no longer be here. And anyway, it's time to put a stop to all this.

Knowing the character of this traveller, I did not try to dissuade him. I helped him get his things together: a razor and, I think, an empty notebook.

– Osip Emelyich! How can you go on a journey? Your underwear hasn't got dry! – He, with the splendid carelessness of one who is departing: – It'll dry in the Crimean sun! – And to me: – You'll see me to the station, won't you?

The station. On my left, above my ear, an agitated Adam's apple on the neck of a camel – he had choked on Alexandrov as though on an apple. Andryusha is trying to escape from Nadya's arms and get under the engine, the 'wheelies'; lyrical Alya, seeing there's a departure, patiently sheds tears: – Is he coming back? He isn't going for ever and ever? Is he just pretending? – Nadya, the nanny, glistening with tears and teeth, is lamenting: – You should have told me last night, Osip Emelyich, I'd have got your socks darned for the journey, I'd have baked you a pie...

The bell. First. Second. Third. Foot on the train step. A turn.

– Marina Ivanovna! Perhaps it's a mistake, to go away.

– Of course (I catch myself in time)... Of course not! Just think: Max, Karadag,[11] Pra[12]... And you can always come back...

– Marina Ivanovna! (the engine is already moving) It's *definitely* a mistake! I've been so... (I walk beside the moving wheels) With you I've been so... so... (the carriage gathers speed and I do too) I've never been so... – Abandoning Mandelstam, I run, overtaking the train and the sentence. End of the platform. A post. I too become a post. Carriages pass: not him, not him, not him – *him*. I wave, as he and I waved to the soldiers only yesterday. He waves. Not with one, with both. Waving something away! A shout is carried in the engine's mane: – I don't want to go to the Crimea!

At the other end of the platform a little orphaned group: Alya weeping: – I knew he wouldn't come back! – Nadya weeping through her smile: – And I didn't darn his socks! – Andryusha howling: his wheelies have gone!

## *Defence of What Was*

Meudon. 1931. Spring. Going through papers. In my hand a newspaper cutting which I was just about to destroy.

> ... Where Russia breaks off
> above a black and alien sea...

–What's that? Alien? Obscure! I should know. And, closing my eyes:

> Doubting the miracle of resurrection,
> we walked about the cemetery.
> Everywhere, you know, the earth
> reminds me of those hills.

> (Two lines missing.)
> Where Russia breaks off
> above a black and obscure sea.
> From the slopes of the monastery

a broad meadow stretches out.
I was so loth to travel south
from the wide spaces of Vladimir.

But staying in this wooden, dark
settlement of holy fools
with such an enigmatic nun
would be asking for disaster.

I kiss a sunburnt elbow
and waxen portion of a brow.
I know it has remained white
under the swarthy-golden tress.

There still remains a band of white
where a turquoise bracelet was.[†]
The fiery summer of Tavrida
brings about these miracles.

How soon you grew to be dark-skinned
and came up to the poor Saviour.
You kissed, you couldn't leave the kissing,
you who in Moscow were so proud!

Only the name remains to us,
a wondrous sound, for a long time,
so accept this sand I've poured
from one palm to the other.[13]

Mandelstam's poem to me, i.e. the first thing that came from him after
that seeing-off.

The sand of Koktebel,[14] which my palms remember so well! Not sand
even – tiny rainbowy stones, with among them amethyst and cornelian, so
the gift was not so beggarly! Tiny stones of Koktebel, a whole bag of which
are kept here in the Kedrov family, who also come from Koktebel.

1911. I'm shaven after measles. I lie on the shore, I dig, beside me is
the poet Max Voloshin. – Max, I'll only marry the man who can guess
which is my favourite stone on the whole sea-shore.

– Marina! (Max's appealing voice) Being in love, as you may already
be aware, makes people stupid. And when the one you've fallen in love
with brings you (he puts on the sweetest of voices)...a cobblestone, you'll
quite sincerely believe it's your favourite pebble.

– Max! Everything makes me cleverer! Even love does!

† Later, an unsuccessful alteration: 'I kiss the wrist where, from the bracelet...'

But it came true about the pebble, for S.Ya. Efron, whom I married a year and a half later, having waited for him to reach the age of eighteen, practically on the first day of our acquaintance dug up and handed me – the greatest rarity! – a Genoese cornelian bead, which is with me to this day.

But I met Mandelstam for the first time in that same Koktebel in the summer of 1915, a year before the visit I have described. I was walking to the sea, and he – from the sea. At the gate of the Voloshin garden, we passed each other by.

I read on:

So this was written in the Crimea, written by a poet who was madly in love.[15]

Madly? I wouldn't have said so.

But if Mandelstam's admirers imagine from these facts (the Crimea, sea, love, poetry) a picture worthy of Aivazovsky's brush (incidentally, Aivazovsky[16] does have a picture like this, a very bad one: *Pushkin bidding farewell to the sea*) – these admirers will be somewhat in error.

Alerted by 'madly in love', I read on:

Mandelstam was living in the Crimea. And as he did not pay for his keep, despite his hosts' insistence that he either pay up or leave...

Stop! stop! What hosts' insistence, when the hosts were Max Voloshin and his mother, a remarkable old lady with the profile of Goethe, who in her childhood was a favourite of the exiled Shamil?[17] And what insistence, when they let rooms for a few pence and people used to owe them money for *years*?

...despite his hosts' insistence that he either pay up or leave, he did not wish to depart, so a special kind of torture was applied to him that was only possible in that 'picturesque corner of Crimea' – they refused him water.

Max and Elena Ottobaldovna – refused someone water? Moreover, a poet?!

Water was brought to Koktebel from far away and was sold in barrels – there was neither river nor well; by cunning and threats Mandelstam managed with difficulty to get some from the stern landlord or the shrew of a servant-woman...

But in Koktebel, where I lived from 1911 to 1917, there never was a servant-woman, there was a half-witted serving-man with a withered hand, owner of the boat *Socrates* which had a hole in it and after which he was named – who would have given the whole house away to the first asker!

They fed him on leftovers...

Who did? Max? Max never ever fed anyone, he found food for *himself* wherever he could. The feeding was done by the most kind-hearted woman in the world who kept an eating-place on some wasteland two versts from the dacha. And as for 'leftovers' – there was only one dish at Koktebel: mutton, a natural leftover and even a 'gnawed-over'. So you might say: in Koktebel there were no *not*-leftovers. Before any revolutions, Koktebel was a hungry place; even leftovers didn't last long there, owing to the threatening number of stray dogs. If Mandelstam ate 'leftovers', everyone did.

When guests came to Koktebel on a Sunday, Mandelstam was evicted from his room – he would spend the night in a lumber-room...

Not in a lumber-room, but in Max's studio containing marvels from all corners of the world – that's to say, a place some wouldn't even dare dream of!

Once he caught a cold while sleeping there...

In Koktebel, with its boiling sea and the earth cracking from heat! In Koktebel, where we all slept in the open air, and more often didn't sleep at all: gazing at the red pillar of the rising Jupiter in the water, or reading poetry in Max's tower. From the rising of Jupiter – to the setting of Venus...

...while sleeping there, and got a terrible gumboil and went around all bandaged up and smeared with iodine, pursued by hallooings from local boys and smiles from the rest of the population 'of that picturesque spot'...

Picturesque – yes, if you get your idea of it from the makers of pictures, from the artists, Max's friends who lived there (Bogaevsky, Lentulov, Kandaurov, Nachman, Lev Bruni, Obolenskaya).[18] But picturesque in inverted commas – no. Bare rocks, the moraine of the shore, no bush or shoot, no greenery except high up in the mountains (huge peonies, child's-head-sized), and apart from that: feathergrass, wormwood, sea, desert. Wasteland. The author clearly took Koktebel (the eastern Crimea, Cimmeria,[19] land of the Amazons, a second Greece) for Alupka, and took the poet Voloshin's dacha for that 'professors' corner', where in the evenings Vyal'tseva would sing on the gramophone: 'I've bedecked our little corner with flow-owers...'

Koktebel: no flowers. A sheer acute angle of rock. (There is a tradition that in one of its rocks, that could only be reached by swimming, is the entrance to Hades. I used to swim there. And go in.)

Incidentally, 'she', especially, used to make fun of him, she to whom he proposed to bring as a pledge of eternal love 'this sand I've poured from one palm to the other'...

'Make fun of him'? I did? I – make fun of a poet? I, who wasn't even in Koktebel, and whom he'd left to go to the Crimea!

She who was very pretty (what?), rather vulgar (what??), a brunette (???), by profession a woman-doctor (wha-a-at???)...was hardly disposed to receive such gifts: she had been brought to Koktebel by the Armenian merchant who kept her, a fat, greasy, swarthy man. He brought her there feeling very pleased: at last he'd found a spot where there was no one to be jealous of except Mandelstam...

A woman doctor, kept by an Armenian merchant? Quite apart from the fact that this woman never existed, these are *not our mores*! A Jewish, that is, Russian, woman-doctor, that is to say an educated woman, is someone who earns her own keep. We didn't let ourselves be kept as easily as that, especially if we were doctors! Moreover, it was 1916, war-time... This is what ten years of emigration does to a person. He forgot not only Mandelstam, but Russia too.

With a gumboil, unfed, and with hurt feelings, Mandelstam would go out of the house, trying not to cross the path of his landlord yet again, or that of the spiteful serving-woman. Dishevelled, with sandals on his bare feet, he would walk on the shore, and little boys along the way snorted in his face and made pig's ears from the skirts of their clothing...

Incidentally, an amusing association: coat-skirt – pig's ear. A Jew in a long-skirted frock-coat to whom people show a pig's ear. But the author of the recollections has little boys making a pig's ear *from their own clothes' skirts*. What skirts? Little boys wear shirts, and shirts don't have skirts, they have a short hem. It's a frock-coat that has a skirt, or an overcoat – anything long that flaps out. Skirt [*pola*] means 'half' [*polovina*]. The author forgot the Crimean boys and forgot the Crimean summer (50 degrees), forgot what any boys are and what any summer is!

He went to the stall where a little old Jewish woman sold matches, cigarettes, rolls and milk...

(which, in brackets, was the greatest rarity in Koktebel, as it was in all the Crimea: bouza – yes; mineral water – yes; 'pasha-tepe' – yes; milk – no).

This old woman...

And it wasn't a little old Jewish woman, but a Greek in his prime, and the only coffee-house in all Koktebel was the 'Tambourine' barrack, scribbled all over with painting and writing by visiting artists and poets. I even recall one verse: there's a depiction of a white-trousered summer-visitor with cane and monocle, whereas we all wore just anything, or nothing –

I'm nature's friend, a tourist meek.
Shame on you all, you naked freaks!

'Tambourine', the poverty-stricken coffee-house with a regal inscription above its log door: 'Tambourine's fame is beyond the mountains!'
    The same thing happened to the author of these recollections, with regard to Koktebel the place, as happened to Igor Severyanin with regard to Koktebel the word: Igor Severyanin, in the days of his youth, saw the word 'Koktebel' under some verses by Voloshin, took the place-name for the name of a poetic form (rondo, ghazal, ritournelle) and derived 'koktebels' from it, something intermediate between cocktails and constables. The author of the recollections replaces wild Koktebel first with dacha-dotted Alupka, and then with a hamlet of the 'West Edge' with its hawkers' trays, its little old women, its boys in long-skirted coats, and so on.

This little old woman, the only person in all Koktebel to behave humanly towards him...

Excuse me, but what about the rest of us? Always giving him the best place in the bullock-cart and the last gulp from the water-flask? Max, his mother, I, my sister Asya, the poetess Maia: every woman his nurse, every man his guardian – *all* the women pitying him, *all* the men admiring him, and *all* of us, both the pitying *and* the admiring, nursing and guarding him from morning till night...In Koktebel, Mandelstam was the general favourite, it may have been the one time, the once in a lifetime, that the poet had good luck, for he was surrounded by *ears* – for his poems, and by *hearts* – for his frailties.

This little old woman (maybe he reminded her of her own grandson, some Yankel or Osip), in the goodness of her heart allowed Mandelstam credit: each morning she let him take a bread-roll and a glass of milk 'on the book'. Of course she knew she wouldn't get a copeck – but the young man needed support – such a nice young man and probably ill: last week he'd been coughing all the time and now, look, a gumboil. Sometimes Mandelstam received a packet of second-class cigarettes from her as well, or matches, or a postage stamp. But if he lost his sensitivity and absentmindedly reached out for something more expensive – a packet of biscuits or a bar of chocolate – the good old woman would politely move his hand aside, saying sadly but firmly: I'm sorry, Mr Mandelstam, but that's beyond your means.

Here is *my* version, obviously unknown to the narrator. Late in the autumn of 1915 Mandelstam left Koktebel in a coat belonging to the landlord of the 'Tambourine', having carelessly, or otherwise, pawned or lost his own. And when, a year later, again at the 'Tambourine', the Greek said to the poet, 'Do you remember, Mr Mandelstam, how it was raining when you went away and I offered you my coat?', the poet said to the Greek, 'You may rejoice: your coat served a poet for a whole year.'

Not to mention the endless chocolate on credit – a fabulous chocolate. This is how much one of the best Russian poets was loved by one of the best places on earth: from the poet Maximilian Voloshin to the semi-literate owner of a poor coffee-house.

Mandelstam walked along the shore that was scorched by the sun and swept by the incessant, melancholy Koktebel wind. Discontented, hungry, proud, ridiculous, hopelessly in love with the woman-doctor, the girlfriend of the Armenian, who at this moment was sitting on her verandah in an attractive pink housecoat, drinking coffee – rich appetizing coffee – and eating hot home-made rolls, as many as she wanted...

Comrade writer of these recollections, I never went about in attractive
pink house-coats, I was never either very pretty or merely pretty, neither
rather nor very vulgar, I was never a woman-doctor, I was never kept by
a swarthy Armenian, the poet Osip Mandelstam was never madly in love
with any such 'me'.

Besides which, I repeat, Koktebel is a place that's empty, there was
never any rich cream in it, only goat's milk, thin (from the feathergrass!)
and somewhat bitter (from the wormwood!), never any hot home-made
rolls, in fact no rolls at all, only dry Turkish boubliks, and not even as many
of those as one wanted. And if the poet was hungry, it wasn't the fault of
the 'cruel landlord' Maximilian Voloshin, but that of our common land-
lady – the earth. In this case the earth of the eastern Crimea, where you,
author of the recollections, never set foot.

You declare these lines of Mandelstam's the best in Russian literature,
yet you've understood nothing in them. These 'Crimean' verses are indeed
written in the Crimea, but in essence they belong to Vladimir. Where in
the Crimea do you find 'wooden, dark settlements of holy fools'? What
'enigmatic nuns'? The poem is written *in fact* in the Crimea, but *in essence*
inside the spaces of Vladimir. Look at it line by line:

> Doubting the miracle of resurrection,
> we walked about the cemetery.
> Everywhere, you know, the earth
> reminds me of those hills.

What hills? As the next two lines are missing (they're replaced in the text
by dots) there are two possibilities: either – at a stretch – he's remember-
ing, even here in the Russian cemetery, the hills of the Crimea; or – far
more likely – even here in the Crimea he cannot forget the hills of
Alexandrov. (A point in favour of the latter guess is the double hilliness
of Alexandrov: hills of the earth and hills of the cemetery.)

Further, in black and white:

> From the slopes of the monastery
> a broad meadow stretches out.
> I was so loth to travel south
> from the wide spaces of Vladimir.

> But staying in this wooden, dark
> settlement of holy fools
> with such an enigmatic nun
> would be asking for disaster.

The nun, I think, is compound: our nanny Nadya with her holy-fool laugh, the actual nun with the shirts, and finally me forever taking us to the cemetery. The enigmatic touch is from this threefold face. But, one way or another, it is because of this nun that he leaves for the Crimea.

> I kiss a sunburnt elbow
> and waxen portion of a brow.
> I know it has remained white
> under the swarthy-golden tress.
>
> There still remains a band of white
> where a turquoise bracelet was.
> The fiery summer of Tavrida
> brings about these miracles.

The 'band' is *still* white, i.e. from the previous Koktebel summer (1915). That's what the Crimean sun is like – it burns you for the whole year. If it were about a Crimean arm, then why 'still' and what miracle?

> How soon you grew to be dark-skinned
> and came up to the poor Saviour.
> You kissed, you couldn't leave the kissing,
> you who in Moscow were so strict.

Not 'strict', but *proud* (see *Tristia*). 'You kissed, you couldn't leave. . .' Kissed what? The crucifix, of course, in front of which I presumably *had* been proud, in Moscow. It's possible to be proud before God in one's youthful stupidity; but strict? Every nun is strict. The present transcription makes it seem that 'she' kissed not an icon, but a person, which makes complete nonsense of the reference to the Saviour and of the whole quatrain. As if one had only to come to God and one would start kissing a man, unable to leave off.

> Only the name remains to us,
> a blissful sound, for a short while...

Not 'short while, blissful sound', but (see *Tristia*)

> a wondrous sound, for a long time...

The author of the recollections obviously read 'for a long' [*na dolgii*] as 'not long' [*ne dolgii*] and thus got 'short'. Poets' memories are not as short as that! But can anyone really quote like this when *Tristia* is on sale in every bookshop?

The article ends with the quotation:

Where Russia breaks off
above a black and alien sea.

Clearly to the writer it is alien, but to Mandelstam and me it is kindred. To all who have lived in it, Koktebel is a second homeland; for many, it's the birthplace of the spirit. And in the present poem it is

Where Russia breaks off
above a black and obscure sea

– making an obscure sound, the same sea as in Mandelstam's poem of genius:

Insomnia. Homer. Tight-drawn sails.
I've read to the middle the list of ships,
this long brood, this train of cranes,
which once rose above Hellas –

Like a wedge of cranes into foreign frontiers!
On the heads of tsars – a divine foam.
Where are you sailing? If not for Helen
what would Troy mean to you, Aegean men?

Sea, Homer – everything's moved by love.
To whom shall I hearken? Homer is silent now,
and the Black Sea is oratorically sounding,
approaching the head of my bed with heavy rumbling.

To avoid possible repetitions of the misunderstanding, I inform the author of the article that in the book *Tristia* the poems 'In the polyphony of a girls' choir' and 'On a sledge carpeted with straw' ('Only the name remains to us, a wondrous sound, for a long time!') belong to me, while the poem 'Solominka' and the following series belong to Salomeya Nikolayevna Halpern,[20] born Princess Andronikova, now thriving in Paris, and resembling that woman doctor just as much as I do.

And that the whole period – from the Germano–Slavic flax to the line 'We walked about the cemetery' – is *mine*, the marvellous days from February to June 1916, when I was giving Mandelstam Moscow. There have not been so many good poems written to me in my life, and, above all, it isn't so often that a poet is inspired by a poet, that one would idly and to no purpose yield this inspiration to the first non-existent girlfriend of a non-existent Armenian.

*This* property – I do defend.

*

But it isn't just a question of me. What does it matter to me? No one is going to believe I am that brunette with an Armenian. And even if they do believe the poem is to her and not me – what of it? When all's said and done, Mandelstam knows and I know.

And if it affected me alone, I would just laugh. But I am not laughing at all now. Because, first, it's a question of a friend (mine, and, as the article makes clear, the author's too. NB! If this is how friends are remembered, how are enemies?); secondly, it's a question of a major poet, who is being made to seem a vulgarian (Mandelstam not only *didn't* love the woman described, but *could not have loved* her); thirdly – of another poet, Voloshin, who is made to appear a skinflint and a monster (refusing to give someone water); and, fourthly, there's the fact that all this is presented in the form of instruction to young poets.

I'll end with the beginning of the article, which reveals the pretext, reason and purpose for which it was written:

> At one of the gatherings of Parisian literary youth a reproach was addressed to me: 'Why do you distort the image of Mandelstam, our favourite poet? Why do you present him in your recollections as a kind of comical eccentric? Could he really have been like that?' That is just what he was like. I have not invented a single word about Mandelstam...

In the present article, as I have shown, *all* the words are invented.

> I am very glad for Mandelstam that young Parisian verse-writers love him, and I'm still gladder for them: this love that many of them feel brings them closer to poetry than their own poems do. But I too, in fact, love Mandelstam's poetry very much and, besides, I also have the advantage that I love him himself no less – the strange, rather weird, ridiculous person, who is indivisible from his poems, and I've known him a very long time and very closely. There were times when we were so inseparable that we had what must have been a unique visiting-card. So and so[†] and O. Mandelstam...And haven't our 'young poets' learnt that the lofty and the ridiculous, the most lofty and the most ridiculous, are often so interwoven that it is impossible to see where one starts and the other ends.

---

† Name of the author of the recollections.

The lofty and the ridiculous – yes; the lofty and the vulgar – never.

– To clarify this, I'll give an example from the life of that same 'eccentric', 'angel' and 'comical figure' – from the life of the poet Mandelstam...

The value of the example – we know.

A long article is known to literary people as a 'cellar' [*podval*]. This is the right word here. The Cimmerian cliffs and my Alexandrov hills, all Koktebel with its high style, all Mandelstam with his high yearning, are here brought low, down to the cellar – of *everyday life* (which never existed!).

I don't know whether poems in general need literal versions in terms of the everyday: who – when – where – with whom – in what circumstances – and so on, like the secondary-school game that everyone knows. The poems grind up everyday life and discard it, then along comes the biographer and, from what remains of the siftings, practically crawling after them on his knees, he strives to recreate what happened. To what purpose? To bring the live poet close to us. Doesn't he know it's *in the poetry* that a poet is alive, that he is distant in *essence*?

However – I won't argue – the biographer has an official right to the true story (to a record). And it is our task to draw the appropriate lesson from this record. One thing alone matters: that the record *be* a record.

If you wish to write the truth about the past, then know it; if you wish to write a lampoon, change the names or wait a hundred years. Whereas we aren't all dead yet! Had the author of the article lived on the same territory as his hero, there'd have been no article. As it was: leagues away and we might never meet again...(while here, close at hand, is the temptation of the anecdote and of easy success with those who prefer gossip about a poet to reading his poems). Irresponsibility of separation and impunity of distance.

*

– Well, if you don't acknowledge literal versions in terms of the everyday, why have you taken it into your head to tell us all this? Why do we need to know how the great poet Mandelstam galloped away from an innocent calf down a green hillside?

Here's my reply:

I was challenged to tell the *true story* of Mandelstam in summer 1916 by the *invention* about Mandelstam in summer 1916. To give *my* literal version of the poem by that *other* literal version. For nowhere and never (1916-1931) have I asserted my right to this property until it came under attack. – Defence! – When, in the Revolution, they took away the money I had in the bank, I didn't question it, as I didn't feel it to be mine. They've robbed my grandfathers! This poem, if only because I care about the poet, is something I have earned.

One thing more: if I had confined myself to merely refuting the invention – that is, to merely catching someone out – I would have put myself in the role I hate most: that of prosecutor. By contrasting the invention with the living reality (and isn't my Mandelstam enchanting, despite his fear of the dead and his passion for chocolate, or, perhaps, because of these?), by affirming life, which is itself an affirmation, I am not leaving the innate condition of a poet – that of defender.

# THE POET AND TIME

'I love art, but not contemporary art': this is said not only by philistines, but sometimes by major artists, though invariably when speaking of some other art than their own – for example, a painter speaking of music. In his own sphere a major artist is always contemporary; why, we shall see later.

Not to like a work is, in the first and most important place, not to recognise it: not to find the pre-cognised in it. The first cause of not accepting a work is not being prepared for it. It's a long time before simple folk in the city will eat our food. Like children not wanting to try anything new. A physical turning away of the head: I see nothing in this picture, therefore I don't wish to look at it. – But, in order to see, one needs to look; in order to really see, one needs to look really closely. Disappointment of an eye that is used to seeing at first glance, which means used to seeing along its old track, that of others' eyes. Used to not an act of cognition, but recognition. The tiredness (which is the backwardness) of the old, the pre-established attitude of the philistine, the chock-full-ness (of head and whole being) of the painter who doesn't like contemporary poetry – chock-full with things of his own. In all three cases it is a fear of effort, forgivable – until they judge.

The only case worthy of respect, the only legitimate non-acceptance of a work, is non-acceptance of it in full knowledge. Yes, I know it; yes, I read it; yes, I acknowledge it – *but* I prefer (say) Tyutchev, who (for I want my own blood and thought) is more akin to me.

Everyone is free to choose his favourites, or rather, no one is free to choose his favourites: I'd be glad, say, to love my own age more than the preceding one – yet I can't. I can't and I'm not obliged to. No one is obliged to love, but every non-loving person is obliged to know – first, what it is he doesn't love, and second, why he doesn't love it.

Let's take the most extreme of extreme cases: an artist's non-acceptance of his own work. My own time may be repulsive to me, I may be repulsive to myself insofar as I am *it*, or even (this does happen!) someone else's work, of another age, may be more desirable to me than

87

my own – not by a sign of power, but by a sign of kinship. Someone else's child may be dearer to a mother than her own which takes after its father, that is, after its age, but I'm doomed to my own child – the child of the age – I cannot give birth to another, much as I'd like to. Fate. I cannot love our age more than the preceding one, but neither can I create any age but my own: you can't create what's been created, and you only create forward.

It isn't given us to choose our children: the given or the assigned.

'I love poetry, but not contemporary poetry.' Like every assertion, this too has its counter-assertion, which goes: 'I love poetry, but only contemporary poetry.' Let's start with the least curious, most frequent, case: that same philistine; and end with the most curious: the major poet.

'Down with Pushkin' is the son's answering shout to the father's 'Down with Mayakovsky', the son yelling less against Pushkin than against his father. 'Down with Pushkin' is the first cigarette smoked in the sight of the father who has given up smoking, and smoked not so much to please oneself as to spite him. It's of the order of family quarrels, which end – in peace. (Neither father nor son really cares, either about Mayakovsky or about Pushkin.) Shouts of warring generations.

A second author of the philistine's shout, 'Down with Pushkin', is the worst of all authors: fashion. We won't dwell on this authoress: fear of being left behind, endorsement of one's sheep-like nature. What can be asked of the philistine if even writers – the tail end of writers – are subject to this sheepishness? Every modernity has two tails: one of restorers and one of innovators, each as bad as the other.

But – a shout, not from a philistine, but from the major writer (eighteen years old at the time) Mayakovsky: 'Down with Shakespeare!'

Self-preservation of creativity. Sometimes, so as not to die, one has to kill (primarily something in oneself). Thus, Mayakovsky – against Pushkin. Not really his enemy, but his ally, the most contemporary poet of his time, as much the creator of his epoch as Mayakovsky is of his – and only an enemy because he's been cast in iron and loaded on to the generations. (Poets, poets, fear statues and anthologies after your death still more than in your lifetime!) A shout that is not against Pushkin, but against his statue. Self-preservation which ends (and did end) once the creator (the fighter) grew mighty. (The wonderful poem about meeting Lermontov, for instance, product of his mature years.)

But except for the *exceptional* example of Mayakovsky, the assertion 'I love poetry, but not contemporary poetry', and its converse, 'I love poetry, but only contemporary poetry', are worthy of each other – worth little – worth nothing.

No lover of poetry (apart from Mayakovsky's innate self-defence) will say such things, no real lover of poetry will hack off yesterday's – and always' – actuality in favour of today's, no real lover will even remember that the word *actual*[1] has any meaning other than *genuine* – in art it has no other meaning, no one will commit – upon art, upon nature – the politicians' sin: of setting up a pole of dissension on a ground of unity.

Anyone who loves *only* something, loves nothing. Pushkin and Mayakovsky would have made friends, they did make friends, essentially never separated. Valleys fight, peaks unite. 'There's room for everyone under the sun':[2] peaks know this best of all. And solitary walkers. And the opinion of the rest – who've fallen behind or got tired or are afraid of falling behind – the opinion and preference of *those who don't know*, doesn't concern us once it's ascertained, and doesn't concern art even before it's ascertained.

An inscription on one of the frontier posts of the contemporary age, 'In the future there'll be no frontiers', has already come true in art – it came true at the very beginning. A universal work is one which, translated into another language and another age, translated into the language of another age – least of all then – loses nothing. Having given everything to its own age and land, it gives everything once again to all lands and all ages. Having revealed its own place and age, up to the furthest bounds, it boundlessly reveals all that is not-place, not-age: for all ages.

There is no non-contemporary art (art which doesn't reveal its time). There is restoration – which is not art – and there are solitary individuals who leap out of their time for as far as, say, a hundred years ahead (NB never backwards), that is, once again, who are contemporaries, even though not of their own time, that is, they are not extra-temporal.

Genius? Whose name do we say when we think of the Renaissance? Da Vinci. A genius gives his name to the epoch, so much is he *it*, even if it is not fully conscious of the fact. We simply say 'The Age of Goethe', conveying both the historical and the geographical age, and even the astral map of that moment. ('In the days of Goethe' – meaning, when the stars stood in a certain way; or, something really definite, 'the Lisbon earthquake', meaning when Goethe first doubted the benevolence of the deity. That earthquake was immortalised and *outweighed* by the seven-year-old Goethe's doubt.)

A genius gives his name to the epoch, so much is it *he*, even if he is not fully conscious of the fact (or allegedly not, for Da Vinci, Goethe, Pushkin, *were* aware). Even in textbooks, we read: 'Goethe and his Time' (that is, a collective noun plus all that's collected in it). A genius has a perfect right to say of his time, what Louis,[3] with no right, said of the state:

'Le temps c'est moi' (or a whole pleiad may say: 'Mon temps – c'est nous'). This is about the genius who outstrips. As for those who are said to come one or three centuries late, I'll mention just one case: the poet Hölderlin, ancient in theme and sources and even vocabulary, thus arriving in his eighteenth century not one but eighteen centuries late, Hölderlin who is only now beginning to be read in Germany, more than a century later, who's been adopted, that is, by our far from ancient age. Someone who was eighteen centuries late in his own century has turned up as a contemporary of the twentieth century. What may this miracle signify? It signifies that in art there is no coming late, that art itself, whatever has nourished it and whatever it has sought to restore, is in *itself* a movement forward. That in art there is no going back; unstopping, therefore unreturning. Not 'no turning', but 'no returning'. Don't watch how the walker turns his head, look at the milestones he has swung past. It's possible to walk with tight-shut eyes – with a blind man's stick – or without any stick. Your feet will take you by themselves, though you're mentally thrice-nine[4]kingdoms away. He looked back, but walked ahead.

Is Tyutchev the only one? And Leskov, dropping into our generation instead of his own? But this way we can reach Esenin who arrived in his country only ten years late. Had he been born ten years earlier, people would have sung *him*, they'd have had the time, *him* and not Demyan. It is he who is the index of the literature of the age, not Demyan, who may be an indicator of something or other but certainly *not* of poetry. Esenin, who perished because he couldn't fulfil our time's command – because of a feeling very close to conscience, in between envy and conscience: perished for nothing, because he did fulfil it – even its civic command (of the multitudes to the one).

I am the last poet of the village.

Every contemporality in the present is a co-existence of times, it is ends and beginnings, it is a living knot, which has only to be cut. Every contemporality is a suburb. The whole Russian contemporality is, at the moment, one sheer unbroken spiritual suburb, with villages that aren't villages and towns that aren't towns – a *place in time*, in which Esenin, who remained after all between village and town, was, even biographically, in place.

I could name dozens of non-contemporary poets who are prospering to this day, but they have either stopped being poets or never were. They've been forsaken, not by their sense of their time, which perhaps they never had in its naked form, but by the gift through which they sensed – revealed – created – the time. Not to go onwards (in verse, as in everything) means to go backwards – that is, to leave the scene. What happens to the philistine after the age of thirty has happened to the trump card of *émigré* literature:[5] he has become contemporary with the preceding generation, which means, in his case, with his own thirty-years-ago authorship. He has fallen behind – not from other walkers, but from the walker he himself ought to be. The reason X doesn't accept contemporary art is that he no longer creates it. X is uncontemporary not because he doesn't accept the contemporary age, but because he has stopped on his creative path – the one thing a creator has no right to do.

The only people who are not contemporary, besides those neutral persons who aren't contemporary with any time, are those who are no longer in the ranks – invalided soldiers, a title of honour since it presupposes validity in the past.

Even this challenge of my own to the time:

For I *bypassed* the age
at my birth. Your demand
is in vain, to no purpose!
Time is king for a day! I bypass you...[6]

is a shout of the time – using my lips, its counter-shout to itself. Were I living a hundred years ago when rivers flowed smoothly...Contemporality of a poet means doomedness to time. Doomed to being driven by it.

You can't jump out of history. Had Esenin realised this, he'd calmly have sung not just of his village, but also of the tree above his cabin, and no axes could have chopped that tree out of twentieth-century poetry.

A poet's contemporality is not a declaration that his time is the best, and not even a simple acceptance of it – no is an answer too! Nor is it even the vital need to give some answer or other to events (the poet is himself an event of his time, and every answer of his to this self-event, every self-answer, will be at once an answer to everything). A poet's contemporality is so little a matter of content ('What did you mean in this work?' – What I *did* in it) that it once befell me, the writer of these lines, to hear with my own ears, after a reading of my poem *The Swain*: 'Is this about the Revolution?' (To say the listener simply hadn't understood is to fail to understand, oneself, for it's not about the Revolution, but *is* it: its footstep.)

I'll say more – that a work's contemporality (in Russia's case, its revolutionariness) not merely doesn't reside in the content, but is sometimes there despite the content, as if jesting with it. Thus, even in Moscow 1920, audiences kept asking me for the poem 'about the Red officer', namely:

And so my heart is gnashing over
the RSFSR – whether fed or not! –
as if I myself were an officer
in the death-days of October.[7]

In poems there is something more important than their meaning: their
sound. And the soldiers of Moscow 1920 were not mistaken: those lines,
in essence, are far more about a Red officer (or even soldier) than about
a White one – who would not have accepted them, who (1922-1932) *did
not accept them*.

I know this from the cheerful, trustful feeling I had when I recited them
there, flung them to my enemies as if to my kin; and from the feeling of
shyness and awkwardness I have when I recite them here, something like:
Forgive me, in the name of Christ. – Forgive you what? – Well, the fact
that I write about you like this, write about you in the wrong way: in their
way, the way that belongs over there. I celebrate you in the language of
the enemy: my language! And, altogether: forgive me, in the name of
Christ, for being a poet, for if I were to write in such a way that you would
not 'forgive' me for myself but instead recognise yourselves in me, I would
not be what I am, a poet.

Once when I was reading my *Swans' Encampment* to a quite inap-
propriate audience, one of those present said: 'None of this matters.
You're a revolutionary poet all the same. You've got our tempo.'

In Russia they forgave me everything because I was a poet; here, they
forgive me for *being* a poet.

I know too that the true listeners to my White *Perekop* are not the White
officers to whom, each time I recite to them, I really sincerely wish I were
reading something in prose, but the Red soldiers whom *Perekop* would
get through to, and will get through to, even including the priest's prayer
before the attack.

If only no politicians stood between poet and people!

Also, despite my isolation, my Russian works – by their will, not mine –
are designed for multitudes. Over here, as a physical fact, there are no
multitudes, only groups. Just as, instead of the arenas and terraces of
Russia, there are little salons, instead of the ethical event of a public
performance – though it be an assault! – there are literary evenings,
instead of the irreplaceable anonymous listener in Russia, there's a
listener with a name, even with a distinguished one. All this belongs to
literature, not to the current of life. The wrong scale, the wrong response.

In Russia, as in the steppes and on the sea, there is room to speak from and into. If they'd let people speak.

The whole thing is simple: over here is – *that* Russia; over there is – all Russia. To people here, in art it's the past that's contemporary. Russia (I mean Russia, not the authorities), Russia the land of those who are in the lead, requires of art that it should lead; the emigration, land of those who have remained behind, requires that art should remain behind too, which means – roll uncontrollably backwards. In the order of things here, I am a disorder of things. There, I wouldn't be published, but I would be read; here, I'm published – and not read. (Incidentally, they've stopped publishing me now as well.) The chief thing in a writer's life (its second half) is writing. Not: to get ahead, but: get it said. Over here, I'm not hindered from writing – doubly not hindered, for it isn't only persecution that hinders, fame (love) does too.

Everything is point of view. In Russia I'll be understood better. But in the next world I'll be understood even better than in Russia. Understood completely. I'll be taught to understand myself completely. Russia is merely the limit of earthly understandability, beyond the limit of earthly understandability in Russia is unlimited understandability in the not-earthly. 'There is a land which is God, Russia borders *with it*' said Rilke, who himself yearned for Russia all his life, everywhere outside Russia. With that land which is God, Russia borders to this day. A *natural frontier*, which politicians can't displace, since it isn't churches that mark it out. Not only now, after all that has come to pass, but always Russia has been the other world to everything that is not-Russia, whether with white bears or with Bolsheviks makes no difference: other. Something like a threat of salvation – of souls – through the perdition of bodies.

And it was not much easier, then, to take the decision to go there – with all the pre-war blandishments – than it is now, through all the prohibitions. Russia was never a country on the earthly map. And those who went there from here really went over the frontier: of the visible.

It's on *that* Russia that poets stake their bets. On Russia-entire, Russia of all time.

But even Russia isn't enough. Every poet is essentially an *émigré*, even in Russia. *Émigré* from the Kingdom of Heaven and from the earthly paradise of nature. Upon the poet – upon all who belong to art, but most especially upon the poet – there's a particular mark of discomfort, by which you'll know him even in his own home. An *émigré* from immortality in time, a non-returner[8] to *his own* heaven. Take the most various of them, line them up in your mind: whose face shows presentness? All of them are – over there. Kinship with soil or people, nationality, race, class, and that contemporality which they create – all this is only surface, the first or the seventh layer of skin, which the poet does nothing but try his utmost to shed. ' "What time is it?"[9] they asked him here, and he answered the curious: "It's eternity" ' – Mandelstam on Batyushkov; and 'What millennium is it, my dears, out there?' – Boris Pasternak on himself. All poets of all times say essentially one thing only. And that one thing remains on the surface of the world's skin in the same way as the visible world itself remains on the surface of the poet's skin. Next to that emigration, what is ours?

And long she languished upon earth
filled with a strange desire,
And could not replace the songs of heaven
with the tedious songs of earth![10]

– no less tedious for being one's own.

Coming back to here: in matters of art the philistine is generally contemporary with the preceding generation – that is, artistically he is his own father, and his grandfather and great-grandfather too. In matters of art the philistine leaves the ranks at around the age of thirty, as soon as he's thirty he starts rolling uncontrollably backwards – through non-understanding of others' youth – to non-recognition of his own youth, to non-acknowledgement of any youth – till he gets to Pushkin, whose eternal youth he transforms into eternal oldness, and whose eternal contemporality he transforms into antiqueness from the word go. At which point he dies. It's to be noted that there is not one ordinary old man who doesn't contrast Pasternak, whom he doesn't know, with Derzhavin, whom he doesn't know either. Pushkin – not merely a great knower of his own time but also the first to defend the authenticity of the 'Lay of the Host of Igor',[11] then newly discovered – is the limit of the philistine's knowledge in any direction, whether looking round or looking back. All ignorance, feebleness and goblinry goes rushing invariably under the shelter of Pushkin – who had knowledge, power, leadership.

Two movements that meet each other: age moving forward in time, and the corresponding awareness of art moving backward; increasing age and decreasing artistic perceptivity.

Thus, to this day, older people in the emigration consider their seventy-year-old coeval, Balmont, almost as a twenty-year-old, still fighting him, or 'forgiving' him as they would a grandson. Others, a bit younger, are still, or already, contemporaries of *that* Igor Severyanin – of their own youth, that is. (Recently there was an 'Igor Severyanin evening' which the emigration attended in order to look at their selves of those days, to look with their own eyes at their own youth and listen to how youth used to sing in those days; but youth – sage fellow! – had grown up and stopped singing, or sang just once – with a grin – at us, at itself...) A third group, finally, are beginning to discover (permit the possibility of) Pasternak, who has been Russia's best poet now for fifteen years (1917, *My Sister Life*) and printed for more than twenty. Those who know and love Pasternak – that is to say, his real contemporaries – are not people of his age, around forty years old, but their children, who will drop behind in their turn one day, get tired and get stuck at that very point – at him, if they don't roll backwards to somewhere beyond Blok, or even further back into the land of their fathers, forgetting that in its time it too was a land of sons. Meanwhile, somewhere, dressed in the protective colouring of non-fame, someone wanders amongst us who is the man of the future, already in being, someone who would be oh *so* much loved by his twenty-year-old coevals, if only they knew! But they don't know him. But he doesn't yet know himself. For the moment, to himself he is still the last of all persons. He is known about only by the gods – and by his empty notebook with the mark of his two elbows going right the way through it. No one is given the chance of knowing Boris Pasternak at twenty.

From all that's been said it is clear that a poet's contemporality is by no means signalled by the timeliness of his general recognition, thus not by the quantity but by the quality of this recognition. General recognition of a poet may even be posthumous. But contemporality (effect on the quality of his time) always happens in his lifetime, for in matters of creativity only quality counts.

'On ne perd rien pour attendre'[12] – Pasternak, for one, lost nothing, but perhaps if that Russian suicide had got caught in some Pasternakian downpour, if he'd been (artistically) capable of perceiving – of surviving – it, he wouldn't have thrown himself off the Arc de Triomphe (in answer to my love, my death: *My Sister Life!*).

We should ask those who went off to war with a volume of Pasternak and Blok in their pockets.

Contemporary Russia, which is almost forcibly – and certainly untiringly and unswervingly – accustoming the philistine to the new art by both the visual and the oral method, has displaced and dislodged all this. Even if not all of them understand, even if they don't understand it all at once, it's enough that they're looking for the cause of this non-understanding in themselves, instead of in the writer. 'Why is it, Vladimir Vladimirovich' – the workers' question to Mayakovsky – 'that when you read we understand everything, but when *we* read...'; 'Learn to read, lads, learn to read'... Russia is a land where, for the first time, people are learning to read the poets – who, however much it's asserted, are not nightingales.

The contemporality of the poet consists in so many heartbeats per second, giving the exact pulse-rate of the age – including its illnesses (NB we all gasp for breath in poems!); it consists in an extra-semantic, almost physical, consonance with the heart of the epoch – which includes my heart and beats in mine, as mine.

I may fall behind in ideas and life, I do fall behind, I defend what's gone, what's remained beyond the edge of the earth, but my poems, without my knowledge or will, carry me out to the front lines. One can't order from God either poems or children – it's they who order fathers!

So when, in Moscow 1920, I first heard that I was an 'innovator', I was not only not pleased, I was indignant – the very sound of the word was repugnant. And it is only now, ten years later – after ten years of emigration, after considering who and what were those who thought like me in the old life, and, especially, who and what are those who accuse me in the new – that I've resolved at last to face up to my 'newness', and adopt it.

Poems are our children. Our children are older than us, because they have longer and further to live. Older than us from the future. Therefore sometimes foreign to us.

To return to the content, and a detail of it – its direction.

Lunacharsky, because he is a revolutionary, didn't become a revolutionary poet; I – because I am *not* – did not become a restoratory poet. Poet of Revolution (*le chantre de la Revolution*) and revolutionary poet – not the same thing. Only once did they merge – in Mayakovsky. And merged all the more because the revolutionary in him was also a poet. Wherefore he is a miracle of our days, the apogee of their harmony. But counter-miracles take place too: Chateaubriand, who was not with the Revolution but against it, paved the way for the revolution of Romanticism in literature, something that would never have happened had the Revolution set him to writing political pamphlets (NB! there are pamphlets of genius – Mayakovsky's, full of all the lyric power he suppressed in himself). Secondly, and this is the main thing: acknowledge, bypass or reject the Revolution, all the same it's in you, and has been since the beginning of time (as the elemental), as well as since 1918 in Russia, which, like it or not, did happen. In a poet all the old could be left by the Revolution just as it was, all except scale and tempo.

And the old Sologub with the bergeries[13] of his dying hours? Precisely

– the *old* Sologub. Poignant as a human document (an old poet in a time of Revolution), exacerbating as an image (an old man who has lost everything, and now look...), but that isn't what art is – 'bergeries' – and 'bergeries' are not what Sologub is! In his bergeries the dark flood of his gift lets him off – lets him down on some arcadian shore. Kuzmin was old *too*, yet in his Byzantine Saint George (1921) there sounds the step of the Revolution; a foreigner listening would say 'It's about a fight'. That is the revolutionary quality I am talking about. There is *no* other, for a poet. Or else (apart from the single miracle of Mayakovsky) there is no *poet*. Pasternak is revolutionary not because he wrote *The Year 1905*, but because he discovered a new poetic consciousness and its inevitable consequence: form. (It's telling that among its contemporaries, those important at the time, the Year Five found no singer, while among the poets important at the time it found no contemporary. There is only one Year Five – Pasternak's, twenty or more years later. The conclusion from this is that an event – like a poet or a poem – may sometimes not merely lose nothing by waiting, but may actually benefit from it. For events and for those who try to hasten them – a great creative lesson in patience.)

There is not a single important Russian poet of the present whose voice hasn't shaken and grown since the Revolution.

The theme of Revolution is the command of the time.

The theme of celebration of the Revolution is the command of the Party.

Does a political party – even the most powerful, even the one with the biggest future in all the world – represent the whole of its time, and can it present its command in the name of the whole of it?

Esenin perished because he took a command that was meant not for him but for others (command of the time to society) as a command to himself (the time to the poet), took one of the commands to be the whole command. Esenin perished because he let others know for him, he forgot that he himself was a conducting wire: the most direct of all!

A political command to a poet (of whatever kind!) has got the wrong address on it; lugging a poet around the Turk-Sib[14] is asking the wrong person; official reports by poets are unconvincing; dragging a poet along after politics is unproductive.

Wherefore: a political command to a poet is not a command of the time, which issues its commands without intermediaries. A command not of contemporality, but of the 'evils of the day'.[15] To the evils of yesterday we owe the death of Esenin.

Esenin perished because he forgot that he himself was just as much an intermediary, herald and leader of the time, he himself was at least as much his time, as those he allowed to deflect and destroy him in the name of and on behalf of the time.

A writer, if he only is
a wave, and the ocean is Russia,
cannot but be roused to wrath
when the elements are roused.

Had the ideologues of proletarian poetry respected poets more and instructed them less, they'd have let those roused elements rouse the poet themselves, let the poet be roused by them in his own way.

Had the ideologues of proletarian poetry respected poets more and instructed them less, they would have pondered the following quatrain:

A writer, if he only is
the nerve of a great nation,
cannot but be defeated when
freedom is defeated...[16]

that is, the very nerve of creativity.

Do not write against us, for you are a force: this is the one legitimate command any government can issue to a poet.

And if you say to me: 'in the name of the future'...well, *I receive commands from the future without intermediaries.*

What is all that pressure (of church, state, society) compared with this pressure from within!

I too have commands from the time. Apart from the martial tempo of the *Tsar-Maiden*, *The Swain*, *On a Red Steed* and much else – apart, that is, from the time's oblique influence – there is the time's direct command, right down to the names of the leaders, but not issued by leaders or counter-leaders, issued by the phenomenon itself. Thus, my poem *Perekop* was ordered by the Perekop bastion. If some White ideologue had ordered it from me, or even just proposed it to me, nothing at all would have come of it, for a third person would have been interfering in a matter of love – invariably destructive, whatever his name, and murderous when there is no name, when the third person is a political programme.

What's more, if my *Perekop* has succeeded, it is only thanks to my writing it without being hampered by anyone's mercenary gratification, in the complete absence of any sympathy, writing it here in the emigration in exactly the same conditions as I would have written it in Russia. As one against all – even against my own heroes, who don't understand my language. In the double estrangement of that *cause perdue*, the Volunteer movement, and that *cause perdue*, the poem about it.

Any group sympathy, party sympathy, mercenary sympathy – is ruin. There is only one sympathy – the people's. But that comes later.

The time's command to me is my tribute to the time. If every creation – that is, every incarnation – is a tribute paid to the human essence, then this is a specially big tribute to the essence and, as such, a specially big sin before God. The only salvation for me and my works is that, in my case, the demand of the time has turned out to be the command of conscience, a thing of eternity. Of conscience concerning all those who were killed, in the purity of their hearts, and who have not been sung and are not going to be sung. And the supremacy, in my works, of the command of conscience over the demand of the time has its guarantee in the supremacy in them of love over hatred. Contrary to all counter-revolutionary Moscow and the emigration, I never hated the Reds as much as I loved the Whites. The badness of the time is, I think, partly redeemed by this love.

Those who in Soviet Russia are called, or modestly call themselves, 'fellow-travellers', are actually the leaders. Creators not only of language, but of the visions of their time.

Not even in Gogol's immortal Russia-troika do I see the poet as trace-horse.

Not 'fellow-travelling', but lonely co-creating. And the poet will best serve his time when he lets it speak, express itself, through him. The poet will best serve his time when he quite forgets about it (when it is quite forgotten). Contemporary is not what shouts the loudest, but sometimes what keeps the quietest.

Contemporality is not the whole of my time. The contemporary is what is indicative of the time, what it will be judged by: not its demand, but its display. Contemporality is in itself a selection. The genuinely contemporary is what is eternal in time, thus not only what is indicative of a given time, but what is timely for ever, contemporary with everything. Pushkin's poem 'To the Sea', for example, with the shades of Napoleon and Byron on the eternal background of the ocean.

Contemporality in art is the influence of the best upon the best – the converse of the topical:[17] influence of worst upon worst. Tomorrow's newspaper is *already* out of date. From which it is clear that the majority of those accused of being 'contemporary' do not deserve this accusation, for their only sin is temporariness, a concept as opposite to contemporariness as is extra-temporariness. Contemporality: omnitemporality. Which of us will turn out to be our contemporary? Something only the future will establish and only the past will have proved. A contemporary: always the minority.

Contemporality is not the whole of my time, but neither is the whole of contemporality one of its phenomena. The age of Goethe is simultaneously the age of Napoleon and the age of Beethoven. Contemporality is the aggregate of the best.

Even if we concede that communism, as an attempt at the best organisation of earthly life, is a good – is it alone in being a good, is it alone all goods, does it include in itself, define through itself, all other goods and powers: of art, science, religion, thought? Include, exclude or – on equal terms – coexist?

On behalf of all the other goods, I stand up for the latter. As one of the movers of contemporality, and precisely as an organiser of earthly life which had been getting more and more disorganised, it deserves an honoured place. But just as earthly organisation is no more all-important than spiritual, just as the science of communal life is no more all-important than a feat of solitude – so even communism, organiser of earthly life, is no more all-important than all the movers of the spiritual life, which is neither a superstructure nor an annexe. The earth is not everything, and even if it were everything, this organising of human communal living is not the whole earth. The earth is worth more and deserves more.

An honoured place – as to everything which knows its honour and its place.

I come to the question I find hardest of all: whether Rilke is indicative of our time, this man who is distant among the distant, lofty among the lofty, lonely among the lonely. If – and of this there can be no doubt – Mayakovsky is indicative of our time.

Rilke is neither a command to our time nor a display of it – he is its counterweight.

Wars, slaughters, churned-up flesh of dissension – and Rilke.

Because of Rilke the earth will be absolved of our time.

As its antithesis, necessity, antidote, Rilke could only have been born in our time.

In this lies his contemporality.

The time did not order him, but summoned him.

The command of the multitudes to Mayakovsky: 'Say *us*'; the command of the multitudes to Rilke: '*Tell* us'. Both commands were fulfilled. Nobody will call Mayakovsky a teacher of life, or Rilke an orator of the masses.

Rilke is as indispensable to our time as a priest on a battlefield: to pray, for the one side and for the other, for them and for us; for the illumination of the still living and the absolution of the fallen.

To be a contemporary is to create one's time, not to reflect it. Or, to reflect it, only not like a mirror but like a shield. To be a contemporary is to create one's time – that is, to do battle with nine-tenths of what's in it, as you do battle with nine-tenths of a first draft.

We remove the scum from the cabbage-soup – shan't we remove it from the boiling cauldron of time?

Gumilyov's

> I am polite to contemporary life
> but there's a barrier between us...

refers, of course, to those who with elbows and hooters prevented him from thinking, to the time's *noises*, not to those who, together with him, were creating the time's silence, of which Pasternak wrote so marvellously:

> Silence, you're the best
> of all I've ever heard.

To the time's favourites and day-labourers, not to his, Gumilyov's, contemporaries.

Now, having cleared my conscience of all omissions, having taken on myself the most difficult task: of establishing the fact of time; having acknowledged my dependence upon time, my boundness to it and boundedness by it, having acknowledged my dependence upon time as my tool of production, as my part-time – and how often private! – employer, I finally ask: Who is my time, that as well as all this I should willingly serve it? And altogether, what is time that it should be served?

My time will have passed tomorrow, as his passed yesterday, as yours will have passed the day after tomorrow, as every time always passes, until time itself will have passed.

A poet's service to the time – which does occur! – is a service that bypasses his will, it is the fated 'I cannot *but*'. It is my fault in God's sight – though a merit in the sight of the age!

A poet's marriage to his time is a forced marriage. A marriage of which – as of any suffered violence – he is ashamed, and from which he tries to tear loose. Poets of the past tear into the past, those of the present into the future, as if time were less time for not being my own! All Soviet poetry is a stake on the future. Solely Mayakovsky, this zealot of his own conscience, this convict of the present day, came to love this present day: overcame, that is, the poet in himself.

The poet's marriage to the time is a forced marriage, consequently an unreliable one. In the best case, *bonne mine à mauvais jeu*,[18] in the worst case, continual and actual, it's one infidelity after another with always the same lover – the One under a multiplicity of names.

However much you feed a wolf, it always looks to the forest. We are all wolves of the dense forest of Eternity.

'There is no marriage.' Yes, there *is* marriage: the same as the wedlock of a convict to his fetters. But when we have thrust upon us not only a marriage with time-in-general, with the concept of time, but also marriage with our own time, *this* time, marriage with some kind of sub-time, and, most important, when this violence is forced on us as a love, when this hard-labour is described as service according to our vocation, when we are fettered spiritually as well...

Violence endured is weakness. Spiritual legitimation of violence endured is a thing without name, of which no slave is capable.

To defend against time what is eternal in time, or to eternalise what is temporary in it – however it's put: to time, the age of this world, another age is counterposed.

Service to time as such is service to change – betrayal – death. You can't keep up with it, you can't oblige it. The present. Is there such a thing? Service to the recurring decimal figure. I think I am still serving the present, but I'm already serving the past and already – the future. Where is it, the *praesens*, and in what?

You may run with someone running, but once you realise that he is running *nowhere*, always running, running because he's running, running in order to run... That his running is an end in itself, or – still worse – a running away from himself: from himself as a wound, a rent into which everything flows away.

'Diese Strecke laufen wir zusammen'[19] ('Let's go together as far as the first turning') is at best a bad travelling-companion, leading us into all the taverns, involving us in all the brawls, deflecting us from even the most modest of our purposes, and, in the final analysis (which comes very, very soon!), abandoning us with an empty purse and head. If we haven't outstripped and abandoned him.

Service to one's time is a command of despair. To the atheist only the age's present moment exists, only this measure of weight, the converse and kindred face of 'seize the moment', for after this you're done for. The Kingdom of Earth from despair of the Kingdom of Heaven.

To the atheist there's nothing left but the earth and its organisation.

Progress? But up to what point? If till the very end of our planet – forward movement towards the pit?

Forward movement not towards an end that is attainment, but towards an end that is annulment. And if ever they teach the planet *not* to end, win the planet from non-being – then one generation of earthly gods after another generation of earthly gods? An end or an endlessness of earthly life, equally dreadful because equally empty.

Lermontov's 'If for a time, then it's not worth the trouble'[20] refers not to love, but to time itself: *time itself* is not worth the trouble.

> Death and time reign upon earth –
> Do not call them masters –
> Everything whirls and goes into the dark,
> Immutable – only the Sun of Love.[21]

## *Afterword*

After I'd set down the last full-stop – after 'of Love' – I read in the newspaper, that very evening: 'In Moscow one "discussion" has ended and another is beginning. The "attention of the writing public is now transferred to the poetry front".'

Aseev, friend and follower of Mayakovsky, gave a talk on poetry. Then a debate began which lasted three days. The sensation of the debate was an appearance by Pasternak. First, Pasternak said: 'There are some things that have not been destroyed by the Revolution'...then he added: 'Time exists for man, not man for time.'

Boris Pasternak over there, and I over here, across all the spaces and prohibitions, external and internal (Boris Pasternak is with the Revolution, I am with nobody), Pasternak and I, not consulting each other, are thinking of the same thing and saying the same thing.

This is – contemporality.

# EPIC AND LYRIC OF CONTEMPORARY RUSSIA

## VLADIMIR MAYAKOVSKY AND BORIS PASTERNAK

If, speaking of the contemporary poetry of Russia, I set these two names side by side, it is because side by side is where they stand. It is possible, speaking of the contemporary poetry of Russia, to mention one of them, either of them without the other, and all poetry would still be conveyed – as it would with any major poet. For poetry doesn't fragment either within poets or into poets; in all its manifestations it is one entire thing, all of it is in each, just as, in essence, there are not poets, there is the poet – one and the same from the beginning of the world to its end – a power which puts on the colours of particular times, tribes, countries, dialects, persons, passing like a river through those who carry it, between these or other banks, under these or other skies, over this or another ground. (Otherwise we would never understand Villon – whom we do, wholly, understand, despite certain words being, purely physically, incomprehensible. We just go back into him as into our native river.)

So, if I set Pasternak and Mayakovsky side by side – set them side by side, not present them together – it isn't because one of them is not enough, it isn't because the one requires the other, or completes the other – each, I repeat, is filled to the brim and Russia is filled with (and conveyed by) each to the brim, and not only Russia but poetry itself. I do it in order to display, twice, something we pray God grant once in fifty years, yet which nature has displayed, here, twice in but five years: the complete and whole miracle of a poet.

I set them side by side because they themselves – in the epoch, at the cornerstone of the epoch – stood side by side and will remain like that.

I hear a voice: 'The Contemporary Poetry of Russia.' 'Well, Pasternak perhaps, but what's this about Mayakovsky, who in 1928...'

First: whenever we speak of a poet, God grant we remember the *age*. Second, and in reverse: when we speak of a particular poet, Mayakovsky,

104

we have to remember not only the age, we've incessantly to *remember* an age in advance. This vacancy – for the world's first ever poet of the masses – won't be filled so very quickly. And to see Mayakovsky, we, and maybe our grandchildren too, shall have to turn round not backwards, but forwards.

When at some French literary gathering I hear every name except that of Proust, and in reply to my innocent surprise: 'Et Proust?' – 'Mais Proust est mort, nous parlons des vivants' – I feel every time that I'm dropping from the clouds: by what sign does one establish a writer's aliveness or deadness? Is X really alive, contemporary and active just because he is able to come to this gathering, while Marcel Proust – since he won't be going anywhere on his feet again – is dead? Only runners can be judged this way.

And an answer comes, so tranquil and genial:

Where shall I find
someone as fast on his feet as I?[1]

With those fast feet of his, Mayakovsky strode far beyond our present age; and somewhere beyond a turning, for a long time yet, he will be waiting for us.

*

Pasternak and Mayakovsky are coevals. Both are Muscovites, Mayakovsky by growth, Pasternak by birth as well. Both came to poetry from something else. Mayakovsky from painting, Pasternak from music. Into their own art both brought something else: Mayakovsky 'the avid rule-of-eye of the simple carpenter',[2] Pasternak – all the ineffable. Both came enriched. Both failed to find themselves straightaway, both found themselves conclusively in poetry. (A passing thought: better fail to find oneself straightaway in something other than one's own; to lose oneself in the alien and find oneself in the kindred. At least this way you can do without 'attempts'.)

For both, the *Irrjahre*[3] ended early. But Mayakovsky came to poetry from Revolution too, and who knows from what else. From revolutionary activity. At sixteen he'd already been in prison. 'That's no merit.' It's an indication, though. Not a merit of the poet, but an index of the human being. And for *this* poet it *is* a merit: he began by settling accounts.

The poetic temper of each was formed and expressed early. Mayakovsky began by showing himself to the world: with display and with thunderous speech. Pasternak – but who can say how Pasternak began? For so long no one knew a thing about him. (Victor Shklovsky, 1922, in a conversation: 'He has such a good reputation: subterranean.') Mayakovsky made his appearance, Pasternak stayed hidden. Mayakovsky revealed himself, Pasternak concealed himself. And if Pasternak now has a name, he could so easily not have had one: the fortuity of an hour and a place propitious to talents: *la carrière ouverte aux talents*, and even more than *ouverte* – *offerte*, if (many poets being maintained, but not mentioned) the talent-bearer is no heterodox.

But Mayakovsky would always have had a name – not always *would* have, but always *did* have. The name was there virtually before he was. He had to catch up with it. Here is what happened to Mayakovsky. The young man sensed a power in himself, what kind it was he didn't know, he opened his mouth and said: I! People inquired: I – who? He replied: I, Vladimir Mayakovsky. – And who is Vladimir Mayakovsky? – I am! – Nothing more for a while. But later came everything. It went on in the same way: 'Vladimir Mayakovsky is the one that is me.' People laughed, but the 'I' stayed in their ears, the yellow jacket stayed in their eyes. (Some, alas, to this day have seen and heard nothing else in him but that: nobody, however, has forgotten him.)

While Pasternak...The name was known, but it was the name of his father: the Yasnaya Polyana artist, the worker in pastels, the painter of women's and children's heads. As late as 1921 I would hear: 'Oh yes, Borya Pasternak, the artist's son, such a well-brought-up boy, very nice indeed. He used to call on us. So he's the one writing poems? I thought he was studying music...' Between his father's painting and his own youthful (very powerful) music, Pasternak was ground away into nothing, like the ravines between meeting mountains. How was the third, the poet, to gain a foothold? Yet Pasternak already had three stops behind him (starting with the last): 1917 – *My Sister Life* (published only in 1922); 1913 – *Over the Barriers*; and the first, the earliest, which even I who am writing this don't know the name of. So what can be expected of others? Till 1920 Pasternak was known only by those few who see the coursing of the blood and hear the growing of the grass. One could apply to him Rilke's words:

...die wollten blühn.
Wir wollen dunkel sein und uns bemühn.[4]

Pasternak did not want fame. Maybe he feared the evil eye: the ubiquitous, uninvolved, objectless eye of fame. Likewise, Russia should beware of foreign tourism.

But Mayakovsky feared nothing. He stood there and yelled, and the louder he yelled the more listeners he had, and the more listeners he had the louder he yelled – till he'd yelled his way to 'War and the World' and the multi-thousand auditorium of the Polytechnic Museum,[5] and then to the 150-million arena of all Russia. (We say a singer has sung himself out – Mayakovsky yelled himself out.)

Pasternak will never have an arena. He will have, has already, a multitude of the lonely, a lonely multitude of the thirsty whom he, a secluded spring, gives to drink. People go *after* Mayakovsky, but go *looking for* Pasternak, like looking for water in an unknown region, going somewhere for something – that's certain enough, but where? and what? – something real, that they grope for and guess at, each on his own patch, all of them separate, always scattered. You can meet by Pasternak, like meeting by a stream, then go off separately again, after each has drunk and each has washed, carrying the stream away in yourself and upon yourself. But on Mayakovsky, as on a public square, people either fight or sing in unison.

There are as many heads as there are Pasternak readers. There's only one Mayakovsky reader – Russia.

In Pasternak you don't forget yourself: you discover both yourself and Pasternak – a new seeing, a new hearing.

In Mayakovsky you forget both yourself and Mayakovsky.

Mayakovsky must be read by everyone at once, almost in a chorus (a clamour, a congregation), anyway aloud, and as loudly as possible, which is what happens to everyone who reads him. The whole hall at once. The whole age at once.

But Pasternak must be carried around with you wherever you go, as a talisman against those who keep yelling in chorus the same two (immutable) Mayakovsky-truths. Or still better – how poets have written and been read in all the ages – alone in a forest, unconcerned as to whether those are the leaves of the forest or the leaves of Pasternak's notebook.

I said: the world's first poet of the masses. I'll add: Russia's first poet-as-orator. From the tragedy *Vladimir Mayakovsky* to the last quatrain –

As they say, 'The incident is closed.'
Love's boat has broken on the daily grind.
Life and I are quits, no need to list
mutual pains, disasters and offences...[6]

– everywhere, over his whole extent, direct speech with a live aim. From grand versifier to market crier, Mayakovsky is tirelessly driving something into our brains, striving to obtain something from us – by all possible methods, including the crudest ones, which are invariably successful. Example of the latter:

And on Alexandra Fyodorovna's bed
Sprawls Alexander Fyodorovich.[7]

Something we'd all known, a consonance of names we had all of us noted, nothing unheard of, and yet – superb! And whatever we may think of Alexandra Fyodorovna and of Alexander Fyodorovich, and of Mayakovsky himself, each one of us feels satisfied by these lines as by a formula. He is the poet for whom everything always succeeds because it must. For in that region where Mayakovsky tirelessly strides, to make a mistake is to be destroyed. Mayakovsky's path is no literary path. Those who go along his paths prove this every day. Power is inimitable, Mayakovsky without power is nonsense. The commonplace raised to greatness: this is often Mayakovsky's formula. In this he resembles – other age, other speech – Victor Hugo, whom, let me remind you, he respected:

In every youth, Marinetti's gunpowder,
In every old man, Hugo's wisdom.[8]

Hugo, deliberately, rather than Goethe, with whom he had no kinship at all.

But to whom does Pasternak speak? Pasternak speaks to himself. One could even say, 'in his own presence', as if in the presence of a tree or a dog, someone who won't betray him. To read Pasternak – and everyone feels this – is to spy on him. We look, not into Pasternak's room (what's he doing?), but directly under his skin, under his ribs (what's happening in him?).

For all his (many years long now) effort to come out of himself, to address certain persons (or even all persons) in such and such a way and about such and such matters, Pasternak invariably speaks in the wrong way about the wrong matters and, above all, to nobody. For this is thinking aloud. Sometimes with us. Other times – he forgets – without us. Speaking in his sleep or his half-sleep. 'The murmuring of the sleepy parca...'[9]

*

(The reader's attempt to converse with Pasternak reminds me of dialogues in *Alice in Wonderland*, where every answer is either late or outstrips the question at a gallop, or else has nothing to do with it – a very accurate answer *if*, but here quite out of place. What explains the resemblance is that in *Alice* another kind of time is introduced, the time of sleep, a time from which Pasternak never emerges.)

\*

Neither Mayakovsky nor Pasternak really has a reader. Mayakovsky has a hearer, Pasternak – an overhearer, a spy, or even a sleuth.

And another thing: Mayakovsky doesn't need the reader's co-creation: he who has ears (even the simplest) – let him hear it, let him bear it.

Pasternak is only there through the reader's co-creation. It is not much easier to read Pasternak, maybe not easier at all, than it is for Pasternak to write himself.

Mayakovsky acts *upon* us, Pasternak – *within* us. Pasternak isn't read by us: he takes place in us.

\*

There is a formula for Pasternak and Mayakovsky. It is the two-in-one line by Tyutchev:

All is in me and I am in all.[10]

All in me is Pasternak. I in all is Mayakovsky. Poet and mountain. For Mayakovsky to be (for him to come true), there need to be mountains. Mayakovsky in solitary confinement is nothing. But Pasternak, for mountains to be, only needed to be born. Pasternak in solitary confinement is everything. Mayakovsky comes true as a mountain. The mountain comes true as Pasternak. Mayakovsky, when he felt he was, let's say, the Urals, *became* the Urals. There is no Mayakovsky. There are the Urals. Pasternak, when he took the Urals into himself, made the Urals – himself. There are no Urals. There is Pasternak. (In extension: no Urals but the Pasternakian Urals, which is how it is: I refer to all readers of *The Childhood of Lyuvers* and the Urals poems.)

Pasternak is a taking in, Mayakovsky is a giving out. Mayakovsky is transmutation of himself in the object, dissolution of himself in the object. Pasternak is transmutation of the object into himself, dissolution of the object in himself – including the most insoluble objects, such as Ural mountain rocks. All the mountain rocks of the Urals have been dissolved in his lyric stream, which is so heavy and cumbersome only because it's, no, not lava even, for lava is a solution of the homogeneously earthly, but a saturated (with the world) solution.

Mayakovsky is characterless, he has become the thing depicted. Mayakovsky, as a noun, is collective. Mayakovsky is the graveyard of 'War and the World', the fatherland of 'October', the column of Vendôme which planned to marry the Place de la Concorde,[11] the cast-iron Ponyatovsky threatening Russia, and someone threatening him from the living pedestal of the crowds (Mayakovsky himself), he's the shout 'Bread!' as it marches on Versailles. He is the last Crimea, he is that last Wrangel...[12] There is no Mayakovsky. There is – epos.

Pasternak will remain in the form of an adjective: Pasternakian rain, the Pasternakian tide, a Pasternakian hazel-grove, Pasternakian – and so on and so forth.

Mayakovsky – in the form of a collective noun: an abbreviative noun.

*

In the life of days, Mayakovsky is one man standing for all (on behalf of all). On the tenth anniversary of the October Revolution, he writes:

Falsely modest – not hiding my joy,
with the conquerors of hunger and darkness I yell:
It's me!
It's us![13]

(There was no false modesty in him, but – read into him! – what real, deep modesty! For the first time a poet is proud of the fact that he's in it *too*, that he's everyone!)

Pasternak: one of all, amongst all, without all:

All my life I wanted to be like all,
but the world in its beauty
wouldn't listen to my whining
and wanted to be – like me![14]

Pasternak is the impossibility of merging.

Mayakovsky is the impossibility of not merging. In enmity he merges more with his enemy than, in love, Pasternak does with his beloved. (I know, of course, that Mayakovsky was lonely too, but his loneliness was only by way of his exceptional power: not the uniqueness of personality, but the personal unity of power.) Mayakovsky is thoroughly human. In his work even mountains speak in human language (as in fairy tales, as in every epic). In Pasternak's the human speaks in mountain language (in that same Pasternakian torrent). There is nothing more touching than when Pasternak tries to imitate a human being, that honesty taken to the point of servility that we find in certain parts of *Lieutenant Schmidt*. He so little knows what it's like for people (what this thing or that thing is like for them) that, like the worst pupil at an exam, he copies everything from his neighbour, right down to slips of the pen. What an eerie contrast: the living Pasternak with his speech, and the speech of his would-be objective hero.

Everything has been given to Pasternak except the other, living human being, the other in all his multiple forms, from just any other to one particular other. For in Pasternak the other is not alive, but is a kind of compendium of proverbs and commonplaces – as when a German wants to boast of knowing Russian. In Pasternak the ordinary person is the most extraordinary. Living mountains, the living sea, are given to Pasternak (and what a sea! an equal of Pushkin's, the first sea in Russian literature since that sea of the 'free element') – why make a list? Everything living is given to him! –

Here even snow is fragrant
and the stone breathes underfoot...

– everything but the living human being, who is either that German or else Boris Pasternak himself, that is to say something individual, not like anything else, thus – life itself, not a living person. (My Sister Life: this is how people *don't* address life.)

In his brilliant story[15] about a fourteen-year-old girl, everything is given but the particular girl, the complete girl: all the Pasternakian knowing (and bestowing) of all that is the soul. All girlhood and fourteen-year-oldness are given, all the girl is given piecemeal (in fractions, one would like to say), all the component elements of a girl are given; yet the given girl, the particular girl, still does not come into being...Who is she? What is she like? No one can say. Because the girl that is given is no particular girl, but is a girl given through Boris Pasternak: it's Boris Pasternak if he'd been a girl, that's to say Pasternak himself, the whole Pasternak, which a fourteen-year-old girl cannot be. (Pasternak does not let *people* come into being through him. In this he is the opposite of a medium or a magnet – if medium and magnet can have an opposite.) What remains for us from this story? Pasternak's eyes.

And more: those eyes of Pasternak remain not only in our consciousness, they remain physically on everything he has ever looked at – as a sign, a mark, a *patent* – so that we can say with exactitude whether any leaf is a Pasternakian one, or merely a leaf. He absorbs it (the leaf) with his eye and returns it with an eye (an eyelet). (I can't resist the following 'reminiscence' – no Russian word for it: the charming, well-known pastel by Pasternak (the father), *Little Eye*. An enormous mug, and above it, covering and concealing the whole face of the drinker, an enormous childish eye: an eyelet...Perhaps Boris Pasternak himself – in his infancy; certainly Boris Pasternak – in eternity. If the father had known who, and, especially, *what*, was drinking like that.)

As I once said quite differently – lyrically, allegorically – about Akhmatova:

And all the icons look with *your* eyes![16]

so I now say, wholly positively and objectively, about Pasternak:

And all the trees look with *your* eyes!

Every lyricist absorbs, but most do so outside the sieve and delay of the eye, directly from the external into the soul, dipping the object into a common-lyrical liquid and giving it back dyed with this common-lyrical soul. But Pasternak *filters* the world through his eye. Pasternak is selection. His eye is a wringer. Past the retina of Pasternak's eye all nature flows, pours in floods. Sometimes even a human fragment slips through (always unforgettable!), but as yet no one complete human being ever penetrated beyond it. Pasternak unfailingly dissolves him too. Not a human being – a human solution.

Poetry! be a Greek sponge with suckers
and amongst the sticky greenery
I'd place you on the wet board
of a green garden bench.
Grow luxuriant frills and farthingales,
absorb clouds and ravines,
and at night, poetry, I'll squeeze you out
to the health of the thirsting paper.[17]

I'll remind you that Pasternak's sponge is highly colouring. Anything it absorbs will never be the same, and we who began by claiming that there never was any such rain as in Pasternak, end with the claim that there never was and never could be any other downpour than the Pasternakian downpour. It's that case in Wilde[18] where art (or the eye) has an influence on nature, that is, above all, on the nature of our eye.

\*

The live human being in Pasternak's work is, as we've said, either a phantom or Pasternak himself – always a substitute. Mayakovsky is just as incapable of conveying the live human being, but not for the same reason. If Pasternak fragments, dissolves, uncreates, Mayakovsky extends, to-the-end-creates – extends him – upwards and downwards and outwards (only, not depthwards!), places beneath him the pedestal of his love or the scaffold of his hatred, so we get, for example, not the loved Lilya Brik, but Lilya Brik elevated to the nth degree of Mayakovsky's love: of all a human being's, a man's, a poet's, love; Lilya Brik the Cathedral of Notre-Dame de Paris. That is, love itself, the great bulk of Mayakovskian love and all love. Or if the subject is a 'White guardsman' (an enemy), Mayakovsky invests him with such expressive attributes that we shan't recall a single live Volunteer of our acquaintance. It will be the White Army in the eyes of the Red Army: a living epic of hatred – a perfect freak (a fiend), not a live (imperfect, meaning with virtues as well) human being. A general will be a monstrously overgrown epaulette and sidewhisker; a bourgeois – a belly strutting towards us, not flesh but a whole promontory; a husband (in the poem 'Love') – Mayakovsky's hatred, which he cannot justify even if a hundred 'husbands' are added together in all their insignificance. No such husband exists. But such hatred does. Mayakovsky's feelings are no hyperbole. But his live human being is a hyperbole. For love – a cathedral. For hatred – a hoarding, namely, the epos of our day: the poster.

\*

In hatred the rule-of-eye of the masses, in love the rule-of-eye of Mayakovsky's *whole mass*. Not only he, his heroes, too, are epic; that is, nameless...Here he's again akin to Hugo who, in the endless and densely populated spaces of *Les Misérables*, did not convey a single living person as such, but Duty (Javert), Goodness (Monseigneur), Misfortune (Valjean), Motherhood (Fantine), Maidenhood (Cosette), and so on and so forth, and conveyed so much more than 'the living person': the living powers that move the world. For – I insist on this with all my weight –

every force, even the purely physical, is conveyed by Mayakovsky, even in his liveliest hatred, as a living force. He distorts only when he despises, when he confronts weakness (albeit of an entire victorious class) instead of power (albeit overpowered). The one thing Mayakovsky does not forgive is, in the final analysis, lack of might. To every might his might accords its due. Remember the lines to Ponyatovsky,[19] and, not far away, the brilliant lines about the last of Wrangel – Wrangel who rises and remains as a last vision of the Volunteer Army over the last of the Crimea, Wrangel whom only Mayakovsky has conveyed in the full height of his human misfortune, Wrangel the height of tragedy.

Facing a *force*, Mayakovsky finds an accurate eye; more accurately, his inordinate eye finds itself here in place: the norm. Pasternak goes wrong as to the human being's make-up; Mayakovsky – as to his size.

\*

When I say 'herald of the masses', I imagine either a time when everyone had the height, stride and power of Mayakovsky, or a time when everyone will have. For the moment, at least in the realm of sentiments, he is, of course, Gulliver among the Lilliputians, who are *exactly the same only very small*. This is what Pasternak speaks of when he greets the prostrate Mayakovsky:

Your shot was like Etna
among the foothills of cowards and cowardesses.[20]

\*

Another reason the 'living human being' does not look like one in both Pasternak and Mayakovsky is that both are poets – the living human being plus something and minus something.

\*

The effect of Pasternak and the effect of Mayakovsky. Mayakovsky sobers us; that is, he wrenches our eyes open as wide as possible, sticking the milepost of his forefinger into the object – and maybe into our eye as well: *Look!* – and makes us see something which was always there and which we didn't see only because we were asleep or unwilling.

Pasternak does not merely print himself on everything by means of his eye, he inserts this eye into us as well.

Mayakovsky sobers, Pasternak spellbinds.

Reading Mayakovsky, we remember everything except Mayakovsky.

Reading Pasternak, we forget everything except Pasternak.

Mayakovsky will remain in the whole external world, cosmically. Impersonally (mergingly). Pasternak remains in us, like an inoculation that has altered our blood.

The wielding of the masses, or even the *massifs* ('les grandes machines' – Mayakovsky himself being the 'Giant' factory). A manifesting through details – Pasternak.[†] Mayakovsky has details too, he is altogether based on them, but each one is the size of a grand piano. Sometimes the physics of Mayakovsky's poems reminds me of the face of Sunday in 'The Man who was Thursday'[22] – too large to be thought. Mayakovsky is wholesale, Pasternak is retail.

Cryptography – Pasternak. Phenography, almost a lesson in orthography[23] – Mayakovsky. 'Don't buy black and white, don't say "yes" and "no" ' – Pasternak. 'Black, white. Yes, no' – Mayakovsky.

Saying it indirectly – Pasternak.[‡] Saying it directly – and, what's more, if you don't follow he'll say it again and again till you drop, till he gets there (he's never exhausted!) – Mayakovsky.

Cipher (Pasternak). Neon signs, or, better, a searchlight, better still a lighthouse [*mayak*].

There's no one who can't understand Mayakovsky. Is there anyone who completely understands Pasternak? (If there is such a person, it *isn't* Boris Pasternak.)

Mayakovsky is all self-awareness, even when he is giving out his strength:

All my resonant, poet's strength
I give up to you, the attacking class!

---

† 'The all-powerful God of love/the all-powerful God of details/Jagiellos and Hedwigas.'[21]

‡ To take an example at random, 'Death of the Poet': 'But there lay on the faces a damp dislocation/As in the folds of a torn dragnet.'[24] A damp tearful dislocation, dislocating the whole face. The dragnet is torn, the water comes through. Tears.

– with the stress on '*All*'. He knows what it is he is giving!

Pasternak is all self-doubt, self-forgetting.

The Homeric humour of Mayakovsky.

The exclusion of humour in Pasternak – at most the beginning of a shy (complex) smile which immediately comes to an end.

Reading a lot of Pasternak is unbearable because of the tension (of brain and eye); like looking through exceedingly powerful lenses, not adapted to your eye (whose eye is he adapted to?).

Reading a lot of Mayakovsky is unbearable because of the sheer physical expenditure. After Mayakovsky you need to eat a lot and for a long time. Or to sleep. Or – stauncher folk – to walk. To catch him up, or – the stauncher folk – to pace it out with him. And here, involuntarily, comes the vision of Peter,[25] as seen by the eighteen-year-old Pasternak:

> How great he was! How a net of convulsions
> covered the cheeks of iron
> when there welled up to Peter's eyes,
> making them water, sedge-grown bays,
> and waves of the Baltic rose to his throat
> like lumps of yearning...

*

This is how Mayakovsky today sees the construction of Russia.

*

With Mayakovsky we always know what it's about, what for, and why. He himself is the account. With Pasternak we can never find our way through to the theme; it's as if we keep catching at a sort of tail disappearing beyond the left edge of the brain, like trying to recall a dream and make sense of it.

Mayakovsky is a poet with a theme.

Pasternak is a poet without a theme. The *theme* is: poet.

The effect of Pasternak is equal to the effect of a dream. We don't understand it. We find ourselves standing in it. We fall and stand under it. We fall – into it. When we understand Pasternak, we understand to one side of him, to one side of the meaning (which does exist and which he struggles to clarify to us); we understand through the intonation, which is invariably precise and clear. We understand Pasternak as animals understand us. We cannot speak Pasternak's language any more than Pasternak can speak ours, but both languages exist and both are intelligible and meaningful, they're only at different stages of development. Uncoupled. The bridge is intonation. Moreover, the more Pasternak seeks to develop and clarify his thought, the more he piles up subordinate clauses (his sentence-formation is always correct and recalls German philosophical and literary prose at the beginning of last century) – the more he obscures the meaning. There is an obscurity of compression, and there is an obscurity of diffusion, but here – I've some of his prose passages in mind – there is the double obscurity of poetic compression and philosophical diffusion. In diffuse prose, such as that of a lecture, there needs to be some water (a shallowing of the inspiration); that is to say, the diffusion must be through repetition, not elucidation: of one image by another, of one thought by another.

Take Mayakovsky's prose: that same contracted muscle of verse, as much the prose of his verse as Pasternak's prose is the prose of Pasternak's verse. Flesh of the flesh and bone of the bone. What is said of Mayakovsky is what I've said about myself:

I take aim – at the word![26]

And with the word I take aim at the object, with the object I take aim at the reader. (We've all been killed by Mayakovsky – if not resurrected!)

An important feature: the whole of Mayakovsky-the-poet is translatable into prose – retellable, that is, in his own words, not just by himself but by anyone. Even the vocabulary doesn't need changing, for Mayakovsky's vocabulary is wholly colloquial, everyday, prosaic (like that of *Onegin*, which its older contemporaries described as 'base'). What's lost is only the power of the poetic speech; the Mayakovskian spacing; the rhythm.

But to translate Pasternak into prose is to get Pasternak's prose, a region far more obscure than his verse: thus the obscurity inherent in the verse itself, and which we legitimise in the verse for this reason, now turns out to be the obscurity of the essence, with no verse to explain or illumine it. For we should not forget: lyric poetry clarifies the obscure, and conceals the obvious. Every poem is an utterance of the Sibyl – infinitely more than was said by the tongue.

Mayakovsky is wholly coherent, while Pasternak's logic is the actual but untraceable interconnection of events in a dream – irrefutable in the dream, but only in the dream. In a dream (reading Pasternak) everything is as it should be, you recognise everything; but just try to give an account of this dream – that is, to convey Pasternak in your own words – and what is left? Pasternak's world is sustained by his magic word alone. 'And through the magic crystal'[27] ...Pasternak's magic crystal is the crystalline lens of his eye.

Let anyone try a retelling of Mayakovsky and I can say in advance that he'll succeed – a good half of Mayakovsky will remain. But only Pasternak can retell Pasternak. Which is what he does in his brilliant prose, which straightaway casts us into dream and dream-vision.

Pasternak is magic.

Mayakovsky is the real, the broadest of daylight.

*

But the fundamental cause of our initial non-understanding of Pasternak lies in ourselves. We humanise nature too much, and so at first, before we've fallen asleep, we can recognise nothing in Pasternak. Between the thing and ourselves is our (or, more accurately, other people's) idea of the thing, our habit which clouds it, our – which means others', which means bad – experience of the thing, all the commonplaces of literature and experience. Between us and the thing is our blindness, our faulty, corrupted eye.

Between Pasternak and the thing there is nothing, which is why his rain is too *close*; it beats at us more than the rain from a cloud which we're used to. We weren't expecting rain from the page – we were expecting a poem *about* rain. Therefore we say: 'This isn't rain!' and 'This isn't a poem!' The rain drums straight onto us:

On the leaves – hundreds of cuff-links,
and the garden dazzles like a sheet of water,
sprinkled, spotted
with a million blue tears.[28]

Nature has revealed itself through the most defenceless, most lunatic, medium-like being: Pasternak.

\*

Pasternak is inexhaustible. In his hand, everything, including his hand, goes from his hand into infinity – and we go with it, after it. Pasternak is solely an *invitation au voyage* of self-discovery and world-discovery, solely a point of departure: a place from which. Our unmooring. Just enough space for weighing anchor. At Pasternak we don't slow down: we linger over Pasternak. Above a line by Pasternak is a very thick and triple aura – of Pasternak's, the reader's, and the thing itself's possibilities. Pasternak comes true above the line. You read Pasternak above the line – a parallel and perpendicular reading. You don't so much read as look (think, walk) *away from*. Something leads you on. Something leads beyond. You might say that the reader himself writes Pasternak.

Pasternak is inexhaustible.

Mayakovsky – exhausts. What is inexhaustible is only that power with which he exhausts the object. A power ready, like the earth, to take on everything afresh each time, and each time once for always.

Beyond the threshold of Mayakovsky's poems is nothing: only action. The only way out from his poems is the way out into action. His poems push us out of poems, like broad daylight pushing us out of our bed of sleep. He is precisely that broad daylight which can't bear anything hidden – 'Die Sonne bringt es an den Tag!'[29] Look at his shadows – aren't they the limited, knife-sharp shadows of noon, which you can't help treading on? Pasternak: the inexhaustibility (non-delimitation) of night.

Above Mayakovsky's lines is nothing; the object is *wholly* there in the line, he is wholly in his line, as a nail goes wholly into a board – and we, too, are directly involved, with a hammer in our hands.

From Pasternak we start thinking.

From Mayakovsky we start doing something.

After Mayakovsky there's nothing to be said.

After Pasternak there's everything.

\*

And, in some terminal final analysis:

'The fighting hindered me from being a poet' – Pasternak.

'Singing hindered me from being a fighter' – Mayakovsky.

For Pasternak's mainstay is the poet.

For Mayakovsky's mainstay is the fighter.

A singer in the camp of Russian warriors – Pasternak in contemporary Russia.

A fighter in the camp of the world's singers – Mayakovsky in contemporary poetry.

And – who knows how far Pasternak might not have gone, to what depth he might not have dug down, were it not for this involuntary mediumistic attraction to the communal cause: to Russia's, the century's, history's present hour. I give all that's due to *The Year 1905*, to Pasternak's genius in *The Year 1905*'s image; but I have to say that Schmidt would still have been Schmidt without Pasternak, Pasternak would still have been Pasternak without Schmidt – and with something other than Schmidt, with something that has no name, he'd have gone further.

If in Russia now the hour is favourable for a poetic career – for a poet's external travel and arrival – for a poet's lonely path it is unfavourable. Events feed, but they also impede, and, in the case of a lyric poet, they impede more than they feed. Events feed only someone who is empty (unfilled, drained, temporarily vacant); someone who is overfilled they will impede. Events feed Mayakovsky, who was filled with but one thing – his powers. Only a fighter is fed by events. A poet has his own events, the own self-event of the poet. In Pasternak this is, perhaps, not broken, but deflected, eclipsed, diverted. Like the diverting of rivers. The altering of riverbeds.

Pasternak, in the nobility of his essence, has himself abolished his rapids – as far as he could. Pasternak, with entirely good conscience, is trying not to flow into the Caspian sea.[30]

Maybe, maybe. But it's a pity about Neyasyt.[31] And that *other* Volga.

*

'Singing hindered me from being a fighter' – Mayakovsky. Yes, for there is a battle more immediate than the battle fought in language – in the flesh! – more active than the one in language – one in deeds, the common cause, the fighting in the ranks. Mayakovsky, though, was never a soldier in the ranks. His gift detached him from all his co-fighters – his comrades – discharged him from every cause but the cause of speech. Mayakovsky, that most straightforward of fighters, had to fight allegorically; that most battling of battlers had to battle roundaboutly. And no matter how much Mayakovsky declares, 'I'm everyone! I'm us!' – he's still, nonetheless, a solitary companion, an unequal equal, the leader of a gang that doesn't exist or whose real leader is somebody else. Here is a poem by a working-man:

I think of you and sing to you
my song that's like resounding steel.
The song rises up to you! to you
and not to anyone else.
You knew no weakness in yourself,
were firm. And therefore
all this youth of mine
I give up to you. We have no man better than you,
and never had in all time.
Spring. And summer's not far off.
The waters seethed, shuddering to the bottom.
The world's streets breathe deeply.
Years passed and years,
but no one ever lived
who loved us so much
as you.
And now you're gone.
But still I stand before you.
You're alive – and will be – so long as the earth
remains. With powerful peal from Kremlin towers
rhythms of the Paris Commune fall.
All hearts in the world that are persecuted
have stretched shared strings in your chest.
On the old stones of Red Square,
one to one with the spring whirlwind,
triumphant and powerful,
a son of the outlying streets
sings you.[32]

These lines are not to Mayakovsky. They are to the man[33] who, hearing of Mayakovsky's national fame, sent for his collected works, read two pages and put the book aside for ever, with the words: 'Pushkin wrote better, whatever they say.'

And I'll assert that, without Mayakovsky, the Russian revolution would have lost a lot, as Mayakovsky would – without the Revolution.

While Pasternak would have gone on growing and growing...

*

If we have but one way out from Mayakovsky's poems – into action, Mayakovsky had but one way out from all his activeness – into poems. Hence their stunning *physicality*, their sometimes overwhelming muscularity, their physical striking-power. The fighter had to cram himself whole into the lines. Hence too the ruptured metres. The poem split all over from Mayakovsky; it burst at the seams and between the seams. And the reader, who at first, in his naive conceit, thought Mayakovsky was acting a part[34] for him (and he *was* a part, was coming apart, like ice at the spring thaw!), soon had to see that these tearings and barings of Mayakovsky were no toy rattle for him, the reader, but a simple matter of staying alive – of having air to breathe. Mayakovsky's rhythms are the physical heartbeat – heart blows – of a horse that has stood still for too long or a man who has been tied up. (One could say of him, in the marvellous market speech of the owner of a troupe of dwarfs envying the next stall: 'What's that to look at? Just an ordinary giant!') No oppression is greater than a power suppressed. And Mayakovsky, even in his seeming freedom, is tied hand and foot. I'm talking of his poems, not of anything else.

Though Mayakovsky's poems were a *deed*, Mayakovsky's deed was not the writing of poems.

There are born poets – Pasternak.

There are born fighters – Mayakovsky.

And for a born fighter – especially fighting for *such* an idea – any path is more favourable than that of a poet.

One more indispensable juxtaposition. Mayakovsky for all his dynamism, is static; he is that uninterrupted, undifferentiated, uttermost mobility which makes for immobility. The motionless column of a top. The top moves only when it is stopping.

But Pasternak is the dynamics of two elbows thrust into a desk and supporting the brow – of a thinker.

Motionlessness of the sea – at the height of a storm.

Dynamics of the sky, with clouds moving across.

In Mayakovsky the static comes from the statuesque. Even that fast-footed runner that he is, is marble. Mayakovsky is Rome. Rome of rhetoric, Rome of action. 'Carthage must be destroyed!' (To swear at him, just say: 'Statue!')[35] Mayakovsky is a live monument. A living gladiator. Closely peer at the bumps of his forehead, peer into the sockets of his eyes, peer at his cheekbones, peer at his jaws. A Russian? No. A worker. In this face proletarians of all lands have not just united, they have been unified, knocked together to make this very face. This face is as much a collective noun as this name. A nameless name. A faceless face. As some faces bear the imprint of international speculation, this face is the very imprint of the Proletariate; with this face the Proletariate could print its money and its stamps.

So much was Mayakovsky at home among the workers of the world, so much was he them, that he could cheerfully puff English tobacco smoke at them out of an English pipe, or gleam at them with the black lacquer of Parisian shoes and his own Parisian car – to them it's sheer pleasure: 'One of *us* has done well' – and address the workers as '*ty*'. (All Pasternak is a tense '*vy*', he used '*ty*' only for Goethe, Rilke and others like them: the '*ty*' of a brother, a fellow-disciple, one of the elect. Mayakovsky's is the common '*ty*' of a comrade.)[36] So much is Mayakovsky at home in communism that despite all his blaming of Esenin and all his mandates to Marusya, the Komsomol girl who took poison for lack of lacquered shoes (because of this her sweetheart had left her!) –

Bear in mind every day that you're a builder
of new loves, new relationships –
and the little love-story of some little Lyuba
and Vova will one day look like nonsense[37]

– he could kill himself for a private love's privations as simply as plunging into a game of cards. One's own kind is permitted everything, an outsider – nothing. At home with one's own kind. Only, those workers are live; this one is stone.

I fear that notwithstanding the national funeral, notwithstanding all the honour paid him and all the laments of Moscow and Russia, Russia to this day hasn't fully understood who was given her in the person of Mayakovsky. Mayakovsky has only one equal in Russia. (I'm not saying: in the world; I'm not saying: in work with words; I'm saying: in Russia.) If that other was 'bread', this one was 'circuses', that is to say the soul's first step away from bread, the first new Russian soul. Mayakovsky is the first new man of a new world, the *first of those to come*. Whosoever has not grasped this, has grasped nothing about him. That is why, listening to a recitation of that worker's poem – 'Spring', the one I quoted above – in which everything pointed to one man: him, the one who had gone, I said straightaway: it's either to Mayakovsky, or.

The Proletariate has only two faces to print. Two faces it must print.

*

Even his well-known limitedness is that of a statue. A statue can only alter its posture: threat, defence, fear, and so on. (The whole ancient world is one statue in various postures.) Modify the posture, but not change the material, which is limited, once for always, which once for always limits the possibilities. The whole statue is contained in itself. It will not come out of itself. That's what makes it a statue. That's why it is a statue. 'In der Beschränkung zeigt sich erst der Meister.'[38] Maybe in this sense Mayakovsky is more *Meister* and *Meisterwerk* than Pasternak, whom it's as absurd to look for in the limited world of craftsmanship as it is to look for Rilke there, and whom it's as natural to find, as it is to find Rilke, in the unlimited world of miracle, which nothing delimits from us.

Laocoon[39] will never climb out of his skin,[40] but is constantly going all out to get out, but he will never get out, and so on *ad infinitum*. The getting out is what he's about: the statics of dynamics. There is a law for him as there is for the sea, and a boundary. This very same fighter's immobility – we see in Mayakovsky.

Now I beg your extreme attention. Out of Mayakovsky only the fighter, only the metre, was trying to climb out. As out of his eye-sockets – the rule-of-eye. Give him a body and a cause a thousand times bigger than those that were set for him, the body and cause that belong to his strength, then all Mayakovsky will fit in himself most excellently, for he'll contain himself in the continuity of living movement and won't be a statue. A statue he became. His tragedy, indeed, is a question of quantity, not one of quality (multiquality). In this he is, once again, alone among poets; for what he was going all out to get out of was words, a skin which had fatally become his own and which he tore at every point. He was going all out to get out into the world of action, whereas what all poets do is go all out to get out of the world of action. All poets: from the physical into the psychical. Mayakovsky: from the psychical into the physical – from our point of view – since, for Mayakovsky, unlike all poets, *word* was body and *deed* was soul. For the lyric poet *even* poetry is too tight; for Mayakovsky it is *precisely* poetry that's too tight. Mayakovsky at a writing-desk is a physical incongruity. It's easier to see him at the *grandes machines* of decorative painting, where – at least – the arm has room to swing up, the foot has room to step back, the eye has something to take in. The painter in him too was going all out, was bursting out of the skin of poetry. The moment Mayakovsky first leaned his elbow on a table was the moment he began to be a statue. (Turned to stone from the elbow *up*.) In that second, Russia gained the most vital, most combative, most *irresistible* of her poets; in that second, whatever fighting ranks there are – the front rank of battle, all front ranks of all the world's battles – lost their best, most combative, most irresistible fighter.

Epic gained, myth lost.

Mayakovsky's suicide, which in another semantic context[41] I present as the poet murdering the citizen, is, in the present context, the fighter taking revenge on the poet. Mayakovsky's suicide was the first blow struck on his live body, that body was the first live stop to the blow, and all this together was his first deed. Mayakovsky slew himself like an enemy.

If, in a lyrical Pasternakian context, Mayakovsky is epos, in the epoch's epical context of action he is lyricism. If among poets he is a hero, among heroes he is a poet. If Mayakovsky's work is epos, then it is only because he, who was meant to be an epic hero, did not become it but took up the whole of the hero into the poet. Poetry gained, but the hero suffered.

An epic hero become an epic poet: this is the strength and the weakness of both the life and the death of Mayakovsky.

Pasternak's case is simpler, this time Pasternak the Obscure can be read from the page. Pasternak, like every lyric poet, feels restricted everywhere but within; he feels restricted in the whole world of action, especially in that very locus of world action – present-day Russia.

Don't I know that, butting at shadows,
the dark would never have come to light,
and I'm a freak and hundreds of thousands'
happiness isn't closer to me
than a hundred's empty happiness?

Don't I measure myself by that,
fall and rise with the five-year plan?
But what shall I do with my rib-cage, what
with the thing more inert than all inertia?

In vain, in the days of the great council
where highest passion is allotted places,
is the poet's vacancy left unfilled:
it's dangerous, when it isn't empty.[42]

Pasternak, who, like every poet and like every great man, doesn't think about happiness, is obliged to lower himself to a numerical comparison between the happiness of a hundred and of hundreds of thousands; to the very concept of *happiness as a value*. He has to handle two magnitudes unknown to him or known to be suspect: happiness and numerical quantity.

Pasternak, who so recently thrust his head through the window and called to the children:

What millennium is it,
my dears, out there?

is obliged – of his own complete goodwill, for which no one is grateful to him (some are vexed, some are sorry, some are moved, all are uneasy) – to measure himself by the five-year plan.

Pasternak, in the contemporary age, is just one large perplexed suffering eye (that very same eye as above the mug, the same eye as through the window, the eye looking directly out of the rib-cage) which he doesn't know what to do with, because, so it seems to him, nobody now needs what is visible and essential in *it*. Pasternak is clambering out of his own eyesockets in order to see what everyone sees and grow blind to everything that isn't *it*. The eye of a seer of mysteries strives to become the eye of an eye-witness. How I should like, on behalf of the world, eternity, the future, on behalf of every tiny leaf he ever looked at like that, to persuade Pasternak in the quiet words of his beloved Lenau ('Bitte'):

Weil auf mir du dunkles Auge,
Uebe Deine ganze Macht.[43]

\*

We come now to the sole measure of things and people at the present hour of the century: their attitude to Russia.

Here Pasternak and Mayakovsky are like-minded. Both are for the new world, and both...but I see that the first 'both' will be the last, as, although Pasternak is manifestly for the new world, he is nothing like so manifestly against the old, which, however much he may condemn the political and economic system of the past, remains for him – above all and after all – his vast spiritual homeland. 'Who isn't with us, is against us.' For Pasternak, 'we' is not limited to the 'attacking class'. His 'we' is all those isolated persons of all the ages who, separately and knowing nothing of one another, are doing one and the same thing. Creation is shared work done by isolated people. I've no doubt that Boris Pasternak would put his name to this. Pasternak is no fighter (*kein Umstürzler!*).[44] Pasternak is a dreamer and a visionary. In his revolutionariness he doesn't differ from all the great lyric poets, all of whom, including the royalist de Vigny and the executed Chénier, stood for liberty: the liberty of others (poets have their own); equality – of opportunity; and fraternity – with which every poet, despite his isolation, or perhaps thanks to his isolation, is filled to the very brim of his heart. His 'left' tendency is no different from that of everyone whose heart is where it should be – on the left.

Here is Pasternak's own confession, a recent confession, after fifteen years of Revolution:

And since from early childhood years
I've been wounded by woman's fate,
And the poet's track is only the track
Of her paths and nothing more,
And since I'm grazed only by her,
And in our land she's given space,
I'm wholly glad to come to naught
In the revolutionary will –[45]

which is just what de Vigny said a hundred years ago: 'Après avoir réfléchi sur la destinée des femmes dans tous les temps et chez toutes les nations, j'ai fini par penser que tout homme devrait dire á chaque femme, au lieu de Bonjour – Pardon!'[46]

And once again from the particular to the general, a roundabout way – a sheer poet's way! – through the detail and the circuitous path of a girl deceived for centuries – through Gretchen, that is! – to reach the Revolution. Like coming to a forest through a leaf. And it is telling that the self-aware, militant, strong-willed Mayakovsky with that so self-aware gift of his –

All my resonant, poet's strength
I give up to you, the attacking class!

– completely dissolves in this choice he makes, with all his will and personality. While Pasternak's confession:

I'm wholly glad to come to naught
In the revolutionary will –

is read by us, in defiance of Pasternak's certainty and the alphabet's
clarity:

I would be glad to come to naught...

That is, in our consciousness, Pasternak, despite *Lieutenant Schmidt* and
everything like it he is yet to write, does not dissolve in this revolutionary
will, nor indeed in any human will; for not only does he not merge into,
he hasn't even met up with, any will at all but the world's – the whole
world's will, acting directly through him. Each is under a power, but each
is under a different power. Someone knows for Pasternak, someone
bigger than he and different from us.

Mayakovsky is led by the masses (I'd like to put it in French) by the
genius of the masses, which is why he leads them. By the masses of the
future, which is why he leads the masses of the present. And to avoid
ambiguity in interpreting this: Mayakovsky is led by history.

Mayakovsky: a leader – and led. Pasternak – only led.

\*

Likemindedness is no measure for comparing two poets. Mayakovsky's
like-minded are, if not all Russia, yet all Russian youth. Every komsomol
member thinks more like Mayakovsky, and in every case more obviously
like him, than does Pasternak. Only once do these two come together
(think alike): in the *themes* of their narrative poems, *October* and *The Year
1905*. One wrote 'October', the other 'December' but *what* an October[47]
and *what* a December![48] And look how 'December' differs from
'October'...And if tomorrow Pasternak writes *his* 'October', it will be,
above all, his own October, with the focus of military activities trans-
ferred to the tops of mutinous trees.

The second, but really the first and only question – of each one's
relation to God, and of God's to each of them – I'm deliberately not
raising here. At the right time.

Towards different estuaries, from different sources, different in the
springs from which they drink, and in the thirsty to whom they give to
drink – why make a list? Not: they are different in everything, but: they
belong to different dimensions, and are equal in one thing only – power.

Power of the creative gift and of giving. Consequently, in the power of their impact on us.

Mayakovsky is our measure of power; Pasternak – our measure of depth, a plummet.

But these two, who are linked by only one presence – of power – are also united in one shared absence: the gap of song. Mayakovsky is incapable of song because he is wholly in a major key, impactive and of thunderous voice. This is how jokes ('not especially good ones') are made and armies commanded. Not how songs are sung. Pasternak is incapable of song because he is overloaded, oversaturated, and – overall – unique. In Pasternak there is no place for song; Mayakovsky is himself out of place in song. Thus, the Blok-Esenin 'vacancy' in Russia is still unfilled. The melodic principle of Russia has flowed off in many small and short-lived streams, and has to find a single river-bed, a single throat.

To be a national poet, you must let a whole nation sing through you. To do this, it isn't enough to be everything: you've got to be everyone – which is just what Pasternak cannot be. You've got to be both the whole nation and merely one particular nation; the particular one and – at the same time – the whole of it. Which is just what Mayakovsky doesn't want to be: that herald of a single class, creator of a proletarian epos.

Neither the fighter (Mayakovsky) nor the visionary (Pasternak) is a composer of songs.

For song we need someone who is, doubtless, already born in Russia, and already growing somewhere, hidden in the great-Russian hubbub. We shall wait.

*

You slept, having made your bed upon gossip,
slept and, were quiet, no longer shuddering.
Handsome, twenty-two-year-old
just as your tetraptych foretold.
You slept, pressing your cheek to the pillow,
slept, cutting your way at full speed,
at full ankle-power, over and over with leaps
into the category of youthful legends.
You cut your way into them all the more notably
for reaching them with a single bound.
Your shot was similar to Etna
in the foothills of cowards and cowardesses.[49]

Pasternak – to Mayakovsky.

# Two Forest Kings

A word-for-word translation of Goethe's 'Erlking':

Who gallops so late through wind and night? It is the father with his child. He firmly presses the boy to himself, the child feels secure and warm with his father. – My son, why do you so fearfully hide your face? – Father, don't you see the Erlking? The Erlking with his crown and tail? – My son, that is a streak of mist! – Dear child, come to me, come with me! I will play wonderful games with you. On my shores there are many colourful flowers, my mother has many golden dresses! – Father, father, don't you hear what the Erlking is promising me in a whisper? – Be calm, my son, don't be afraid, my son, it's the wind rustling in the dry leaves. – Tender boy, will you go with me? My daughters will wonderfully cherish you, my daughters are dancing the round-dance of night – they will lull you and dance you and sing you to sleep. – Father, father, don't you see, there in that gloomy darkness, the Erlking's daughters? – My son, my son, I see plainly – it's the old willow trees glowing so greyly. – I love you, your beauty is wounding me! If you're not willing, I'll take you by force! – Father, father, he's got me in his grip! The Erlking has done me a hurt! In dread, the father gallops fast, he holds the moaning child in his arms – he galloped home with all his might – in his arms the child was dead.

I know it is an ungrateful task to give a forced and literal translation in prose when we possess a free poetic translation of genius;[1] however, this is needed for my present task.

Let us first look at concepts that are untranslatable and therefore unconveyable. There's a number of them. We'll start with the first: tail. In German 'tail' is both *Schwanz* and *Schweif*; for example, a dog has a *Schwanz*, while a *Schweif* is what a lion, a devil, a comet – and the Erlking – have. So my 'tail' [*khvost*] degrades and disparages the Erlking's tail. A second word is *fein*, which I have translated 'tender' [*nezhnyi*] – a poor translation, as the word signifies, above all, something lofty: some elect, very genuine, exquisite quality, something noble and high-born in a person or thing. Here, it means both noble and high-born, and tender, and exceptional. A third word – the verb *reizt, reizen* – has a primary meaning of irritate, stir up, incite to, drive to (always to something bad: anger, trouble, and so on). 'To charm' is only its secondary meaning. It cannot be translated here in either its complete or its primary meaning. To go by its root, the closest would be: 'I am provoked (irritated) by your beauty' – in the sense of 'wounded' [*uyazvlyon*]. A fourth word, in the same line, is *Gestalt*: figure, bodily frame, external shape, form. Appearance, spread over the whole person. The way a person is outwardly manifested. A fifth is *scheinen*, meaning both to seem and to shine; to glimmer and to be only-imagined. A sixth untranslatable word is *Leids*. 'Has done me a hurt' [*mne sdelal bol'no*] is something less than *Leids gethan*, which all at once, all in one, signifies pain and harm and damage: in Goethe's use, here, an irreparable damage – death.

Now that we've listed everything Zhukovsky could not convey, or could convey only with great and perhaps unjustified labour, let's turn to what he substituted wilfully (so far as this word can be used about poetry). From the very first stanza we find things that we don't find in Goethe: the rider is described as an old man, and the child as exhausted from shivering, already shivering before he first glimpses the Erlking, which immediately gives us the idea that the Erlking is his delirium – an idea which is not in Goethe's poem, where the child shudders from the *reality* of the Erlking. (He saw because he shuddered – he shuddered because he saw.) The father's gesture is changed too: in Goethe he holds the child firmly and warmly; in Zhukovsky he warms him in response to his shivering. So the father's surprise, too, loses its point: 'Child, why do you press against me so fearfully?' – surprise which in Goethe is justified and heightened by the child's excellent well-being *before* the vision. In the second stanza every line is altered. The first vision of the Erlking is descriptive – in the child's words: 'Father! the Erlking has flashed into my eyes!' – whereas in Goethe's ('Don't you see the Erlking?') it is imperative, hypnotic: the child can't imagine how it is possible not to see the Erlking and tries to make his father see it. There is all the difference between 'I see' and 'Don't you see?' Now let's turn to the vision itself. In Zhukovsky we see an old man, majestic, 'in a dark crown, with a thick beard', a kind of *bedarkened* king – Saul through the eyes of the shepherd David. At the sight of him, as at the sight of any majesty, we feel calm despite everything. In Goethe we see an undefined – indefinable! – being, of uncertain age, without any age, all lion's tail and crown – a *daemon*, whose tailedness is closely reflected in the 'streak' (the tatter, shred, scrap, *Streif*) of mist, just as Zhukovsky's 'beard' is reflected in the mist-in-general over the water-in-general.

What sort of temptations does the Erlking use to try to entice the child? We can say right away that Goethe's Erlking was a better knower of the childish heart. The wondrous games he is going to play with the child are more alluring than the indefinite 'much that is joyful in my land', just as the golden garment the Erlking's mother will robe him in is more tempting than cold golden palaces. The two fourth stanzas diverge even more. The child's enumeration of the Erlking's temptations (and what temptations they *are* – 'gold, pearls, joy...' – like some pasha trying to tempt a Turkish woman...) is incomparably less exciting to us than the child's mere mention of, mere hinting at, them, his silence about them, in 'Father, father, don't you hear what the Erlking is whispering and promising me?' And this *what*, intensified by the quietness of the promise, by his not naming the things that are promised, expands in us to visions of such power, horror and bliss as are not even dreamt of by the idyllic author of 'pearls and streams'. Likewise the father's answers: in Zhukovsky the answer is a serene one: 'Oh no, my child, you have misheard, it is the wind waking up and shaking the leaves'; in Goethe it's a deathly frightened, frightening answer: 'Be calm, my child! Don't be afraid, my child! It's the wind rustling in the dry leaves.' An answer of which every word sounds the heart's alarm. An answer which, in a single word, tells us the season of the year, here as important and inevitable as the time of day, the season richest in possibilities and impossibilities.

We've come now to the peak of the temptation and of the ballad, the place where the Erlking, bridling his savagery, uses deeper than fatherly tones: motherly tones take us through the whole scale of feminine influence, the whole gamut of womanly intonation, from feminine cajoling to maternal tenderness – we've come to the stanza which, apart from its sense, is a cradle song by its very sound. And once again, how much more intimate and detailed Goethe's 'Erlking' is than Zhukovsky's, if only for the antiquated folk-word *warten* ('to cherish' [*nyanchit'*], translated by most Russian readers as 'wait'), which Zhukovsky leaves out altogether, replacing it with: 'You shall know my lovely daughters.' In Zhukovsky – 'lovely'; in Goethe – simply 'daughters', since Goethe's Erlking cannot think of anyone's loveliness at this moment except the little boy's. Zhukovsky has *beautiful daughters*; in Goethe the daughters will *beautifully cherish*.

And, once again, just as before: in Zhukovsky – a paraphrase of the vision; in Goethe – the thing itself. 'Dear father, the Erlking has gathered his daughters, I can see them nodding to me from the dark boughs...' (had he only put 'do you see...?'), and: 'Father, father, don't you see – over there in that dreadful dark, the Erlking's daughters?' An intonation in

which we recognise the impatience that we feel when we can see some-
thing and another can't. And such different answers, so well corres-
ponding to the questions: Zhukovsky's Olympian: 'Oh no, everything's
calm in the night's depth. It's the old grey willows standing to one side',
an answer which doesn't even convey the willows' swaying, i.e. not even
an illusion of visibility! And Goethe's shaken, heart-pounding answer:
'My son, my son, I see plainly...', the answer of a man who begs, who
entreats the other to believe, so as to believe himself, and, by talking of
plainly visible willows, persuades us still more of the opposite vision.

And at last, the last – an outburst, all cards on the table, the mask torn
off, a threat, ultimatum: 'I love you! Your beauty has wounded me! If
you're not willing, I'll take you by force!' And Zhukovsky's passive: 'Child!
I am captivated by your beauty!', like a pampered pasha to his slave-girl,
a pasha who is himself taken captive, that same pasha of the turquoise
and pearl bribe. Or it's seventy-year-old Goethe moving from contem-
plation of Roman engravings to contemplation of a fifteen-year-old girl.
In narrative, contemplative, painterly mode, as if moving on to a painting.
And even his brilliant rendering – a formula – of the following line,
'Willing or unwilling, you shall be mine!' is weaker than Goethe's 'If you're
not willing, I'll take you by force!', as the very form of words – 'You'll be
taken by me' – does less *taking* than 'I shall take you'; it weakens and
distances the act of seizing by the Erlking's hand – which is already seizing
and from which there's less than a single step, less than a galloping step
of the steed, to the child's cry, 'He's hurting me.' In Zhukovsky this cry is
not there: 'Father, the Erlking wants to catch us up! He's here, I'm stifled,
I can hardly breathe!' In Goethe, between the Erlking's shout – 'I'll take
you by force!' – and the child's cry – 'He's hurting me!' – there is nothing
but the repeated 'Father, father!' and the very gasp of the seizure, while
in Zhukovsky there's all the distance of an intention. In Zhukovsky the
Erlking remains on the horse's withers.

And, as an afterword (for the work ends here), what we all already
knew, from the first line of the second stanza: death, the one thing which
in Zhukovsky coincides almost word for word, since the dynamic of the
work is now past.

I repeat: it is an ungrateful task to compare my captious, literal,
arhythmical, non-artistic translation with Zhukovsky's brilliant free rend-
ering. Good poetry is always better than prose, even the best, and
Zhukovsky's superiority over me is all too obvious. However, I haven't
been comparing prose with poetry, but the exact text of the original with
the exact text of the translation: Goethe's 'Erlking' with Zhukovsky's
'Erlking'.

Now, conclusions.

The two works are equally great. It is impossible to translate the 'Erlking' better than Zhukovsky has done it. Nor should it be attempted. Having been with us for a century, it is no longer a translation, it's an original. It is simply a different 'Erlking' – the Russian 'Erlking' – that of the anthology and of children's nightmares.

The two works are equally great. And completely different. Two 'Erlkings'.

Not only two 'Erlkings', but also two Erlkings: an ageless, burning demon and a majestic old man. And, as well as two Erlkings, two fathers: a young horseman and, again, an old man (Zhukovsky has two old men, Goethe – none). Only the child remains the same.

Two variations on one theme, two ways of seeing one thing, two testimonies to one vision.

Each saw it with his own eyes.

Goethe, with the blackness of his fiery eyes, *saw*, and we see with him. Our feeling during the dream-period of 'The Erlking': how is it the father doesn't see?

Zhukovsky, with the smoothness of his brown, kind, intelligent eyes, did not see, and we do not see with him. He believed in the mist and the willows. Our feeling in the course of 'The Erlking': how is it the child doesn't see that it's the willows?

In Zhukovsky the child dies of fear.

In Goethe – of the Erlking.

In Zhukovsky the matter is simple. The child took fright, the father couldn't calm him, the child imagined it was being seized (maybe a branch whipped at him), and because of all these seeming things the child really died. Like that madman who thought he was made of glass and responded to the dissuasive jolt of commonsense with a heart attack and a tinkling sound! (The analogy could take us a long way.)

Just once, at the very end, as if having doubts, Zhukovsky departs from his good sense, with a single word: 'the *frightened* rider…', but then gets frightened himself and quickly passes over it.

Zhukovsky's Erlking (Zhukovsky himself) is infinitely kinder: kinder to the child – his child isn't hurt, he's only 'stifled'; kinder to the father – a grievous, but none the less natural, death; kinder to us – the order of things is not disturbed. For to allow the existence of the Erlking, even for a moment, is to displace us from all our places. So, a regrettable case, but not unprecedented. And the vision itself is kinder: an old man with a beard, a grandfather, 'turquoise streams' ('flowers of turquoise, streams of pearls'). You even wonder what the child was afraid of.

(Of the dark crown? Of the force of love?) A terrifying tale for the night. Terrifying, but a tale. A terrifying tale of an unterrifying grandfather. After the terrifying tale you can still go to sleep.

A terrifying tale not of a grandfather at all. After Goethe's terrifying non-tale you cannot live – as you did. (Into that forest! Home!)

...More kind and cold, more majestic and unreal. A beard is more majestic than a tail; seen daughters are more majestic, more cold and unreal than cherishing daughters. Zhukovsky's whole poem is on the threshold between life and dreams.

Goethe's vision is wholly life or wholly dream, it makes no difference what it is called, since *each is more terrifying than the other*; and it isn't the naming that's important, but the breath-taking.

Which is more art? Debatable.

But some works are more than art.

More terrifying than art.

# POETS WITH HISTORY AND POETS WITHOUT HISTORY†

...What is the 'I' of a poet? It is – to all appearances – the human 'I' expressed in poetic speech. But only to appearances, for often poems give us something that had been hidden, obscured, even quite stifled, something the person hadn't known was in him, and would never have recognised had it not been for poetry, the poetic gift. Action of forces which are unknown to the one who acts, and which he only becomes conscious of in the instant of action. An almost complete analogy to dreaming. If it were possible to direct one's own dreams – and for some it is, especially children – the analogy would be complete. That which is hidden and buried in you is revealed and exposed in your poems: this is the poetic 'I', your dream-self.

The 'I' of the poet, in other words, is his soul's devotion to certain dreams, his being visited by certain dreams, the secret source – not of his will, but of his whole nature.

The poet's self is a dream-self and a language-self; it is the 'I' of a dreamer awakened by inspired speech and realised only in that speech.

This is the sum of the poet's personality. This is the law of his idiosyncrasy. This is why poets are all so alike and so unalike. Like, because all without exception have dreams. Unlike, in what dreams they have. Like – in their ability to dream; unlike – in the dreams.

All poets can be divided into poets with development and poets without development. Into poets with history and poets without history. The first could be depicted graphically as an arrow shot into infinity; the second – as a circle.

Above the first (the image of the arrow) stands the law of gradual self-discovery. These poets discover themselves through all the phenomena

---

† [The reader is reminded that the original of this essay has not survived, and that the translation has been made from a translation; see Introduction and Notes. – A.L.].

they meet along their way, at every step and in every new object. Mine or others', the vital or the superfluous, the accidental and the eternal: everything is for them a touchstone. Of their power, which increases with each new obstacle. Their self-discovery is their coming to self-knowledge through the world, self-knowledge of the soul through the visible world. Their path is the path of experience. As they walk, we physically sense a wind, the air they cleave with their brows. A wind blows from them.

They walk without turning round. Their experience accumulates as if by itself, and piles up somewhere behind, like a load on the back which never makes the back hunch. One doesn't look round at the sack on one's back. The walker knows nothing of his rucksack until the moment he needs it: at the stopping-place. The Goethe of *Götz von Berlichingen* and the Goethe of the *Metamorphosis of Plants* are not acquainted with each other. Goethe put in his sack everything he needed from *himself of that time*, left himself in the wondrous forests of young Germany and of his own youth, and went – onward. Had the mature Goethe met the young Goethe at a crossroads, he might actually have failed to recognise him and might have sought to make his acquaintance. I'm not talking of Goethe the person, but of Goethe the creator, and I take this great example as an especially evident one.

Poets with history (like people with history in general and like history itself) do not even renounce themselves: they simply don't turn round to themselves – no time for it, only onward! Such is the law of movement and of pressing forward.

The Goethe of *Götz*, the Goethe of *Werther*, the Goethe of the *Roman Elegies*, the Goethe of the *Theory of Colours*, and so on – where is he? Everywhere. Nowhere. How many are there? As many as there are strides. Each step was taken by a different person. One set out, another arrived. *He* was no more than the tirelessness of the creative will, the muscle that lifted the walker's foot. The same is true of Pushkin. Maybe this is what genius is?

The loneliness of such walkers! People look for a person you yourself would no longer recognise. They fall in love with the one of you whom you have already disavowed. They give their trust to one you have outgrown. From Goethe, until he was eighty-three (the year of his death), people went on demanding *Götz* (Goethe at twenty!). And – a smaller but nearer example – from the Blok of *The Twelve* they still demand 'The Unknown Woman'.

This is what our Russian Goethean, the poet and philosopher Vyacheslav Ivanov, now living in Padua, meant when he wrote his fine lines:

The one whose name you trumpet
has taken another name,
the one you love today
has already ceased being loved.[1]

It isn't a question of age; we all change. The point is that the mature
Goethe didn't understand his own youth. Some poets grow young in their
old age: Goethe's *Trilogy of Passion* was written by a seventy-year-old!
It's a question of one thing replacing another, of opening horizons, of
previously concealed spaces. It's a question of the quantity of minutes, of
the infinity of tasks, of the immensity of his Columbus-like strengths. And
the rucksack on the back (Goethe really did walk about with a bag for
collecting stones and minerals) gets heavier and heavier. And the road
keeps stretching ahead. And the shadows grow. And you can neither
exhaust your strength nor reach the end of the road!

Poets with history are, above all, poets of a theme. We always know
what they are writing about. And, if we don't learn where they were going
to, we do at least realise, when their journey is completed, that they had
always been going somewhere (the existence of a goal). Rarely are they
pure lyricists. Too large in size and scope, their own 'I' is too small for
them – even the biggest is too small – or they spread it out till nothing is
left and it merges with the rim of the horizon (Goethe, Pushkin). The
human 'I' becomes the 'I' of a country – a people – a given continent – a
century – a millennium – the heavenly vault (Goethe's geological 'I': 'I live
in the millennia'). For such a poet a theme is the occasion for a new self,
and not necessarily a human one. Their whole earthly path is a sequence
of reincarnations, not necessarily into a human being. From a human to
a stone, a flower, a constellation. They seem to incarnate in themselves
all the days of creation.

Poets with history are, above all, poets of will. I don't mean the will to
fulfil, which is taken for granted: no one will doubt that a physically huge
bulk like *Faust*, or indeed any poem of a thousand lines, cannot come into
being by itself. Eight, sixteen or, rarely, twenty lines may come about by
themselves – the lyric tide most often lays fragments at our feet, albeit the
most precious ones. I mean the will to choose, the will to have choice. To
decide not merely to become another, but – this particular other. To decide
to part with oneself. To decide – like the hero in the fairy tale – between
right, left and straight on (but, like that same hero, never backward!).
Waking up one morning, Pushkin makes a decision: 'Today I shall write
Mozart!' This Mozart is his refusal to a multitude of other visions and
subjects; it is total choice – that is, a sacrifice. To use contemporary

vocabulary, I'd say that the poet with history rejects everything that lies outside his general line – the line of his personality, his gift, his history. The choice is made by his infallible instinct for the most important. And yet, at the end of Pushkin's path, we have the sense that Pushkin could not have done otherwise than create what he did create, could not have written anything he did not write...And no one regrets that in Gogol's favour he refused the *Dead Souls* project, something that lay on Gogol's general line. (The poet with history also has a clear view of others – Pushkin had, especially.) The main feature of poets of this sort is the striving towards a goal. A poet without history cannot have a striving towards a goal. He himself doesn't know what the lyric flood will bring him.

Pure lyric poetry has no project. You can't make yourself have a particular dream or feel a particular feeling. Pure lyricism is the sheer condition of going through something, suffering something through, and in the intervals (when the poet is not being summoned by Apollo²to holy sacrifice), in the ebbs of inspiration, it is a condition of infinite poverty. The sea has departed, carried everything away, and won't return *before its own time*. A continual, awful hanging in the air, on the word of honour of perfidious inspiration. And suppose one day it lets you go?

Pure lyric poetry is solely the record of our dreams and feelings, along with the entreaty that these dreams and feelings should never run dry...To demand more from lyricism...But what *more* could be demanded from it?

The lyric poet has nothing to grasp hold of: he has neither the skeleton of a theme nor obligatory hours of work at a desk; no material he can dip into, which he's preoccupied with or even immersed in, at the ebb times: he is wholly suspended on a thread of trust.

Don't expect sacrifices: the pure lyricist sacrifices nothing – he is glad when anything comes at all. Don't expect moral choice from him either – whatever comes, 'bad' or 'good', he is so happy it has come at all that to you (society, morality, God) he won't yield a thing.

The lyric poet is given only the will to fulfil his task, just enough for sorting out the tide's offerings.

Pure lyricism is nothing but the recording of our dreams and sensations. The greater the poet, the purer the record.

A walker and a stylite. For the poet without history is a stylite or – same thing – a sleeper. Whatever may happen around his pillar, whatever the waves of history may create (or destroy), he sees, hears and knows only what is his. (Whatever may be going on around him, he sees only his own dreams.) Sometimes he seems to be really great, like Boris Pasternak, but the small and the great draw us equally irresistibly into the enchanted circle of dream. We too turn into stone.

To exactly the extent that other people's dreams, when they tell us them, are inexpressive and uninfectious, these lyric dreams are irresistible, affecting us more than our own!

Now beyond the slumbering mountain
the evening ray has faded.
In a resounding stream the hot
spring faintly sparkles...[3]

These lines by the young Lermontov are more powerful than all my childhood dreams – and not only childhood, and not only mine.

It could be said of poets without history that their soul and their personality are formed in their mother's womb. The don't need to learn or acquire or fathom anything at all – they know everything from the start. They don't ask about anything – they make manifest. Evidence, experience are nothing to them.

Sometimes the range of their knowledge is very narrow. They don't go beyond it. Sometimes the range of their knowledge is very wide. They never narrow it to oblige experience.

They came into the world not to learn, but to say. To say what they already know: everything they know (if it is a lot) or the only thing they know (if it is just one thing).

They came into the world to make themselves known. Pure lyricists, only-lyricists, don't allow anything alien into themselves, and they have an instinct for this just as poets with history have an instinct for their own general line. The whole empirical world is to them a foreign body. In this sense they have the power to choose, or more exactly, the power to select, or more exactly still, the power to reject. But the rejection is done by the whole of their nature, not by their will alone. And is usually unconscious. In this, as in much, maybe in everything, they are children. Here is how the world is for them: 'That's the wrong way.' – 'No, it's the right way! I know! I know better!' What does he know? That any other way is impossible. They are the absolute opposite: I am the world (meaning the human world – society, family, morality, ruling church, science, commonsense, any form of power – human organisation in general, including our much-famed 'progress'). Enter into the poems and the biography too, which are always a single whole.

For poets with history there are no foreign bodies, they are conscious participants in the world. Their 'I' is equal to the world. From the human to the cosmic.

Here lies the distinction between the genius and the lyric genius. There do exist purely lyric geniuses. But we never call them 'geniuses'. The way this kind of genius is closed upon himself, and doomed to himself, is expressed in the adjective 'lyrical'. Just as the boundlessness of the genius, his impersonality even, is expressed by the absence, even impossibility, of any adjective whatever. (Every adjective, since it gives an exact meaning, is limiting.)

The 'I' cannot be a genius. A genius may call itself 'I', dress itself in a certain name, make use of certain earthly tokens. We must not forget that among ancient peoples 'genius' signified quite factually a good higher being, a divinity from *above*, not the person himself. Goethe was a genius because above him there hovered a genius. This genius distracted and sustained him up to the end of his eighty-third year, up to the last page of *Faust* Part Two. That same genius is shown in his immortal face.

A last, and perhaps the simplest, explanation. Pure lyric poetry lives on feelings. Feelings are always the same. Feelings are not regular or consistent. They are all given to us at once, all the feelings we are ever to experience; like the flames of a torch, they are squeezed into our breast from birth. Feeling (the childhood of a person, a nation, the planet) always starts at a maximum, and in strong people and in poets it remains at that maximum. Feeling doesn't need a cause, it itself is the cause of everything. Feeling doesn't need experience, it knows everything earlier and better. (Every sentiment is also a presentiment.) Someone in whom there is love, loves; someone in whom there is anger, gets angry; and someone in whom there is a sense of hurt, is hurt, from the day he is born. Sensitivity to hurt gives rise to hurt. Feeling doesn't need experience, it knows in advance that it is doomed. There's nothing for feeling to do on the periphery of the visible, it is in the centre, is itself the centre. There's nothing for feeling to seek along any roads, it knows that it will come – will lead – into itself.

An enchanted circle. A dream circle. A magic circle.

Thus once again:

Thought is an arrow.
Feeling is a circle.


This is the essence of the purely lyrical sort of poet, the nature of pure lyricism. And if they sometimes seem to develop and change – it is not *they* that develop and change, but only their vocabulary, their linguistic equipment.

Few lyricists are given the right words, their own words, from the start! From helplessness, they often begin with others' words – not their own, but universal ones (and often it's precisely at that stage that they please the majority, which sees in them its own nothingness). Then, when they start talking their own language, sometimes very soon, we think they have changed and grown up. Yet it's not they who have grown, but their language-self, which has reached them in its growth. Not even the greatest musician can express himself on a child's keyboard.

Some children are born with a ready-made soul. No child is born with ready-made speech. (Or just one was – Mozart.) Pure lyricists, too, learn to talk, for the language of poets is the physics of their creativity, their soul's body, and each body has got to develop. The hardest thing of all for a lyric poet is to find his own language, not his own feeling, as he has that from his birth. But there is no pure lyricist who hasn't already conveyed himself in his childhood – his definitive and fated self – announced his whole self in some fairly complete and exhaustive stanza of four or eight lines, one that he will never offer again and that could stand as an epigraph to the whole of his work, a formula for his whole fate. A first stanza, which could also be the last: a pre-life stanza which could also be a pre-death one (inscription on a tombstone).

Such is Lermontov's 'The Sail'. Pure lyric poets, the majority of them, are children of very early development (and of very short life, both as persons and as writers) – or rather of very early insight, with a present-iment of their being doomed to poetry – *Wunderkinder* in the literal sense, having a wide-awake sense of fate, that is to say of themselves.

The poet with history never knows what is going to happen to him. It is his genius that knows this, guiding him and revealing to him only as much as he needs for free movement: a proximate goal, a sense of direction, constantly keeping the main thing hidden round a turning. The pure lyricist always knows that nothing is going to happen to him, that he will have nothing but himself: his own tragic lyric experience.

Take Pushkin who began with his *lycée* verses, and Lermontov who began with 'The Sail'. In Pushkin's first poems we discern nothing of Pushkin whatsoever – only the genius Derzhavin was able to glimpse the future genius in the living face, voice and gesture of the youth. But in the eighteen-year-old Lermontov's 'The Sail' all Lermontov is present, the Lermontov of turbulence, offence, duel, death. The young Pushkin could not have had such a poem as the 'The Sail' – but not because his talent was undeveloped: he was no less gifted than Lermontov. Simply, Pushkin, like every poet with history, and like history itself, began at the beginning – like Goethe too – and then spent all his life *im Werden* ('in becoming') while Lermontov – immediately – 'was'. To find himself, Pushkin had to live not one life, but a hundred. While Lermontov, to find himself, had only to be born.

Of our contemporaries I will name three exceptional cases of per-
fection in the innate lyrical quality: Anna Akhmatova, Osip Mandelstam
and Boris Pasternak, poets born already equipped with their own vocab-
ulary and with maximum expressiveness.

When in the first poem of her first book, the young Akhmatova conveys
the confusion of love in the lines:

I drew my left-hand glove
onto my right hand – [4]

she conveys at one blow all feminine and all lyric confusion (all the
confusion of the empirical!), immortalising with one flourish of the pen
that ancient nervous gesture of woman and of poet who at life's great
moments forget right and left – not only of glove, but of hand, and of
country of the world, suddenly losing all their certainty. Through a patent
and even penetrating precision of detail, something bigger than an emo-
tional state is affirmed and symbolised – a whole structure of the mind.
(A poet lets go the pen, a woman lets go her lover's hand, and immediately
they can't tell the left hand from the right.) In brief, from these two lines
of Akhmatova's, a broad, abundant flow of associations comes into being,
associations which spread like the circles from a flung pebble. The whole
woman, the whole poet is in these two lines; the whole Akhmatova,
unique, unrepeatable, inimitable. Before Akhmatova none of us por-
trayed a gesture like this. And no one did after her. (Of course,
Akhmatova is not only this gesture; I'm giving just one of her main
characteristics.) 'Again or still?' was what I asked in 1916, about
Akhmatova who in 1912 had begun by dipping the same jug into the same
sea. Now, seventeen years later, I can see that then, without suspecting it,
she had provided the formula for a lyric constant. Listen to the image: it
has a depth. Look at its movement: it conveys roundness. The roundness
of the dipping gesture, essentially deep. A jug. A sea. Together they
constitute volume. Thinking about it today, seventeen years later, I might
say: 'the same bucket into the same well', preferring an accurate image
to a beautiful one. But the essence of the image would be the same. I offer
this as yet another instance of lyric constancy.

I've never heard anyone say, about Akhmatova or Pasternak: 'Same
thing over and over again – boring!' Just as you cannot say 'Same thing
over and over again – boring!' about the sea, of which Pasternak wrote
the following:

All becomes dull, only you never grow familiar –
days pass, years pass, thousands and thousands of years... [5]

For, both Akhmatova and Pasternak scoop not from the surface of the sea (the heart), but from its depth (the fathomless). They can't become boring, just as sleep can't be boring – which is always the same, but with always different dreams. Just as dreaming can't be boring.

When you approach something, you need to know what you may expect from it. And you must expect from it its own self, that which constitutes its being. When you approach the sea – and the lyric poet – you are not going for something new, but for the same again; for a repetition, not a continuation. Lyric poetry, like the sea, even when you're discovering it for the first time, is something you invariably re-read; while with a river, which flows past, as with Pushkin, who walks past – if it's on their banks you've been born – you always read *on*. It is the difference between the crossways, lulling, lyrical motion of the sea, and the linear, never-returning movement of a river. The difference between being somewhere and passing by. You love the river because it is always different, and you love the sea because it is always the same. If you desire novelty, settle by a river.

Lyric poetry, like the sea, rouses and calms itself, happens within itself. Not in vain did Heraclitus say: 'Nobody steps twice into the same river', taking, as his symbol of flowing, not the sea which he saw before him every day and knew well, but – a river.

When you go to the sea and to the lyricist, you are not going for the never-returning flow of the current, you're going for the ever-returning flow of the waves; not for the unrepeatable moment, not for the intransient, but precisely for the repeatability of the unforeseen in sea and in lyric, for the invariability of changes and exchanges, for the inevitability of your amazement at them.

Renewal! This is where their power over us lies, the might which sustains all worship of the divine, all sorcery, all magic, all invoking, all cursing, all human and non-human unions. Even the dead are summoned three times.

Who will say to the great and the genuine: 'Be different!'

Be! – is our silent prayer.

To the poet with history we say: 'Look further!' To the poet without history: 'Dive deeper!' To the first: 'Further!' To the second: 'More!'

And if some poets seem dull because of their monotony, then this comes from the shallowness and smallness (the drying up) of the image, not from the fact that the image remains the same. (A dried up sea is no longer a sea.) If a poet bores us with monotony, I'll undertake to prove that he is not a great poet, his imagery is not great. If we take a saucer for a sea, that is not its fault.

Lyricism, for all that it is doomed to itself, is itself inexhaustible. (Perhaps the best formula for the lyrical and for the lyric essence is this: being doomed to inexhaustibility!) The more you draw out, the more there remains. This is why it never disappears. This is why we fling ourselves with such avidity on every new lyric poet: maybe he'll succeed in drawing out all that essence which is the soul, thereby slaking our own? It's as if they were all trying to get us drunk on bitter, salty, green sea-water and each time we believe it is drinking-water. And once again it turns out bitter! (We must not forget that the structure of the sea, of the blood, and of lyricism – is one and the same.)

What's true of dull people is true of dull poets: what's dull is not the monotony, but the fact that the thing repeated – though it may be very varied – is insignificant. How murderously identical are the newspapers on the table, with all their various dissonances; how murderously identical are the Parisian women in the streets with all their variety! As if these things – advertisements, newspapers, Parisian women – were not varied, but were all the same. At all the crossroads, in all the shops and trams, at all auctions, in all concert-halls – innumerable, and yet, however many, they all amount to one thing! And this one thing is: everyone!

It is boring when, instead of a human face, you see something worse than a mask: a mould for the mass production of facelessness: paper money with no security in gold! When, instead of a person's own words, no matter how clumsy, you hear someone else's, no matter how brilliant (which, by the way, straightaway lose their brilliance – like the fur on a dead animal). It is boring when you hear from the person you're talking to not his own words, but somebody else's. Moreover, if a repetition has bored you, you can be pretty sure it's a case of someone else's words – words not created, but repeated. For one cannot repeat oneself in words: even the slightest change in the speech means it is not a repetition but a transformation with another essence behind it. Even if one tries to repeat a thought of one's own, already expressed, one will involuntarily do it differently every time; the slightest change and something new is said. Unless one learns it by heart. When a poet is obviously 'repeating himself', it means he has abandoned his creative self and is robbing himself just as if he were robbing someone else.

In calling renewal the pivot of lyricism, I don't mean the renewal of my own or others' dreams and images, I only mean the return of the lyric wave in which the composition of the lyrical is constant.

The wave always returns, and always returns as a different wave.

The same water – a different wave.

What matters is that it is a *wave*.

What matters is that the wave *will return*.

What matters is that it will *always* return *different*.

What matters most of all: however different the returning wave, it will always return as a wave of the *sea*.

What is a wave? Composition and muscle. The same goes for lyric poetry.

Similarity, variation on the same, is not repetition. Similarity is in the nature of things, at the basis of nature itself. In the renewing (the constant developing) of the given forms of trees, not one oak repeats its neighbour, and on one and the same oak not one leaf repeats a preceding one. Similarity in nature: creation of the similar, not of the same; the like, not the identical; new, not old; creation, not repetition.

Each new leaf is the next variation on the eternal theme of the oak. Renewal in nature: infinite variation on a single theme.

Repetition does not happen in nature, it is outside nature, thus outside creativity too. That is the way it is. Only machines repeat. In 'poets who repeat', the machine of memory, separated from the springs of creativity, has become a mere mechanism. Repetition is the purely mechanical reproduction of something which inevitably turns into someone else's, even when it is one's own. For, if I've learnt my own thought by heart, I repeat it as though it were someone else's, without the participation of anything creative. It may be that only the intonation is creative, is mine, the feeling, that is, with which I utter it and change its form, the linguistic and semantic vicinity in which I place it. But when, for example, I write on a blank page the bare formula I once found: 'Etre vaut mieux qu'avoir ('it's better to be than to have'), I repeat a formula which doesn't belong to me any more than an algebraic one does. A thing can only be created once.

Self-repetition, that is self-imitation, is a purely external act. Nature, creating its next leaf, does not look at the already created leaves, doesn't look because it has in itself the whole form of the future leaf: it creates out of itself by an inner image and without a model. God created man in his own image and likeness without repeating himself.

In poetry, every self-repetition and self-imitation is, above all, imitation of form. One steals from oneself or from one's neighbour a certain verse-form, certain phrases, certain public figures or even a theme (thus

everyone steals rain from Pasternak, for example, but no one loves it
except him and no one serves it except him). No one has the power to
steal the essence (their own or another's). Essence cannot be imitated.
Therefore, all imitative poems are dead. If they're not dead but stir us
with live agitation, then they're not an imitation but a transformation. To
imitate means to annihilate in every case – it means destroying the thing
to see how it is made; stealing from it the secret of its life, and then
reinstating everything except the life.

*

Some poets start with a minimum and end with the maximum, some start
with a maximum and end with the minimum (drying up of the creative
vein). And some start with a maximum and stay at this maximum right up
to their last line – among our contemporaries, Pasternak and Akhmatova,
mentioned already. These never gave either more or less, but always
stayed at a maximum of self-expression. If for some there is a path of self-
discovery, for these there is no path at all. From their birth, they are here.
Their childish babble is a sum, not a source.

The soft careful break
of a fruit off a tree
amidst ceaseless music
of deep forest quietness.[6]

This quatrain by the seventeen-year-old Osip Mandelstam has in it the
whole vocabulary and metre of the mature Mandelstam. A formula for
himself. What was the first thing to touch the ear of this lyricist? The sound
of a falling apple, the acoustic vision of roundness. What signs are there
here of a seventeen-year-old? None. What is there here of Mandelstam?
Everything. To be precise: this ripeness of the falling fruit. The stanza is
that very falling fruit which he depicts. And, just as from the two lines by
Akhmatova, there are unusually wide circles of associations. Of round
and warm, of round and cold, of August, Augustus (the emperor), the
Hesperides, Paris, Eden, Adam (the throat): Mandelstam gives the read-
er's imagination all this in a single stanza. (Evocative power of lyricists!)
Characteristic of the lyrical: in conveying this apple, the poet did not
explicitly name it. And, in a sense, he never departed from this apple.
    Who can talk of the poetic path of (to take the greatest, most indis-
putable lyricists) Heine, Byron, Shelley, Verlaine, Lermontov? They have
covered the world with their feelings, laments, sighs and visions, drenched

it with their tears, set fire to it on all sides with their indignation.

Do we learn from them? No. We suffer for them and because of them.

It is the French proverb, retailored in my Russian style: 'Les heureux n'ont pas d'histoire.'[7]

One exception, a pure lyricist who did have development and history and a path: Alexander Blok. But, having said 'development', I see that I've not only taken the wrong direction but used a word that contradicts Blok's essence and fate. Development presupposes harmony. Can there be a development which is – catastrophic? And can there be harmony when what we see is a soul being torn completely apart? Here, without playing with words, but making a severe demand on them and answering for them, I assert: Blok, for the duration of his poetic path, was not developing, but was tearing himself apart.

One could say of Blok that he was trying to escape from one himself to another. From one which tormented him. To another which tormented him even more. The peculiarity is this hope of getting away from himself. Thus a mortally wounded man will run wildly from the wound, thus a sick man tosses from land to land, then from room to room, and finally from side to side.

If we see Blok as a poet with history, then it is solely the history of Blok the lyric poet, of lyricism itself, of suffering. If we see Blok as a poet with a path, then the path consists of running in circles away from himself.

Stopping to draw breath.

And entering the house, to meet oneself there once again!

The sole difference is that Blok started running at birth, while others stayed in one place.

Only once did Blok succeed in running away from himself – when he ran onto the cruel road of the Revolution. That was the leap of a dying man from his bed, of a man fleeing from death into the street, which won't notice him, into the crowd, which will trample him. Into Blok's physically collapsing and spiritually undermined personality rushed the elemental force of the Revolution, with its songs and demons – and it crushed that body. Let us not forget that the last word of *The Twelve* is 'Christ', which was one of the first words Blok spoke.

Such were this pure lyric poet's history, development and path.

# ART IN THE LIGHT OF CONSCIENCE

'Art is holy', 'holy art': however much a commonplace, this does have a certain meaning, and one in a thousand does think what he is saying and say what he is thinking.

That one in a thousand who consciously affirms the holiness of art is the person I am addressing.

What is holiness? Holiness is a condition the reverse of sin. Our contemporary age does not know sin, it replaces the concept 'sin' with the concept 'harm'. It follows that for an atheist there can be no question of the holiness of art: he will speak either of art's usefulness or of art's beauty. Therefore, I insist, what I say is addressed exclusively to those for whom God – sin – holiness – *are*.

If an atheist starts speaking of the loftiness of art, then what I say will partly concern him too.

## *What is art?*

Art is the same as nature. Don't seek in it other laws than its own (don't look for the self-will of the artist, which isn't there – only look for the laws of art). Perhaps art is just an offshoot of nature (a species of its creation). What is certain: a work of art is a work of nature, just as much born and not made. (And all the labour towards its realisation? But the earth labours too – in French, 'la terre en travail'.[1] And isn't birth itself labour? Female gestation and the artist's gestation of his work have been talked of so often they don't need insisting on: all know – and all know correctly.)

So what is the difference between a work of art and a work of nature, between a poem and a tree? There's none. Whatever the paths of labour and miracle, yet it *is*. I am!

That means the artist is the earth, which gives birth, and gives birth to everything. For the glory of God? And spiders? (There are some in works of art too.) I don't know for the glory of whom, and I think the question here is not of glory but of power.

Is nature holy? No. Sinful? No. But if a work of art is the same as a work of nature, why do we ask something of a poem but not of a tree? At most we'll regret that it grows crooked.

Because earth, the birth-giving, is irresponsible, while man, the creating, is responsible. Because the sprouting earth has but one will – to sprout – whereas man has got to will the sprouting of the good which he knows. (It is telling that the only thing that can be called 'wicked' is the notorious 'individual' quality, the unipersonal; there is no 'wicked epic' or 'wicked nature'.)

The earth didn't eat the apple in Paradise, Adam ate it. It didn't eat and doesn't know, he did eat and does know, he knows and is answerable. And insofar as the artist is a human being and not a monster, an animated bone-structure and not a coral bush, he has to answer for the work of his hands.

So, a work of art is the same as a work of nature, but one that is supposed to be illumined by the light of reason and conscience. Then it serves the good, as a stream turning a mill-wheel serves the good. But to call every work of art 'a good' is like calling every stream 'useful'. It is sometimes useful and sometimes harmful, and how much oftener harmful!

It is good when you take it (take yourself) in hand.

The moral law can be introduced into art, but can a mercenary corrupted by so many changes of master ever make a soldier of the regular army?

## Poet and elements

Poetry is God in the holy dreams of the earth[2]

There is an ecstasy in battle
and on the sombre chasm's edge.[3]

Ecstasy, that is to say, intoxication, is a feeling that is not good in itself, it is outside goodness, and anyway – intoxication with what?

Whatever threatens us with doom
hides in itself, for mortal hearts,
unspeakable pleasures...

Whenever you mention art's holiness call to mind this confession of
Pushkin's.
  – Yes, but further on it says...
  – All right. Let's dwell on that line, then, the one trump card for
goodness: '...guarantee/perhaps of immortality!'
  What kind of immortality? In God? In such vicinity the very sound of
the word is wild. A guarantee of the immortality of nature itself, of the
elements themselves – and of us insofar as we are they, are it. A line, if
not blasphemous, at least manifestly pagan.
  And further on, in black and white:

And so, all praise to thee, O Plague!
We're not afraid of murky tombs,
we're not confounded by your call!
As one we lift our frothing cups
and drink the rose maiden's breath
although that breath be – breath of Plague!

Not Pushkin, the elements. Nowhere and never have the elements spoken
out so strongly. Visitation of the elemental – upon whom, doesn't matter,
this time upon Pushkin. It is written in tongues of flame, in ocean waves,
in desert sands – in anything you like, only not in words.
  And this capital letter for Plague: plague no longer as a blind elemental
force, but as a goddess, the proper name and face of *evil*.
  The most remarkable thing is that we all love these lines, none of us
judges them. If one of us said this in real life or, better, did it (set fire to
a house, for instance, blew up a bridge), we'd all come to and shout
'Crime!' Yes, come to – from a spell, wake up – from a sleep, that dead
sleep of conscience, with nature's powers, our own, awake within it, that
sleep into which we were cast by these few measured lines.

## Genius

Visitation of the elemental, upon whom? Doesn't matter. Today upon
Pushkin. Pushkin, in the little song of the Wilson tragedy, is a genius
primarily because it *came upon* him.

Genius: the highest degree of subjection to the visitation – one; control of the visitation – two. The highest degree of being mentally pulled to pieces, and the highest of being – collected. The highest of passivity, and the highest of activity.

To let oneself be annihilated right down to some last atom, from the survival (resistance) of which will grow – a world.

For in this, this, this atom of resistance (resistivity) is the whole of mankind's chance of genius. Without it there is no genius – there is the crushed man who (it's still the same man!) bursts the walls not only of the Bedlams and Charentons but of the most well-ordered households too.

There is no genius without will, but still more is there none, still less is there any, without the visitation. Will is that unit to the countless milliards of the elemental visitation thanks to which alone they *are* milliards (realise their milliardness) and without which they are noughts – bubbles above a drowning man. While will without the visitation is – in creativity – simply a post. Made of oak. Such a poet would do better to go for a soldier.

## Pushkin and Walsingham

Walsingham was not the only one visited by the plague. To write his *Feast in Time of Plague* Pushkin had to *be* Walsingham – and cease to be him. Repentant? No.

To write the song of the *Feast*, Pushkin had to fight down in himself both Walsingham and the priest, and pass through into some third thing as through a door. Had he dissolved himself in the plague, he could not have written this song. Had he warded off the plague with signs of the Cross, he could not have written this song (the link would have snapped). From the plague (the element) Pushkin escaped, not into the feast (the plague's, that is, Walsingham's, triumphal feast over him) and not into prayer (the priest's), but into song.

Pushkin, like Goethe in *Werther*, escaped from the plague (Goethe from love) by giving his hero the death he himself longed to die. And by putting into his mouth a song that Walsingham could not have composed.

Had Walsingham been *capable* of that song, he would have been saved, if not for life everlasting, at least for life. But Walsingham, as we all know, is long since upon the black cart.

Walsingham is Pushkin with no way out into song.

Pushkin is Walsingham with the gift of song and the will to sing.

*

Why do I arbitrarily identify Pushkin with Walsingham and not with the priest, whose creator he also is?

This is why: in the *Feast*, the priest doesn't sing. (– Priests never do sing. – Yes, they do: prayers.) Had Pushkin been the priest as much (as powerfully) as he was Walsingham, he could not have helped making him sing; he'd have put into his mouth a counter-hymn – a prayer to the plague – just as he put the delightful little song (of love) into the mouth of Mary, who is in the *Feast* (while Walsingham is what Pushkin *is*) what Pushkin loves.

The lyric poet betrays himself by song, and always will, for he cannot help making his favourite (his double) speak in his own, poet's, language. A song, in a dramatic work, is always love's give-away, an unwitting sign of preference. The author tires of speaking for others and gives himself away – in song.

What remains to us of the *Feast* (in our ears and souls)? Two songs. Mary's and Walsingham's. A love-song and a plague-song.

Pushkin's genius lies in his not giving a counterweight to Walsingham's 'Hymn', an antidote to plague, a prayer. Had he done so, the work would have been stabilised, and we satisfied, from which no increase of good would have come; for by slaking our thirst for a counter-hymn Pushkin would have extinguished it. And so, with only the 'Hymn to the Plague', God, the good and prayer remain – outside, as the place we not only aspire to but are thrown back to; the place to which the plague throws us back. The prayer Pushkin doesn't give is there, unavoidable. (The priest in the *Feast* speaks in the performance of his duty and we not only feel nothing, we don't even listen, knowing in advance what he will say.)

Pushkin could hardly have thought of all that. One can only plan a work backwards from the last step taken to the first, retracing with one's eyes open the path one had walked blindly. Think the work *through*.

A poet is the reverse of a chess-player. He not only doesn't see the pieces and the board, he doesn't see his own hand – which indeed may not be there.

*

In what lies the blasphemy of Walsingham's song? There is no reviling of God in it, only praise of the plague. Yet is there any blasphemy stronger than this song?

Blasphemy, not because from fear and despair we feast in a time of plague (thus children laugh from fear!), but because in the song – the apogee of the feast – we have lost our fear; because we turn punishment into a feast, turn punishment into a gift; because we dissolve not in the fear of God, but in the bliss of annihilation. If (as everyone believed, in those days, and we do too while reading Pushkin) the plague is God's will to punish and vanquish us; if it really is God's scourge.

We throw ourselves under the scourge, as foliage under sunbeams, as foliage under the rain. Not joy in the teaching, but joy in the beating. Pure joy in the blow as such.

Joy? More than that! Bliss, with no equal in all the world's poetry. Bliss of complete surrender to the elemental – be it Love, or Plague, or whatever else we may call it.

For after the 'Hymn to the Plague' there was no longer any God. And having come in ('enter Priest'), what else is there for the priest to do, but to go out.

The priest went away to pray, Pushkin – to sing. Pushkin goes away after the priest, he goes away last, tearing himself with effort (as if by the roots) from his double, Walsingham; or rather, at this moment Pushkin divides: into himself as Walsingham and himself as poet, himself doomed and himself saved.

But Walsingham sits at the table eternally. But Walsingham rides on the black cart eternally. But Walsingham is dug in with a spade eternally.

For that song by which Pushkin was saved.

\*

A terrible name – Walsingham. It's no wonder Pushkin named him only three times in the whole play (named as if invoking him, and, like an invocation, thrice). The anonymous 'President', which lends the work a sinister modern relevance, is still closer to us.

\*

Walsinghams aren't needed by the elements. They defeat them in their stride. To conquer God in Walsingham is, alas, easier than to conquer song in Pushkin.

The plague, in *Feast in Time of Plague*, coveted not Walsingham but Pushkin.

And – *wonder of wonders!* – Walsingham, who is to the plague only an occasion for getting hold of Pushkin, Walsingham, who is for Pushkin only an occasion for his own elemental (his plaguey) self, that very Walsingham rescues Pushkin from the plague – into song, without which Pushkin cannot be his elemental self. By giving him the song and taking upon himself the end.

The last atom of resistance to the elemental, to the glory of the elemental, is what art is. Nature conquering herself to her own glory.

\*

So long as you are a poet, you shall not perish in the elemental, for everything returns you to the element of elements: the word.

So long as you are a poet, you shall not perish in the elemental; for that is not to perish but to return to the lap of nature.[4]

The poet perishes when he renounces the elemental. He might as well cut his wrists without ado.

\*

The whole of Walsingham is an exteriorisation (a carrying outside his limits) of the elemental Pushkin. You cannot live with a Walsingham inside you: either a crime or a poem. Even if Walsingham *existed*, – Pushkin would still have *created* him.

\*

Thank the Lord the poet has the hero, the third person – *him* – as a way out. Otherwise, what a shameful (and uninterrupted) confession.

Thus, at least the appearance is saved.

\*

The 'Apollonian principle', the 'golden mean': don't you see that this is nothing more than bits of Latin stuck in a schoolboy's head?

Pushkin, who created Walsingham, Pugachov, Mazeppa, Peter, who created them from inside himself, who didn't create them but disgorged them...

The Pushkin of the sea 'of the free element'.

– There was also another Pushkin.

– Yes, the Pushkin of *Walsingham's deep thought.*

(Exit Priest. The President remains, sunk in *deep thought.*)

\*

November 1830. Boldino. A hundred and one years ago. A hundred and one years later.

\*

## Art's lessons

What does art teach? Goodness? No. Commonsense? No. It cannot teach even itself, for it is – given.

There is no thing which is not taught by art; there is no thing the reverse of that, which is not taught by art; and there is no thing which is the only thing taught by art.

All the lessons we derive from art, *we* put into it.

A series of answers to which there are no questions.

All art is the sole givenness of the answer.

Thus, in *Feast in Time of Plague*, it answered before I asked, plied me with answers.

All *our* art is in managing (in time) to put, to each answer before it evaporates, *our* question. This being outgalloped by answers is what inspiration is. And how often – a blank page.

\*

One reads *Werther* and shoots himself, another reads *Werther* and, because Werther shoots himself, decides to live. One behaves like Werther, the other like Goethe. A lesson in self-extermination? A lesson in self-defence? Both. Goethe, by some law of the particular moment in his life, *needed* to shoot Werther; the suicidal demon of the generation needed to be incarnated precisely through Goethe's hand. A twice fateful necessity, and as such – without responsibility. And *very* fraught with consequences.

Is Goethe guilty of all the subsequent deaths?

He himself, in his profound and splendid old age, replied: no. Otherwise we wouldn't dare say a single word, for who can calculate the effect of any one word? (I'm putting it my own way, this is the substance of it.)

I too shall reply for Goethe: no.

He had no evil will, he had no will at all except the creative one. Writing his *Werther*, he not only forgot all others (that is, their possible troubles), but forgot himself too (his own trouble!).

All-forgetfulness, forgetfulness of everything which is not the work: the very basis of creation.

Would Goethe have written *Werther* a second time, after everything that had happened, if (improbably) he had again had just as urgent a need to? And would he then have been indictable? Would Goethe have written – knowingly?

He'd have written it a thousand times if he had needed to, just as he would not have written even the first line of the first one if the pressure had been the tiniest bit lighter. (Werther, like Walsingham, is a pressure from within.)

– And would he then have been indictable?

As a man, yes. As an artist, no.

Moreover, as an artist Goethe would have been both indictable and condemned if he had immolated Werther in himself with the aim of preserving human lives (fulfilment of the commandment: Thou shalt not kill). Here the law of art is exactly the reverse of the moral law. An artist is guilty in two cases only: in that refusal I have mentioned to create the work (for whoever's benefit), and in the creation of an inartistic work. Here his lesser responsibility ends, and his boundless responsibility as a human being begins.

Artistic creation is in some cases a sort of atrophy of conscience – more than that: a necessary atrophy of conscience, the moral flaw without which art cannot exist. In order to be good (not lead into temptation the little ones of this world), art would have to renounce a fair half of its whole self. The only way for art to be wittingly good is – not to be. It will end with the life of the planet.

## *Tolstoy's crusade*

'An exception in favour of genius.' Our whole relation to art is an exception in favour of genius. Art is itself that genius in whose favour we are excepted (excluded) from the moral law.

What is our whole relation to art if not this: conquerors are not judged; and who else *is* it – this Art – but a notorious conqueror (seducer) of, above all, our conscience.

The reason why, despite all our love for art, we respond so warmly to Tolstoy's clumsy, extra-aesthetic challenge to art (for he went, and he led, against his own grain) is that this challenge comes from the lips of an artist, seduced and seducing lips.

In Tolstoy's call for the annihilation of art, what is important are the lips that do the calling; if it did not sound from such a dizzying artistic height – if it were one of *us* calling us – we would not even turn our head.

In Tolstoy's crusade against art, what is important is Tolstoy: the artist. We *forgive* the artist the shoemaker. *War and Peace* cannot be eradicated from our relation to him. Ineradicable. Irreparable.

Through the artist we *consecrate* the shoemaker.

In Tolstoy's crusade against art, we are seduced once again – *by* art.

\*

All this is no reproach to Tolstoy, but a reproach to us, the slaves of art. Tolstoy would have given his soul to make us listen – not to Tolstoy, but to *the truth*.

\*

An objection.

Whose preaching of poverty is more convincing (that is to say, more deadly to wealth): the poor man's, poor from birth, or the rich man's who has renounced his riches?

The latter, of course.

The same applies to Tolstoy. Whose condemnation of pure art is more convincing (more deadly to art): that of the Tolstoyan who has been nothing in art, or that of Tolstoy himself who has been everything?

So we start by placing our eternal credit with Tolstoy the artist, and end by recognising the complete discrediting – by Tolstoy the artist – of art itself.

*

When I think of the moral essence of that human individual, the poet, I always recall the definition of the Tolstoy father in *Childhood and Boyhood*: 'He belonged to that dangerous breed of people who can narrate one and the same action as the greatest baseness and as the most innocent joke.'

## The sleeper

Let us return to Goethe. Goethe, in his *Werther*, is just as innocent of the bad (the destruction of lives) as (example of the second reader who because of *Werther* decides to live) innocent of the good. Both – death and desire to live – are consequence, not purpose.

Whenever Goethe had a *purpose*, he realised it in his life: he built a theatre, proposed a series of reforms to Karl-August, studied the customs and soul of the ghetto, worked at mineralogy. In short, when Goethe had some purpose or other, he realised it directly, without this great roundabout way of art.

The sole purpose of a work of art during its making is that it should be completed, and not even that the whole work should be completed, but each individual particle of it, each molecule. The very work itself, as a whole work, steps back before the realisation of this molecule; or rather, each molecule *is* this whole, whose purpose is everywhere in its entire length and breadth, ubiquitous, omnipresent – and it itself, as a whole, is an end-in-itself.

At its completion it may turn out that the artist has made something bigger than he planned (was able to do more than he thought he could!), something other than he'd planned. Or others will say so, as they did to Blok. And Blok was astonished every time, he always agreed with everyone, agreed almost with the first comer, so new to him was all this (that is, the presence of any purpose whatsoever).

Blok's *The Twelve* arose under a spell. The demon of that hour of the Revolution (who is Blok's 'music of Revolution')[5] inhabited Blok and compelled him.

Then the naive moraliser, Z. G.,[6] spent a long time wondering whether or not to shake hands with Blok, while Blok patiently waited.

Blok wrote *The Twelve* in one night and got up in complete exhaustion, like one who has been ridden.

Blok did not know *The Twelve*, never read it from a stage. ('I don't know *The Twelve*. I don't remember *The Twelve*.' Truly, *he did not know*.)

And one can understand his terror when in 1920 on the Vozdvizhenka[7] he seized his companion's hand: 'Look!' And only five paces later: 'Katka!'[8]

In the Middle Ages (yet what *extreme* ones!), whole villages were possessed by a demon and suddenly started talking Latin.

A poet? A sleeper.

## *Art in the light of conscience*

One woke up. A man sharp-nosed and waxen-faced[9] who, in the hearth of the Sheremetev house, burned a manuscript. The second part of *Dead Souls*.

Lead not into temptation. A more than medieval – *propriomanual* – casting of one's creation into the flames. Self-judgment, which I say is the only judgment.

(The shame and failure of the Inquisition lies in the fact that it itself did the burning, instead of leading people to do their own burning; burned manuscripts, when it should have burned out the soul.)

– But Gogol was mad by that time.

A madman is one who burns down a temple (not built by him) to achieve fame. Gogol, burning the work of his hands, burned his fame as well.

And I recall the words of a shoemaker (Moscow 1920), a case where the shoemaker really is higher than the artist: 'You and me, Marina Ivanovna, are not out of our minds, but them – they're short of mind.'

*

That half-hour of Gogol's at the fireplace did more for good, and against art, than all Tolstoy's many years of preaching.

For here is a deed, a visible deed of the hands, that movement of the hand which we all thirst for, and which is not to be out-weighed by any 'movement of the spirit'.

*

Maybe we would not have been tempted by the second part of *Dead Souls*. Certainly we'd have been glad to have it. But that gladness of ours would have been nothing in comparison with our actual gladness in Gogol, who, out of love for our living souls, burned his *Dead* ones. On the fire of his own conscience.

The first were written with ink.

The second – in us – with fire.

## Art without artifice

Yet in the very heart of art, and at the same time on its heights, there are works that make you say: 'This is not art any more. It's more than art.' Everyone has known works of this sort.

Their sign is their effectiveness despite their inadequacy of means, an inadequacy which nothing in the world would make us exchange for any adequacies and abundances, and which we only call to mind when we try to establish: how was it done? An essentially futile approach, for in every born work the ends are hidden.

Not yet art, but already more than art.

Such works often come from the pens of women, children, self-taught people – the little ones of this world. Such works often come from no pen at all, being unwritten but kept (or lost) orally. Often they are the sole works of a lifetime. Often – the very first. Often – the very last.

Art without artifice.[10]

Here is a verse by a four-year-old boy who did not live long.

Over there, lives a white bird.
Over there, walks a pale boy.
Surely! Surely! Surely!
There *is* – far away.

(*Vedno* ['surely'] – a childish and folk form of *vedomo* ['known'] which
here sounds like both *verno* ['right'] and *zavedomo* ['wittingly']: wittingly
right. While *tam-ot* ['far away'] is a nanny's word for distance.)

Here is the last line of a poem by a little girl of seven who has never
walked, and who prays to be able to stand up. I heard the poem only once,
twenty years ago, and have kept only the last line: 'So that I may *stand up*
to pray!'

And here is a poem by a little nun at the Novo-Devichii Monastery.[11]
There were a lot – she burned them all before she died. One remained
and is alive today solely in my memory. I pass it on, as a good deed.

Whatever life may keep in store,
Dear children, there will be much sorrow,
The crafty nets of temptation,
The darkness of burning repentance,
The yearning of hopeless desires,
And cheerless unending toil,
And a dozen moments of happiness,
Paid for with years of suffering –
Yet do not weaken in spirit,
In time of tribulations
Mankind is solely alive
Through the round robin of good!
Wherever your heart bids you live,
In world's bustle or country quiet,
Pour out fearlessly and freely
The treasures of your soul!
Don't seek or expect a return,
Nor let cruel jibes disturb you.
Mankind is solely rich
In the round robin[12] of good!

Take the rhymes[13] – they are obviously commonplace [...], obviously weak
[...] Take the metre – again nothing to make you prick up your ears. By
what means was this obviously great deed done?

– By no means at all. By the bare soul.

This unknown nun of an irretrievable nunnery gave the fullest
definition of goodness that has ever existed: '*goodness as a round robin*',
and flung the most unmalicious challenge to evil that has ever been heard:

Wherever your heart bids you live,
In world's bustle or country quiet...

(the words of a nun, who lives in confinement!)

Pour out fearlessly and freely
The treasures of your soul!

To say that these lines have 'genius' would be blasphemy, and to judge them as a literary work would be mean-minded, so far is all that beyond the threshold of this *great* (as earthly love) *trifle of art*.

I've quoted what I remember. I'm convinced there is more. (I deliberately pass over the poems of my six-year-old daughter,[14] some of which were published at the end of my book *Psyche*, as I mean to speak of them separately some time.) But even suppose there were not! Here, in *my* memory alone, are three poems, more than poems.

And perhaps such poems are the only real poems?

\*

A sign of such works is their unevenness. Take the nun's poem.

'Whatever life may keep in store/Dear children, there will be much sorrow/The crafty nets of temptation/The darkness of burning repentance' (so far all cliché)/'The yearning of hopeless desires/And cheerless unending toil' (still the same)/'And a dozen moments of happiness/Paid for with years of suffering' (this last bit is almost a parlour song)/'Yet do not weaken in spirit/In time of tribulations', and – here it comes! –

Mankind is solely alive
Through the round robin of good!

Then on, up a now continuous line of ascent that never falters, in one great profound sigh to the very end.

This at first glance (a glance I've already spoken of) commonplace beginning was needed by her as a run-up, so that she could talk her way up to the round robin of good. Inexperience of the non-professional. A real poet – the kind our capitals teem with – if, contrary to expectation, he'd written his way up to the round robin (which he never would!) – would have dropped that beginning and tried to fit everything to one common level of loftiness.

Whereas the nun did not even notice the insufficiency of the beginning, for neither did she notice the round robin; she was, perhaps, vaguely glad of it as something very *like*, but no more. For my nun is not the professional poet who would sell his soul to the devil for an effective turn of phrase (though the devil would not take it – there's nothing there to take), but a pure vessel of God, just the same as that four-year-old with his 'far away'; all of them – the nun, the little girl without legs, the little boy, and all the nameless girls, boys, nuns of the world – all say one thing, speak of one thing, or rather, that one thing speaks through them.

These are my favourite poems of all I have ever read, or ever written, my favourites among all poems on earth. When I read (or write) my own after reading them, I feel nothing but shame.

I'd also place among such poems the poem 'Thought' (its thought has been stoned to death many a time) by an unknown author, marked, in all the collections where it was reprinted, with the single letter D.

Thus, with this large D (D for *dobro* ['goodness']), these poems went on their way.


## Attempt at a hierarchy

Major poet. Great poet. Lofty poet.

A major poet is what anyone – any major poet – can be. To be a major poet, it is enough to have a major poetic gift. To be a great poet, even the most major gift is too small: he needs an equivalent gift of personality – of mind, soul, will – and the aspiration of this whole towards a definite aim; that is, its organisation. But a lofty poet is something that even a quite minor poet, bearer of the most modest gift, can be – such as Alfred de Vigny, who wins our recognition as a poet by the power of his inner worth alone. In his case, the gift just reached to the brim. A little less and he'd have been merely a hero (that is to say, immeasurably more).

The great poet includes – and counterbalances – the lofty poet. The lofty poet does *not* include the great one, otherwise we'd call him 'great'. Loftiness as the sole sign of existence. So, there is no poet bigger than Goethe, but there are poets who are loftier – his younger contemporary Hölderlin, for instance, an incomparably poorer poet, yet a *dweller* upon those highlands where Goethe is but a guest. And the lofty is after all less than the great, even if they are of equal height. Thus: the oak is great, the cypress lofty.

The earthly foundation of genius is too vast and stable to let it disappear into loftiness. Shakespeare, Goethe, Pushkin. If Shakespeare, Goethe, Pushkin, had been loftier they would have left many a thing unheard, unanswered, would simply not have condescended to many things.

Genius: a resultant of counteractions, that is, ultimately, equilibrium, that is, harmony; while the giraffe is a freak, creature of a single dimension, his own neck; the giraffe is neck. (Every freak is a part of itself.)

'The poet soars among the clouds' – true, but true of only one breed of poet: the only-lofty, the purely-spiritual. And he doesn't even soar, he sojourns. The humpback pays for his hump, the angel too pays for his wings while on earth. Fleshlessness, so close to fruitlessness, rarefied air, thought instead of passion, utterances instead of words – these are the earthly signs of heavenly guests.

A single exception: Rilke. A poet not only equally lofty and great (this can be said of Goethe too), but one who has that same exclusive loftiness which here excludes nothing. As if God, who, when giving other poets of the spirit their one gift, took everything else away from them, left to Rilke that everything else. Into the bargain.

*

Loftiness does not exist as parity. Only as primacy.

*

For the merely major poet, art is always an aim in itself – that is, a mere function without which he cannot live and for which he is not responsible. For the great and for the lofty, it is always a means. He himself is a means in someone's hands – as is, indeed, the merely major poet, in other hands. The whole difference, apart from the basic difference of which hands, is in the degree of consciousness the poet has of being held. The spiritually greater the poet – that is, the loftier the hands that hold him – the more powerfully conscious he is of this being-held (being in service). Had Goethe not known a higher force above himself and his work, he would never have written the last lines of the last *Faust*. Only to the innocent is it *given* – or to the one who knows *everything*.

In essence, a poet's whole labour amounts to a fulfilment, the physical fulfilment of a spiritual task (not assigned by himself). And a poet's whole will – to the labouring will to realisation. (No such thing as individual creative will.)

The will to embody physically what already exists spiritually (the eternal) and to embody spiritually (to inspirit) what doesn't yet exist spiritually and desires to, regardless of the qualities of this desirer. To embody the spirit that desires a body (ideas), and to inspirit the bodies that desire a soul (the elements). The word is body to ideas, soul to the elements.

Every poet is, in one way or another, the servant of ideas or of elements: sometimes, (as already mentioned) of ideas alone; sometimes, of both ideas and elements. Sometimes, of the elements alone. But even in this last case, he is still the first low sky of something: of those same elements and passions. Through the element of the word, which alone among all elements, is – from its very beginning – made sense of, that is to say, made spirit of. *The low close sky of the earth.*

*

In this ethical approach (the demand for idea-content, for loftiness, in a writer) may lie the whole solution to something at first glance incomprehensible: the nineties' preferring Nadson to Pushkin, who, if not obviously idea-less is certainly less clearly idea-ful than Nadson, and the previous generation's preferring Nekrasov-the-citizen to just Nekrasov. All that fierce utilitarianism, all the Bazarovism,[15] is only the affirmation of and demand for loftiness as the basic principle of life – it is *only the Russian form of loftiness*. Our 'usefulness' is only conscience. Russia, to her honour – or rather, to the honour of her conscience, not the honour of her artistry (two things that don't need each other) – always approached writers – rather, always *went* to writers – the way the peasant went to the Tsar – for the truth. And it was excellent when that Tsar turned out to be Lev Tolstoy and not Artsybashev. For Russia also learned to live from Artsybashev's *Sanin!*

## Prayer

What can we say about God? Nothing. What can we say *to* God? Everything. Poems to God are prayer. And if there are no prayers nowadays (except Rilke's and those little ones', I know of none), it is not because we don't have anything to say to God, nor because we have no one to say this anything to – there is something and there is someone – but because we haven't the conscience to praise and pray God in the same language we've used for centuries to praise and pray absolutely everything. In our age, to have the courage for direct speech to God (for prayer) we must either not know what poems are, or forget.

Loss of trust.

*

The cruel thing Blok said about the early Akhmatova: Akhmatova writes poems as if a man were watching her, but you should write them as if God were watching you – adapting the first, denunciatory half of the sentence to fit every one of us – holily, in the end. As if before God, *standing in the divine presence*.

But what in us shall then withstand, and who among us?

## *Point of view*

In relation to the spiritual world: art is a kind of physical world of the spiritual.

In relation to the physical world: art is a kind of spiritual world of the physical.

Starting from the earth, it is the first millimetre of air over it (of sky, that is, for the sky begins right from the earth, or else there is no sky at all. Check this by distances, which clarify phenomena).

Starting from the top of the sky, it is that same first millimetre above the earth, but the last when seen from the top; that is, it is almost earth from there, and from the very top it is entirely earth.

*Where you look from*.

*

In the same way, the soul, which the common man supposes to be the peak of spirituality, is for the spiritual man – almost flesh. The analogy with art is not accidental, for poetry – which I never take my eyes off when I say 'art', the whole *event* of poetry, from the poet's visitation to the reader's reception – takes place entirely within the soul, that first, lowest sky of the spirit. Which is in no way contradictory to art as nature. There is no soul-less nature; there is only uninspired – spirit-less – nature.

Poet, poet! The most soul-animated – and how often (perhaps just *because* of that) the most uninspired object!

\*

'Fier quand je me compare' – no! Because whatever is below the poet does not even count: there is still enough pride not to level oneself down. For I look up – from below, – and my point of support is not in my own lowness, but in that height.

'Humble quand je me compare, inconnu quand je me considère',[16] for in order to contemplate something one must rise above the contemplated thing; place between oneself and the thing all the vertical, the refusal, of height. For I look down – from above! The highest in me – at the lowest in me. And what remains to me of this confrontation – but amazement... or recognition.

> She took the faded pages
> And gazed upon them strangely
> As souls look from on high
> At bodies they've cast off.[17]

This is how I too shall one day (indeed, I already do) look at my poems...

## Poet's heaven

– A priest serves God in his way, you in yours.

– Blasphemy. When I write my poem *The Swain* – about a vampire's love for a girl and hers for him – I don't serve any God: I know what God I serve. When I describe Tatars in open spaces, I again don't serve any God except the wind (or a wizard: a forefather).[18] All my Russian works[19] are elemental, that is, sinful. One has to distinguish what forces are *im Spiel*.[20] And when shall we finally stop taking power for truth, and magic for holiness?

Art is a temptation, perhaps the last, subtlest, most insuperable of the earth's seductions, that last cloud in the last sky, at which gazed the dying *brother of a brother*, Jules Goncourt – no longer looking at anything, yet attempting to get its colouring into words – having by then forgotten all words.

A third kingdom with its own laws, from which we so seldom escape into the higher one (and how often into the lower!). A third kingdom, the first sky from the earth, a second earth. Between the heaven of the spirit and the hell of the species, art is a purgatory which no one wishes to leave for paradise.

When, at the sight of a priest, a monk, even a nurse, I – invariably, irresistibly!– lower my eyes, I know why I lower them. My shame at the sight of a priest, a monk, even a nurse – this shame is visionary.

– You are doing God's work.

– If my works release, enlighten, purify – yes; if they seduce – no, and it would be better to hang a stone round my neck.

But how often in one and the same work, on one and the same page, in one and the same line, they both release *and* seduce. Like the dubious swill in a witch's cauldron – what *hasn't* been heaped into it and boiled?

*

How many it has ruined; how few, saved!

*

And the immediate riposte of the accused:

Dark power!
Craft of *Mra*!
How many – ruined!
How few – saved!

I fear that even when dying...*Mra*,[21] by the way, I take here as a feminine noun, a feminine ending, the sound of death. *Mor* (masculine), *Mra* (feminine). Death could have had this name; perhaps at some time, somewhere, it did have this name: *Mra*. Word-creation, like any creation, only means following the track of the hearing ear of nation and nature. A journey by ear. 'Et tout le reste n'est que littérature.'[22]

*

Polytheism of the poet. I'd say our Christian God is at best *one* among the host of his gods.

Never an atheist. Always a polytheist, with the sole difference that the higher knows the older (knows what there was in pagan times too). But the majority don't know even this, and blindly alternate Christ with Dionysus, not realising that the very juxtaposition of these names is blasphemy and sacrilege.

Art would be holy if we lived then, or those gods now. The poet's heaven is just on a level with the pedestal of Zeus: the summit of Olympus.

## *Kernel of the kernel*

> …and you send reply.
> But to you there is no response…
> Such, poet, are you as well![23]

Not-poet, above-poet, more than poet, not only poet: but where and what is the *poet* in all this? *Der Kern des Kernes*, the kernel of the kernel.

A poet is an answer.

From the lowest level of the simple reflex to the highest level of Goethe's great answer, the poet is a definite and invariable mental-artistic reflex. To what? may be simply a question of brain capacity. Pushkin said: to everything. A genius' answer.

This mental-artistic reflex is the kernel of the kernel which unites the anonymous author of a chastushka[24] with the author of *Faust* Part Two. Without it there is no poet, or rather, it *is* the poet. Miracle of the poet, not explicable by any convolutions of the brain.

A reflex before thought, even before feeling, the deepest and fastest – as by electric current – spearing of the whole being by a given phenomenon, and the simultaneous, almost preceding, answer to it.

An answer not to the blow, but to a quivering of the air – of a thing that has not yet moved. Answer to the pre-blow. Not an answer, but a pre-answer. Always to a phenomenon, never to a question. The phenomenon itself is the question. The thing self-strikes the poet – with itself; self-questions him – with itself. The command for an answer, coming from the phenomenon itself – which is not yet manifest and is manifested only through the answer. Command? Yes, if 'SOS' is a command (the most unrepulsable of all).

Before it existed (well, it always existed, only hadn't yet reached time;

thus the opposite shore has not yet reached the ferry). Why the poet's hand so often hangs in mid-air is that its support – in time – does not yet exist (*nicht vorhanden*).[25] The poet's hand – even if hanging in mid-air! – creates the phenomenon (completes its creation). This hand hanging in the air is, in fact, the poet's imperfect, despairing, yet nonetheless creative, '*be*'. (Who called me?[26] – Silence. – I must create, that is, name, the one who called me. Such is the poet's 'responding'.)

One more thing. 'Mental-artistic reflex'. Artistic-vulneral,[27] for the soul is our capacity for pain – pure and simple. (For pain which is not headache, not toothache, not throatache, not…not…not, etc. – pain pure and simple.)

This is the kernel of the kernel of the poet, leaving aside the *indispensable* artistry: the *strength of anguish*.

## Truth of poets

Such then is the truth of poets, the most elusive, most invincible, most convincing and most unproven truth; truth that lives in us only for some primary *glimmer* of perception (what was that?) and remains in us only as a trace of light or loss (*was* it something?). Truth irresponsible and inconsequential, which – for God's sake – one should not even attempt to pursue, because it is irretrievable even for the poet. (A poet's truth is a path where all traces are straightaway overgrown. Untraceable even for the poet, were he to follow in his own wake.) He didn't know he was about to *pronounce*, often didn't know what it was he was pronouncing. Didn't know it before the pronouncing, and forgot it immediately after. Not one of innumerable truths, but one of the innumerable faces of the truth, which destroy each other only when set side by side. Once-only aspects of the truth. Simply – a thrust in the heart of Eternity. The means: juxtaposition of two most ordinary words, which stand side by side just so. (Sometimes – separation by a single hyphen!)

There is a lock which opens only through a certain combination of figures: if you know this, opening it is nothing; if you don't, it's a miracle or chance. A miracle-chance which happened to my six-year-old son who, in one go, twisted and unfastened a fine chain of this sort that had been locked around his neck, to the horror of the chain's owner. Does the poet know, or not know, the combination of figures? (In the poet's case – since all the world is locked up and everything is waiting to be unlocked – it is different every time, to each thing its own lock; and behind the lock is a particular truth, different every time, once-only – like the lock itself.) Does the poet know *all* the combinations of figures?

\*

My mother had a peculiarity: she would set the clock during the night, whenever it stopped. In response to not its ticking but its not-ticking – doubtless what woke her up – she would set it in the dark without looking. In the morning the clock showed *it* – the absolute time, I assume – which was never found by that unhappy crowned contemplator[28] of so many contradictory clock-faces and listener to so many uncoinciding chimes.

The clock showed *it*.

\*

Chance? Chance that is repeated every time is, in the life of a man, fate; in the world of phenomena, law. This was the law of her hand. The law of her hand's *knowledge*.

Not: 'my mother had a peculiarity', but: her *hand* had the peculiarity – of truth.

Not playing like my son, not self-assured like the owner of the lock, and not visionary like the supposed mathematician – but both blind and visionary, obeying only his hand (which, itself, obeys what?): thus the poet opens the lock.

He lacks only one gesture: the self-assured, sure of self and of lock alike, gesture of the owner of the lock. A poet does not possess a single lock as his own. That is why he unlocks them all. And that is why, unlocking each at the first try, he won't open any of them a second time. For he is not the owner of the secret, only its passer-by.

## Condition of creation

The condition of creation is a condition of entrancement. Till you begin – *obsession*; till you finish – *possession*.[29] Something, someone, lodges in you; your hand is the fulfiller not of you but of *it*. Who is this *it*? That which through you wants to be.

Things always chose me by the mark of my power, and often I wrote them almost against my will. All my Russian works[30] are of this sort. Certain things of Russia wanted to be expressed, they chose me. And how did they persuade, seduce me? By my own power: only you! Yes, only I. And having given in – sometimes seeingly, sometimes blindly – I would obey, seek out with my ear some assigned aural lesson. And it was not I who, out of a hundred words (not rhymes! but in the middle of a line), would choose the hundred and first, but *it* (the thing), resisting all the hundred epithets: that isn't *my* name.

The condition of creation is a condition of dreaming, when suddenly, obeying an unknown necessity, you set fire to a house or push your friend off a mountain-top. Is it your act? Clearly it *is* yours (after all, it is you sleeping, *dreaming!*). Yours – in complete freedom. An act of yourself without conscience, yourself as nature.

A series of doors, behind one of which someone, something (usually terrible), is waiting. The doors are identical. Not this one – not this one – not this one – *that* one. Who told me? Nobody. I recognise the one I need by all the unrecognised ones (the right one by all the wrong ones). It's the same with words. Not this one – not this one – not this one – *that* one. By the obviously *not-this* I recognise *that*. Native to every sleeper and writer is the *blow of recognition*. Oh, the sleeper cannot be deceived! He knows friend and he knows enemy, knows the door and knows the chasm behind the door, and to all this – both friend and enemy, and door and pit – he is doomed. The sleeper cannot be deceived, even by the sleeper himself. Vainly I say to myself: I won't go in (through the door), I won't look (through the window) – I know that I shall go in, and even while I am saying I won't look, I am looking.

Oh, the sleeper is not to be saved!

There is a loop-hole, though, even in sleep: when it gets too terrible, I'll wake up. In sleep, I'll wake up; in poetry, I shall resist.

Someone said to me about Pasternak's poems: 'Splendid poems when you explain them all like that, but they need a key supplied with them.'

No, not supply a key to the poems (dreams), but the poems themselves are a key to understanding everything. But from understanding to accepting there isn't just a step, there is no step at all; to understand is to accept, there is no other understanding, any other understanding is non-understanding. Not in vain does the French *comprendre* mean both 'understand' and 'encompass' – that is, 'accept' and 'include'.

There is no poet who would reject any elemental force, consequently any rebellion. Pushkin feared Nicholas, deified Peter, but loved Pugachov.[31] It wasn't by chance that all the pupils of one remarkable and wrongly forgotten poetess, who was also a teacher of history, answered the question put by the district administrator: 'Well, children, and who is your favourite tsar?' – (the whole class together) 'Grishka Otrepyev!'[32]

Find me a poet without a Pugachov! without an Impostor! without a Corsican![33] – *within*. A poet might lack the power (the means) for a Pugachov, that's all. *Mais l'intention y est toujours.*[34]

What doesn't accept (rejects, even ejects) is the human being: will, reason, conscience.

In this realm the poet can have only one prayer: not to understand the unacceptable – let me not understand, so that I may not be seduced. The sole prayer of the poet is not to hear the voices: let me not hear, so that I may not answer. For to hear, for the poet, is already to answer, and to answer is already to affirm, if only by the passionateness of his denial. The poet's only prayer is a prayer for deafness. Otherwise there is the most difficult task of choosing what to hear according to its quality; that is, of choosing the forcible stopping of his own ears to a number of calls, which are invariably the stronger. Choice from birth, that is, to hear only what is important, is a blessing bestowed on almost no one.

(On Odysseus' ship there was neither hero nor poet. A hero is one who will stand firm even when not tied down, stand firm even without wax[35] stuck in his ears; a poet is one who will fling himself forward even when tied down, who will hear even with wax in his ears, that is – once again – fling himself forward.

The only things non-understood by the poet from birth are the half-measures of the rope and the wax.)

Thus Mayakovsky failed to vanquish the poet in himself, and the result was a monument to the Volunteer leader raised by the most revolutionary of poets. (The poem 'Crimea', twelve immortal lines.) One can't help remarking the devilish cunning of whatever those forces are that pick themselves a herald from among their very enemies. The end of the Crimea just *had* to be depicted by Mayakovsky!

When, at the age of thirteen, I asked an old revolutionary: 'Is it possible to be a poet and also be in the Party?', he replied, without a moment's thought: 'No.'

So I too shall reply: no.

\*

What element was it then, what demon, that lodged in Mayakovsky at that hour and made him describe Wrangel?[36] For the Volunteer movement, as everyone now recognises, was not elemental. (Unless – the steppe they went over, the songs they sang...)

Not the White movement, but the Black Sea; into which, kissing the Russian earth three times, stepped the Commander-in-chief.

The Black Sea of that hour.

\*

I don't want to be a springboard for others' ideas, a loudspeaker for other people's passions.

Other people's? But is anything 'other' to a poet? In *The Covetous Knight* Pushkin made even miserliness his own, in *Salieri*[37] even untalentedness. And it was not through being other, but precisely through being *related*, that Pugachov knocked at me.

So I'll say: I don't want anything that isn't wholly mine, wittingly mine, most mine.

And what if the most mine (revelation of dream) is indeed Pugachov?

I don't want anything that I won't answer for at seven o'clock in the morning and won't die for (won't die without) at any hour of day or night.

I won't die for Pugachov – that means he is *not mine*.

\*

The reverse extreme of nature is Christ.

The other end of the road is Christ.

Everything in between is – halfway along the road.

And it is not for the poet, from birth a man of many roads, to give up his many roads – the native cross of his crossroads!– for the halfway roads of social issues or whatever else.

To lay down one's soul for one's friends.

Only this can overpower the elemental in a poet.

# Intoxiqués [38]

> When I find myself among literary people,
> artists and so on...I always have the feeling
> that I am among...*intoxiqués*. – Yes, but
> when you are with a great artist, a great
> poet, you won't say that; on the contrary, all
> the rest will seem to you poisoned.
>
> (Conversation after a literary meeting)

When I speak of the possessed condition of people of art, I certainly don't
mean they are possessed *by art*.

Art is that through which the elemental force holds – and overpowers:
a means for the holding (of us – by the elements), not an autocracy;[39] the
condition of being possessed, not the content of the possessed condition.

A sculptor is not possessed by the deed of his own hands, nor a poet
by the deed of his one.

Being possessed by the work of our hands means being held in some-
one's hands.

This is about major artists.

But possession by art does happen, for there does exist – and in immensely
greater numbers than the poet – the pseudo-poet, the aesthete, the one
who has taken a gulp of art, not of the elemental, a creature lost both to
God and to man – and lost for nothing.

The demon (the elemental) pays its victim. You give me blood, life,
conscience, honour, and I will give you such consciousness of power (for
power is mine!), such power over everyone (except over yourself, for you
are mine!), such freedom (within my grip), that every other power will be
laughable to you, every other might will be small, every other freedom will
be constricting, and every other prison – spacious.

Art does not pay its victims. It doesn't even know them. The worker is
paid by the master, not by the lathe. The lathe can only leave you without
an arm. How many I've seen, poets without an arm. With an arm no good
for any other labour.

*

Shyness of the artist before the object. He forgets that it is not *himself* writing. Vyacheslav Ivanov said to me (in Moscow, 1920, persuading me to write a novel): 'Just make a start! By the third page you'll be convinced there is no freedom' – meaning I shall find myself in the power of things, in the power of the demon, merely a humble servant.

To forget oneself is, above all, to forget one's weakness.

Who has ever been *able* to do anything with his own two hands?

Let the ear hear, the hand race (and when it doesn't race, *let it stop*).

Not without reason does each of us say at the end: 'How marvellously my work has come out!' and never: 'How marvellously well I've done it!' And not: 'It's come out marvellously', but it's come out by a marvel, always by a miracle; it's always a blessing, even if sent not by God.
    – And the amount of will in all this?
    – Oh, enormous. If only not to despair when you wait by the sea for good weather.
    Of a hundred lines, ten are given, ninety assigned: unyielding, then yielding, surrendering like a fortress – lines I got by hard work, that is, by dint of listening. And listening is what my will *is*, not to tire of listening until something is heard, and not to put down anything that wasn't heard. To be afraid not of the rough-work page (criss-crossed in vain searches), nor of the blank page, but of one's *own* page: self-willed.

Creative will is patience.


## Parenthesis about a species of hearing

This hearing is not allegorical, though not physical either. So far is it from being physical that you don't actually hear any words at all, or if you do you don't understand them, like someone half-asleep. The physical hearing either sleeps or fails to carry, replaced by another hearing.
    I hear, not words, but a kind of soundless tune inside my head, a kind of aural line, from a hint to a command – but this is too long to tell now, it is a whole distinct world, and to tell of it is a whole distinct duty. But I

am convinced that here too, as in everything, there is a law.

In the meantime, it is authentic hearing without ears, one more proof that:

There *is* – far away.

\*

The pseudo-poet considers art to be God, and makes this God himself (while expecting Him to send rain!).

The pseudo-poet always does it himself.

Signs of pseudo-poetry: absence of *given* lines.

There are great experts among them.

\*

But that happens to poets and geniuses too.

In 'Hymn to the Plague' there are two lines that are solely the author's – namely:

And happy the one who finds and knows
those pleasures mid this turbulence.

Pushkin was released by the demon for a second, and did not have enough patience. This and only this is what has happened when we discover in our own or other people's work a stop-gap line, that poetic 'water' which is nothing other than the *shallows of inspiration*.

Take the whole passage:

There is an ecstasy in battle
and on the sombre chasm's edge,
and in the ragings of the ocean,
the dreadful waves and thundering dark,
and in the Arabian hurricane,
and in the breathing of the Plague.
Whatever threatens us with doom
hides in itself, for mortal hearts,
unspeakable pleasures – guarantee

perhaps of immortality!
And happy the one who finds and knows
those pleasures mid this turbulence.

Take it word by word: 'and happy the one' – too small! small and limp
after those absolutes of pleasure and ecstasy, an obvious repetition, a
weakening, a lowering; 'mid this turbulence' – what kind of? and again
what a small word (and thing)! After all the hurricanes and abysses! An
allegory of worldly turbulence after the authentic ocean waves. '...the one
who finds and knows' – finds inexpressible delights – is this German? It's
certainly not Pushkinian and not Russian. Next: 'and knows' (a repetition,
for if you've found, you already know). And how, in a situation like *that*,
could one help finding them? A gallicism: 'Heureux celui qui a pu les
connaître',[40] and altogether it's a piece of philosophising, *preposterous* in
such a whirlwind.
 That is what happens when the hand overtakes the hearing.

*

Returning to pseudo-poets.
 Pseudo-poet. Poet. Victim of literature. Victim of the demon. Both are
lost to God (to the cause, to the good) – but if you're to be lost, then let
it be honourably; if you're to accept subjugation, let it be beneath the
highest yoke.
 Unfortunately you cannot choose your masters.

## Parenthesis about poet and child

The poet is often compared to the child, for their innocence only. I would
compare them for their irresponsibility only. Irresponsibility in everything
except play.
 When you enter this playing with your human (moral) and man-made
(social) laws, you only disturb the game and perhaps bring it to an end.
 By bringing your conscience into it, you will confuse our (creative)
conscience. 'That isn't the way to play.' Yes, it *is* the way to play.
 Either the playing should be forbidden altogether (children's by us,
ours by God), or it shouldn't be interfered with.
 What to you is 'play' is to us the one thing that is serious.
 We shall not even die more seriously.

## Whom to judge, to judge for what, and who should judge

A demon lodges in a person. Will you judge the demon (the elemental)? Will you judge the fire that is burning the house down?

Judge me, for instance?

For what? For lack of conscience, will, strength: for *weakness*?

I'll answer with a question:

Why, out of all who walk along the streets of Moscow and Paris, is it just me that it comes upon, and outwardly comes in such a way that I do not foam at the mouth, and I do not fall down on flat ground, and they do not take me either to the hospital or to the police-station?

Why – if I am possessed – this outward innocence (invisibility) of my possessed state (what is more innocent than writing poems!) and why – if I am a criminal – this decorousness of my criminality? Why – if all this is so – is there no mark upon me? God brands the scoundrel; why doesn't God brand *this* scoundrel?

Why, on the contrary, instead of attempts to bring me to my senses, is there encouragement, and, instead of a prison sentence, the affirmation that I am beyond jurisdiction?

Why, even the most ideological government in the world shot a poet not for his poems (the essence), but for deeds which could have been done by anyone.

Why have I got to be my own doctor, tamer, guard?

Isn't it asking too much of me?

I'll answer with an answer:

Everything knowing is wittingly guilty. Because I am given a conscience (knowledge), I am – once for all – in all cases of contravening its laws, whether by weakness of will or by strength of gift (of the blow struck at me), guilty.

Before God, not before men.

Who should judge? One who knows. People do not know; indeed so little do they know, that they will beat from me the last of my knowledge. And if they judge, then, like the government mentioned above, it will be not for my poems but for my deeds (as if a poet *had* other deeds!), for the chance happenings of life, which are only consequences.

People judge me, for instance, for not sending my six-year-old son to school (six hours on end of morning school!), not realising that I don't send him because I write poetry, as follows:

(from the poem to Byron)

Accomplished! He is alone between sky and water...
Here is a school for you, oh you – hater of schools!
And into the fated breast, pierced by a star,
Aeolus, king of fateful winds, tears his way in.[41]

– and I write such lines because I don't send him to school.

Praise me for my poems and judge me for my son?

Oh, you lickers of cream!

\*

A reflection on literature teaching in secondary schools. They give the younger ones *The Drowned Man* [42] and are surprised when they are frightened. They give the older ones Tatyana's letter[43] and are surprised when they fall in love (shoot themselves). They put a bomb in their hands and are surprised when it explodes.

And to finish with the subject of school: if you like these poems, let the children go (that is, meet the cost of your 'liking'), or else recognise that 'liking' is no measure of things and poems, is a measure not of things and poems but only of your own lowness (and the author's), our common weakness before the elemental, for which at some hour, while still here upon earth, we shall answer.

Either let the children go.

Or tear the poems out of the book.

\*

I allow no one the right of judgment over a poet. Because no one knows. Only poets know, but they will not judge. And the priest will absolve.
   The only judgment over a poet is self-judgment.[44]

\*

But apart from judgment, there is struggle – mine, with the element; yours, with my poems – not to give in, I to it, you to me. That we may not be seduced.

\*

Where shall I at last find a priest who will not absolve me of my poems?

## Conclusion

Whether a command or a plea, whether it's by fear or by pity that the elements overcome us, there are no reliable approaches, neither Christian nor civic nor any other kind. There is no approach to art, for it is a seizure. (While you are still approaching, it has already seized you.)

Example: Boris Pasternak in entire purity of heart, surrounding himself with all the materials, writes, copies from life – right down to its inadvertencies! – *Lieutenant Schmidt*; and yet the main character in his work is: trees at a meeting. They are the leaders, over Pasternak's Square. Whatever Pasternak writes, it is always elements, not characters, as in 'Potemkin'[45] it is the *sea*, not the sailors. Glory to Pasternak (Boris' human conscience) for the sailors, and glory to the sea, glory to his gift – the sea, that insatiable sea for which all our gullets are too small and which will always cover us, with all our stories and consciences.

Therefore, if you wish to serve God or man, if in general you wish to serve, to work for the good, then join the Salvation Army or something of that sort – and *give up poetry*.

But if your gift of song is indestructible, don't flatter yourself with the hope that you serve, even after you've finished *A Hundred And Fifty Million*. It is only your gift of song that has served you: tomorrow *you* will serve *it* – that is, you'll be hurled by it thrice-nine kingdoms or heavens away from the goal you have set.

Vladimir Mayakovsky, who for twelve years on end served loyally and truly, body and soul –

All my resonant, poet's, strength
I give up to you, the attacking class!

– ended more powerfully than with a lyric poem: with a lyric shot. For twelve years on end Mayakovsky the man killed in himself Mayakovsky the poet; in the thirteenth the poet arose and killed the man.

If there is a suicide in that life, it is not where people see it; and its duration was not the pressing of a trigger, but twelve years of life.

No imperial censor[46] dealt with Pushkin as Vladimir Mayakovsky dealt with himself.

If there is a suicide in that life, there is not one but two; and both are non-suicides, for the first is an act of valour, the second a celebration. The overcoming of nature and the glorifying of nature.

He lived like a human being, and he died like a poet.

*

To be a human being is more important, because it is more needed. The doctor and the priest are more needed than the poet because they, not we, are at the deathbed. Doctor and priest are humanly more important, all the rest are socially more important. (Whether the social is itself important is another question, which I shall have the right to answer only from a desert-island.) With the exception of parasites in all their various forms, everyone is more important than we are.

And knowing this, having put my signature to this while of sound mind and in full possession of my faculties, I assert, no less in possession of my faculties and of sound mind, that I would not exchange my work for any other. Knowing the greater, I do the lesser. This is why there is no forgiveness for me. Only such as I will be held answerable at the Judgment Day of Conscience. But if there is a Judgment Day of the Word, at that I am innocent.

# TWELVE POEMS

## I

Every poem a love-child,
Pauper, illegitimate,
First-born, laid at a road's
Rut, to beg of the winds.

For the heart it's hell and a shrine.
For the heart it's heaven and shame.
The father? Maybe a king,
A king or maybe a thief.

# II

Words are traced in black sky,
Splendid eyes are blinded...
And we do not fear the bed of death,
Nor enjoy the bed of passion.

You who write in sweat, you who plough in sweat!
We – know another ardour:
The light flame dancing above our hair
Is the breeze of inspiration!

# III

Any soul that's been born with wings –
What does it care for mansions or huts!
Genghis Khan or the Mongol Horde!
I've two enemies in this world,
Two twins inseparably united:
Pangs of the hungry, fat of the sated!

# IV

I spoke, and another heard,
Murmured to a third, the third
Understood, a fourth took
Oaken staff and strode off
Into the night - to a great deed.
The world made up a song of this:
That song is on my lips – oh life! –
As I encounter death.

# V

My day is aimless and absurd:
I ask the beggar alms for bread,
I give the rich man poor man's coins,

I thread a needle with a ray,
I trust the robber with my key,
I rouge my pallid skin with bleach.

The beggar doesn't give me bread,
The rich man doesn't take my coins,
The sunbeam won't go through the needle,

The robber enters without a key,
And the fool weeps three streams of tears
Over the senseless, inglorious day.

# VI

Verses grow like stars, like roses,
Like beauty - useless in a family.
'How has this come to me?' is my sole
Reply to wreaths and apotheoses.

We sleep – and see: through the stone floor
A heavenly guest, a quatrefoil.
World, understand! Poets in their sleep discover
The flower's formula, the star's law.

# VII

Who hasn't built a house
Doesn't deserve the earth.

Who hasn't built a house
Shall not be earth:
Straw and ash…

I haven't built a house.

# VIII

There's a certain hour, like a thrown-down load,
The hour of our tamed pride, the hour
Of discipleship. In every life
It's undeflectable and solemn.

The high hour when, laying down our weapons
At the feet of one a finger points to,
We take off our warrior's purple and put on
Camel's fur, on the sea shore.

That hour! It lifts us – like a voice –
From days of self-will to a great deed!
That hour when, like the ripened corn,
We bend with our own heaviness.

The corn has grown, the joyful hour has struck,
And the grain is longing for the millstone.
The law! The law! Yoke I already yearned for,
Lying in the womb of the earth.

Hour of discipleship! Yet we behold
And know another light, another kindled dawn.
Blessed is the hour to come afterward,
You, supreme hour – of solitude!

# IX

A poet – takes up speech from far.
A poet – is taken far by speech.

By way of planets, signs… circuitous
Parables' tracks… Between a *yes* and a *no*
He'll – even casting widely from a bell tower –
Conjúre a hook… For the path of comets

Is the poet's path. Causality's links
Wind-scattered are his sole connection!
Brow upward, you'll despair! No calendar
Can foreguess a poet's eclipses.

He's the one mixing up the cards,
Getting the better of weight and count,
He's the one asking from the school-bench,
The one who wholly confounds Kant,

The one who, in the Bastilles' stone tombs,
Is like a tree in all its beauty.
The one whose tracks have always cooled,
The train that everyone arrives
Too late to catch…
                              – for a comet's path

Is the path of poets: burning, not warming,
Tearing, not tending – outburst, break-in –
Maned curve, the trail you make
Isn't foretold by the almanac!

# X

Some extra, superfluous people exist,
They don't fit in to the range of the eye.
(Not numbered in your directories –
A rubbish tip is home for them).

Some hollow, jostled people exist,
They don't say anything: they are dung
Or a nail catching your silken hem!
Mud, squeamish, from under wheels!

Some unreal, invisible people exist
(Sign: spots of the lepers' hospice),
Some Jobs exist in the world who would have
Envied Job, provided –

Poets are what we are and we rhyme
With pariahs, but when we flood our banks
We contend with a god for goddesses,
And for a virgin, with gods!

# XI

What shall I do, being blind and a step-child,
In a world where they all have father and sight,
Where over anathemas, as over embankments,
Passions pass! Where a cold in the head
Is how they describe weeping!

What shall I do, by rib and by trade
A singer – like sunburn! A wire! Siberia!
Crossing my own entrancements like crossing a bridge!
With their weightlessness
In a world of weights.

What shall I do, being a singer and first-born,
In a world where the very blackest is grey!
Where they keep inspiration as though in a thermos!
With this measurelessness
In a world of measures!

# XII

Opened my veins – unhaltable,
Unrestorable gush of life.
Place your plates and dishes under it:
Every plate will be too shallow,
Every bowl too flat.
                              It flows
Over the rim and *past* the rim –
Into black earth to feed the reed.
Unrestorable, unhaltable,
Irretrievable gush of verse.

# NOTES TO ESSAYS

I have translated seven of the eight essays in this book from the Russian texts in the two-volume edition of Tsvetaeva's prose: Marina Tsvetaeva, *Izbrannaya proza v dvukh tomakh, 1917-1937*, edited by Alexander Sumerkin (New York, 1979); 'Poets with History...' is translated from the text given in Marina Tsvetaeva, *Sochineniya*, Vol. 2, ('Proza'), edited by A. Saakyants (Moscow, 1980), and has been checked closely against the Serbian text in *Ruskii arkhiv* (see below). I have occasionally used both the Sumerkin and the Saakyants editions for help with references.

The title of each essay is followed by the place and date of its first publication.

(Tsvetaeva's quotations: except for those in 'Downpour of Light', she usually quotes poetry by heart, and often inaccurately. In the course of 'Two Forest Kings', she quotes inaccurately from her own prose translation of 'Der Erlkönig'.)


## DOWNPOUR OF LIGHT [Svetovoi liven']

*Epopeya* (Berlin), 1922, No. 3

1. **his first book:** Tsvetaeva later realised she was mistaken about this – see her footnote , p. 25.
2. **Polytechnic Museum:** many public readings of poetry took place here in the years after the Revolution.
3. **Silence...:** from the poem 'Zvyozdy letom'. All Tsvetaeva's quotations of verse in this essay are from Pasternak's *My Sister Life*.
4. **'Durch Leiden – Freuden':** 'Through sufferings – joys'.
5. **Pelion on Ossa:** two youths piled mountains on top of one another in the hope of gaining the love of goddesses (Greek mythology).

6. **hunt for bread:** in the Civil War years, people went by train to the South of Russia in search of bread or flour.

7. *Serment:* the oath sworn in the Salle du Jeu de Paume at Versailles by members of the newly self-proclaimed 'Assemblée Nationale' on 17 June, 1789 ('ne jamais se séparer et se rassembler partout où les circonstances l'exigeront jusqu'à ce que la constitution du royaume soit établie...').

8. *durch:* through(out).

9. **Kerensky:** Alexander Kerensky became head of the 'Provisional Government' which took power in Russia after the February 1917 Revolution, and was ousted by the Bolsheviks in October.

10. **Slavonic sun:** a god of the early Slavs was called Dazhbog, meaning 'god grant'.

11. **has written nature:** *pisat'* means both 'to write' and 'to paint'; the thing 'painted' is the direct object of the verb, in the latter sense. I have preferred to sound un-English by using one and the same verb for 'write (about)' and 'paint ( + direct object)' rather than forfeit Tsvetaeva's slight play on this word.

12. **Lebedyan:** a place, south of Tula.

# The Poet on the Critic [Poet o kritike]

*Blagonamerennyi* (Brussels), 1926, No. 2

(The title of this essay could equally well be translated 'The Poet on Criticism'.)

1. *Souvienne vous:* 'Remember the man who, when he was asked why he took so much trouble in an art which could become known to almost no one, replied: "A few are enough for me – one is enough for one – none is enough for me." '

2. **impudently-breaking:** for the sake of Tsvetaeva's argument, I am preserving a punctuation that is odd in English though normal in Russian.

3. **Series of...:** lines from a poem by Fet.

4. **Bazarovism:** Bazarov – hero of Turgenev's *Fathers and Children* – scorned the spiritual and metaphysical, brought everything down to earth, to materialism.

5. **Rheingold, Dichtergold:** gold of the Rhine, gold of poets.

6. **We mustn't presume**: lines from Griboedov's play, *Woe from Wit*.

7. **Kokoshkin**: lawyer and statesman, early twentieth century.

8. **Podgaetskii-Chabrov**: actor, later a priest, early twentieth century.

9. **thrice-ninth**: a well-known phrase from Russian fairy tales.

10. **attitude, relation**: *otnoshenie*.

11. *Alles...*: 'Everything transient is but a likeness.' From the ending of Goethe's, *Faust* Part II.

12. *Ça ne tient...*: 'It won't stay upright', or 'It won't hold water'.

13. *Je suis de ceux...*: 'I am one of those to whom the visible world exists'.

14. *J'entends...*: 'I hear voices, she said, which command me...'

15. **a whole book**: *Swan's Encampment*.

16. **Volunteer**: the White army, opposing the Bolsheviks, in the South of Russia.

17. **hurrying...**: line by the poet Vyazemskii, used by Pushkin as epigraph to Chapter 1 of *Evgenii Onegin*.

18. *Etre salué...*: 'To be hailed by a lot of people you don't know'.

19. *Qu'en dira-t-on?*: 'What will people say?'

20. *Ich, der...*: 'I who live in the millennia'.

21. *Orientirungssin*: sense of orientation.

22. **Gurzuf**: place in the Crimea where Pushkin lived in 1820.

23. **Mikhailovskoe**: Pushkin's family estate.

24. **the role of...Lensky**: Tsvetaeva refers to operas by Chaikovsky based on narrative works by Pushkin.

25. **Sytin**: (Ivan D.) 1851-1934, Russian publisher, who published a series of illustrations to well-known works by Pushkin; he also published cheap editions of the Russian classics, including the works of Pushkin.

26. **Repin**: (Ilya E.) 1844-1930, Russian realist painter.

27. **false-Pushkin couplet**: two lines in Pushkin's 1836 poem, *Exegi monumentum*, were re-written by the tsarist censor (to be affixed to the statue of Pushkin) in the form given here by Tsvetaeva. A translation of the *true* third line of that stanza of which the first three lines are quoted here (in the first line the word-order was altered to accommodate the false third line) would run: 'That in my cruel century I glorified freedom'.

28. **'The Sail'**: a well-known poem by Lermontov.

29. *Wer kennt...*: 'Who knows you not, O great Goethe! Firmly built in the earth!'

30. *Pugachov*: see under 'Pushkin' in 'List of Writers', p. 213.

31. **The Poet and the Mob**: presumably a reference to Pushkin's poem, 'The Poet and the Crowd'.

32. **Poetry is agreeable to you...**: from Derzhavin's poem, 'Felitsa'.

## HISTORY OF A DEDICATION
## [Istoriya odnogo posvyashcheniya]

Not published in Tsvetaeva's lifetime. First published in *Oxford Slavonic Papers*, XI, (Oxford, 1964). (Only the second and third parts of this three-part essay are given here in translation.)

1. ***pood***: 36 lbs.
2. **Rasputin**: the debauched pseudo-monk who gained disastrous influence in the imperial household of Nicholas II; murdered by palace nobles in 1916.
3. **capital**: the ancient capital of Russia was Moscow; Petersburg became the capital in 1712. (In 1918 Moscow became capital again.)
4. **a rustic version...**: literally – '*obvorozhaet* the Tsaritsa (not *obvorazhivaet*, but precisely, in the rustic way: *obvorozhaet'*).
5. **boundless**: *neobozrimoi* = which the eye cannot encompass; the letters 'zr' suggest *zarya*, 'dawn'.
6. **Novo-Devichii ('New Virgin') Monastery**: in Moscow; many famous persons are buried here.
7. **with a band**: *venchikom* – suggests a corpse
8. **It will suddenly...**: line from a well-known children's song.
9. **Red Steer**: A reference to her unfinished narrative poem *The Red Steer*, written 1928-9.
10. **angle...coals**: *uglom... ugli*.
11. **Karadag**: a mountain.
12. **Pra**: nickname of Elena Ottobaldovna Voloshina, mother of the poet Voloshin.
13. **Doubting...**: this poem of Mandelstam's, addressed to Tsvetaeva, became part of his verse-collection *Tristia*.
14. **Koktebel**: see under Voloshin in 'List of Writers', on p. 214.
15. **So this...**: Tsvetaeva quotes from an essay by the poet Georgii Ivanov, 'Kitaiskie teni' (Chinese shades) in the Russian Parisian newspaper *Poslednie novosti* (22 Feb. 1930).
16. **Aivazovsky**: mediocre but popular painter of the nineteenth century.
17. **Shamil**: 1797-1871; leader of the mountain people of Daghestan and Chechnya in their struggles against the Tsarist colonisers; captured in 1859.

18. **Bogaevsky, Lentulov, Kandaurov, Nakhman, Bruni, Obolenskaya**: Russian artists working around the turn of the century.

19. **Cimmeria**: Tsvetaeva follows Voloshin in calling Koktebel by this name (from the Cimmerians, an ancient legendary people on the shores of the Black Sea).

20. **Salomeya Halpern**: a friend of Tsvetaeva's (1888-1982); Mandelstam wrote a number of poems to her.

## THE POET AND TIME [Poet i vremya]

*Volya Rossii* (Prague), 1932, No. 1-3

1. **actual**: *nastoyashchee* means both 'present' and 'real'.

2. **There's room...**: line from Lermontov's poem 'Valerik'.

3. **Louis**: Louis XIV, King of France, claimed 'L'état c'est moi': 'The state is myself'.

4. **thrice nine**: see note 9 to 'The Poet on the Critic'.

5. **trump card of émigré literature**: Tsvetaeva apparently means the writer Ivan Bunin.

6. **For I bypassed...**: from Tsvetaeva's poem 'Khvala vremeni'.

7. **And so my heart...**: from Tsvetaeva's poem 'Yest' v stane moyom...' 1920.

8. **non-returner**: *nevozvrashchenets* – a person who left Russia after the Revolution and did not return.

9. **"What time is it?"**: from Mandelstam's poem 'Batyushkov'.

10. **And long she languished**: from Lermontov's poem 'Angel'.

11. **Lay of the Host of Igor**: The damaged manuscript of this now-famous epic was found and published in 1800, but perished in the Moscow fire of 1812. Its authenticity as a fifteenth-century work was doubted by some. Pushkin wrote a defence of it in 1836.

12. *On ne perd...*: One loses nothing by waiting.

13. **bergeries**: pastorals – subtitle of a 1922 volume of poems by Sologub.

14. **Turk-Sib**: the construction of the Turkestan-Siberia railway was one of the largest achievements of the early Soviet government.

15. **evils of the day**: see note 17, below.

16. **A writer, if...**: from a poem by Polonsky, 'V al'bom k Sh'.

17. **the topical**: *zlobodnevnoe* – literally, 'the evils of the day'.

18. *bonne mine...*: making the best of a bad situation.

19. *Diese Strecke…*: We'll run together for this stretch (of the road) – Tsvetaeva does not give an exact translation.

20. **if for a time…**: line from Lermontov's poem 'I skuchno, i grustno…' saying that since love is temporary it's not worth going in for it.

21. **Death and time…**: from a poem by V. Solovyov, 'Bednyi drug, istomil tebya put'…'

# EPIC AND LYRIC OF CONTEMPORARY RUSSIA
## [Epos i lirika sovremennoi Rossii]

*Novyi grad* (Paris), 1932 and 1933, Nos. 6-7

1. **Where shall I find…**: from Mayakovsky's poem 'Gorod'.

2. **the avid rule-of-eye…**: a line from Mandelstam's poem 'Admiral-teistvo'.

3. *Irrjahre*: years of erring, wandering.

4. *die wollten blühn*: they wanted to blossom, we want to be dark and work with effort. Lines from Rilke's poem 'Im Saal' which should run: '…Sie wollten blühn/und blühn ist schön sein; doch wir wollen reifen/und das heisst dunkel sein und uns bemühn.'

5. **Polytechnic Museum**: see note 2 to 'Downpour of Light'.

6. **As they say…**: from the poem 'Uzhe vtoroi, dolzhno byt', ty legla', which formed part of Mayakovsky's suicide-note.

7. **And on Alexandra…**: from the play *Moskva gorit* (*Moscow is Burning*).

8. **In every youth…**: from 'War and the World'.

9. **The murmuring…**: line from Pushkin's poem 'Stikhi, sochinyonnye noch'yu vo vremya bessonnitsy'.

10. **All is in me…**: from Tyutchev's poem 'Teni sizye smesilis'.

11. **Vendôme…Concorde**: reference to the poem 'Gorod'.

12. **Wrangel**: reference to the flight of Wrangel, a Commander of the White Army, in the poem 'Khorosho!'

13. **Falsely modest…**: from the poem 'Avtobusom po Moskve'.

14. **All my life…**: lines from Pasternak's long poem *Vysokaya bolezn'*.

15. **brilliant story**: *Detstvo Lyuvers* (*The Childhood of Lyuvers*).

16. **And all the icons…**: line from Tsvetaeva's poem to Akhmatova, 'U tonkoi provoloki nad volnoi ovsov'.

17. **Poetry! be…**: from the poem 'Vesna'.

18. **Wilde**: reference to Oscar Wilde's *Portrait of Dorian Gray*.

19. **Ponyatovsky**: reference to the poem 'Chugunnye shtany'; Ponyan-tovsky – a military man in the service of Napolean.

20. **Your shot...**: see last note to this essay.

21. **The all-powerful God of love...** [Footnote]: from Pasternak's poem 'Davai ronyat' slova...'

22. **'The Man who was Thursday'**: a story by G. K. Chesterton.

23. **Cryptography...Phenography...orthography**: 'Tainopis'...Yavn-opis'...propis''.

24. **But there lay on the faces...** [Footnote]: lines from Pasternak's poem 'Smert' poeta', of which the concluding twelve lines are quoted at the end of this essay.

25. **Peter**: Peter the Great. Lines from Pasternak's poem 'Peterburg'.

26. **I take aim...**: from Tsvetaeva's poem 'Yest' v stane moyom – ofitserskaya pryamost'.

27. **And through the magic crystal**: from Pushkin's *Evgenii Onegin*.

28. **On the leaves...**: lines from Pasternak's poem 'Ty v vetre, vetkoi probuyushchem'.

29. *Die Sonne...*: 'The sun brings it to light'. From a poem by German poet Chamisso (1781-1839).

30. **not to flow into the Caspian sea**: normally this would mean 'not to do the obvious'; here it appears to mean 'not to do what is natural to him', or even 'to do the impossible'.

31. **Neyasyt**: a river.

32. **I think of you...**: an unknown, and clearly bad, poem.

33. **the man**: Lenin.

34. **that Mayakovsky was acting a part**: 'chto Mayakovskii eto dlya nego lomaetsya (deistvitel'no lomalsya: kak lyod v ledokhod!)'.

35. **Statue!**: Tsvetaeva uses an irregular, masculine form (*statui*) of the word for statue which is feminine: *statuya*.

36. *vy...ty...*: cf. French '*vous...tu*'.

37. **Bear in mind each day...**: from the poem 'Marusya otravilas''.

38. *In der Beschränkung*: 'It's only in (self-) limitation that the master is revealed.' Quoted from Goethe's poem 'Natur und Kunst' (1800).

39. **Laocoon**: famous Greek sculpture of Laocoon and his two sons struggling with the snakes which were sent by the gods to strangle him for his disobedience.

40. **Out of his skin**: 'Laokoon iz kozhi ne vylezet, no vylezaet vsegda': play on this idiom continues through the next paragraph.

41. **another semantic context**: see 'Art in the Light of Conscience', p. 183.

42. **Don't I know...**: Pasternak's poem 'Drugu'.

43. *Weil auf mir...*: 'Rest on me, you dark eye, exercise your whole power.' From Lenau's poem 'Gebet'.

44. *kein Umstürzler*: no overturner.

45. **And since from my early...**: from Pasternak's poem 'Vesenneyu poroyu l'da'.

46. *Après avoir réfléchi...*: 'After having reflected on the destiny of women in all the ages and in all the nations, I've come to think that every man should say to every woman, not "Good day" but "I'm sorry!"'

47. **October**: The Bolshevik Revolution took place in October 1917, and was the subject of many poems by Mayakovsky, including one entitled 'October' (1926).

48. **December**: The worker's uprising in Moscow in December 1905, subject of the last section ('Moscow in December') of Pasternak's long poem *The Year 1905* (1926).

49. **You slept...**: from Pasternak's poem 'Smert' poeta', on the death of Mayakovsky.


# Two Forest Kings [Dva lesnykh tsarya]

*Chisla* (Paris), 1934, No. 10

1. **a free poetic translation of genius**: that by Zhukovsky, which she proceeds to analyse. Here is a rough English translation of Zhukovsky's Russian version of Goethe's poem:

Who gallops, who speeds through the cold darkness?
A belated rider, with him his young son.
The child, tired from shivering, leans close to his father,
Embracing him, the old man holds and warms him.

– Child, why do you press against me so fearfully?
– Dear Father, the Erlking has flashed into my eyes;
He's in a dark crown, with a thick beard.
– Oh no, that's the mist looking white over the water.

– Child, look round; little one, come to me;
There's much that is joyful in my land:
Flowers of turquoise, streams of pearl;
My palaces are made of gold.

– Dear Father, the Erlking is talking to me:
He's promising gold and pearls and joy.
– Oh no, my child, you have misheard:
It's the wind waking up and shaking the leaves.

– To me, little one; in my leafy grove
You shall know my beautiful daughters:
They will play and flit in the moonlight,
Playing and flitting, they'll lull you to sleep.

– Dear Father, the Erlking has gathered his daughters:
I can see them nodding to me from the dark boughs.
– Oh no, everything's calm in the night's depth:
It's the old grey willows standing to one side.

– Child, I am captivated by your beauty:
Willing or unwilling, you shall be mine.
– Father, the Erlking wants to catch us up:
Here he is: I'm stifled, I can hardly breathe.

The frightened rider doesn't gallop, he flies;
The little boy pines, the little boy cries out;
The rider rides faster, the rider arrives.
In his arms lay the dead little boy.

# Poets with History and Poets without History
[Poety s istoriei i poety bez istorii]

*Russkii arkhiv* (Belgrade), 1934, Nos. XXV-XXVII, published there in a
Serbian translation by B. Kovačević; the original manuscript has been
lost. It has been translated back into Russian twice – the better translation
is that by O. Kutasova, published in Marina Tsvetaeva, *Sochineniya*, ed.
A. Saakyants, Vol. 2 (Moscow, 1980).

(Only the first two parts of this six-part essay are given here in English
translation, and the translation of the first part starts with its sixth
paragraph.)

1. **The one whose name...**: from V. Ivanov's poem 'Lichinu obvet-
shaluyu'.

2. **summoned by Apollo**: reference to Pushkin's poem 'Poet'.

3. **Now beyond...**: from Lermontov's poem 'Svidanie'.

4. **I drew my left-hand glove...**: from Akhmatova's poem 'Pesnya poslednei vstrechi'.

5. **All becomes dull...**: from Pasternak's epic *1905 -yi god* (*The Year 1905*).

6. **The soft careful break...**: the whole of a poem by Mandelstam (1908).

7. **Les heureux...**: Happy people have no history.


ART IN THE LIGHT OF CONSCIENCE
[Iskusstvo pri svete sovesti]


*Sovremennye zapiski* (Paris), 1932 and 1933, Nos. 51 and 52

1. **la terre en travail**: the earth in labour.

2. **Poetry is God...**: last line of Zhukovsky's play *Camoens*.

3.**There is an ecstasy...**: These and subsequent lines come from Pushkin's dramatic fragment in verse *Pir vo vremya chumy* (*Feast in Time of Plague*) which is based on part of a play by the English playwright John Wilson (1789-1854), *The City of the Plague*. In the fragment, people feast in the street during a plague, with a Master of Ceremonies called Walsingham. They speak of dead friends; the black cart passes, carrying bodies; a woman called Mary sings a song lamenting the devastation brought by the plague: but the dramatic climax is the song sung by Walsingham, which he introduces as a 'Hymn to the Plague'. The fragment ends with a priest calling the feasters 'godless madmen' and begging Walsingham to remember his dead mother and his wife. The closing stage-directions are: 'The Feast continues. Its President remains, sunk in deep thought.'

4. **lap of nature**: *lono*.

5. **music of Revolution**: in many of his writings Blok used the metaphor 'music' for the elemental force that makes history and change.

6. **Z.G.**: Meeting Blok in a tram, by chance, after the Revolution (and after his poem *The Twelve*), Zinaida Gippius agreed to shake hands with him only 'personally', not 'socially'.

7. **Vozdvizhenka**: a main road in Moscow.

8. **Katka**: character in Blok's poem *Dvenadtsat'* (*The Twelve*).

9. **A man sharp-nosed and waxen-faced**: Gogol.

10. **Art without artifice**: *Iskusstvo bez iskusa* – there are several ways of translating *iskus*: see discussion at end of Introduction.

11. **Novo-Devichii**: see note 6 to 'History of a Dedication'.

12. **round robin**: *krugovaya poruka* – lit. a 'circular guarantee' (each person in a group takes responsibility for all the others).

13. **rhymes**: I omit, as untranslatable, Tsvetaeva's examples of banal rhymes in the quoted poem by the nun. They are: *tishi-dushi*; *deti-seti*; *dushoyu-odnoyu*.

14. **six-year-old daughter**: Ariadna; she did not become a poet, but worked for years after her mother's death, editing her manuscripts.

15. **Bazarovism**: see note 4 to 'The Poet on the Critic'.

16. *Fier quand...Humble quand...*: Proud when I compare myself... Humble when I compare myself, unknown when I consider myself.

17. **She took the faded pages**: from Tyutchev's poem 'Ona sidela na polu'.

18. **A wizard: a forefather**: *libo chura: prashchura*. *Chur* means 'limit' or 'circle' and is used in magical contexts.

19. **Russian works**: Tsvetaeva means her works about Russia, using Russian folk-themes.

20. *im Spiel*: in play, i.e. at work.

21. *mra*: Tsvetaeva has invented this word, from the stem of the Russian words for 'death' and 'darkness'.

22. *Et tout le reste...*: 'And all the rest is only literature.' Last line from Verlaine's poem 'Art poétique' (quoted inaccurately).

23. **and you send reply...**: from Pushkin's poem 'Ekho'.

24. **chastushka**: chastushki are four-line poems made up, and sung, by peasants or people at work, in response to current events.

25. *nicht vorhanden*: not present (not to hand).

26. **Who called me?**: Tsvetaeva has in mind the Earth Spirit's words to Faust (in *Faust* Part I) who has just summoned it up: 'Wer rief mir?'

27. **vulneral**: I have made up this word, to translate *bolevoi*.

28. **unhappy crowned contemplator**: probably Paul I of Russia, who collected clocks.

29. *obsession...possession*: these words are in French in the original.

30. **Russian works**: see above, note 19.

31. **Pugachov**: see 'Pushkin' in 'List of Writers' on p. 213.

32. **Grishka Otrepyev**: the runaway monk Grigorii who obtained the Russian throne in 1605 and is one of the heroes of Pushkin's play *Boris Godunov*. Tsvetaeva calls him the 'Impostor' in the next paragraph.

33. **Corsican**: Napoleon.

34. *Mais l'intention*...: But the intention is always there.

35. **wax**: Odysseus's companions stuck wax in their ears to avoid being enticed by the singing of the sirens, while Odysseus had himself lashed to the mast of his ship.

36. **Wrangel**: see note 12 to 'Epic and Lyric...'

37. *Salieri*: the hard-working but insufficiently talented composer who, in Pushkin's play, poisons Mozart.

38. *Intoxiqués*: poisoned, or drugged, people.

39. **not an autocracy**: *ne samoderzhavie* – i.e. art is not itself a holder of absolute power.

40. *Heureux celui*...: Happy the one who was able to know them.

41. **Accomplished!**...: from Tsvetaeva's poem 'Ya bereg pokidal tumannyi Al'biona' (1918).

42. **The Drowned Man**: Pushkin's much anthologised poem 'Utoplennik'.

43. **Tatyana's letter**: in Pushkin's novel in verse, *Evgenii Onegin*, Tatyana declares her love for Onegin by letter.

44. **self-judgment**: *samosud* (a word that normally means 'lynchlaw').

45. **'Potemkin'**: part of Pasternak's epic *The Year 1905*.

46. **censor**: after the 1825 Decembrist uprising, Pushkin's works were subjected to censorship by the tsar himself.

# NOTES TO POEMS

**Every poem...** (p. 184)

'Kazhdyi stikh – ditya lyubvi' (1918).

**Words are traced...** (p. 185)

'V chornom nebe slova nachertany' (1918).

**Any soul...** (p. 186)

'Esli dusha rodilas' krylatoi' (1918).

**I spoke...** (p. 187)

'Ya skazala, a drugoi uslyshal' (1918).

**My day...** (p. 188)

'Moi den' besputen i nelep' (1918).

**Verses grow...** (p. 189)

'Stikhi rastut, kak zvyozdy i kak rozy' (1918).

**Who hasn't built...** (p. 190)

'Kto doma ne stroil' (1918).

**There's a certain hour...** (p. 191)

'Est' nekii chas, kak sbroshennaya klazha' (1921). This poem forms part of a cycle entitled *The Disciple* (*Uchenik*).

**A poet takes up speech...** (p. 192)

'Poet izdaleka zavodit rech'' (1923). In the fifth stanza Tsvetaeva doubtless has in mind the poet André Chénier, imprisoned in the Bastille and guillotined in 1794.

**Some extra...** (p. 193)

'Est' v mire lishnye, dobavochnye' (1923); 'squeamish' translates *brezguyet* ('is squeamish') which by its sound suggests *bryzgaet* ('splashes').

**What shall I do...** (p. 194)        'Chto zhe mne delat', sleptsu u pasynku' (1923). 'Wire, sunburn, Siberia': perhaps suggesting that a poet is a fast communicator, like a telegraph wire, which can take words both to very hot places and to very cold. 'by trade' translates as *promyslom*, which is the instrumental case of both *promysel* (skill, trade, business) and *promysl* (with capital P = Providence), so an alternative, biblical-sounding translation might be 'by rib and design'. NB *rebrom* ('by rib') also means both 'point-blank' and 'edgewise'.

These three poems of 1923 constitute a cycle entitled *The Poet* (*Poet*).

**Opened my veins...** (p. 195)        'Vskryla zhily: neostanovimo' (1934).

# LIST OF WRITERS MENTIONED BY TSVETAEVA

(Details of their work and lives are given only insofar as these are useful for understanding Tsvetaeva's references to them.)

**Adamóvich, Georgii V.** (1884-1972) literary critic; left Russia 1922.

**Afanásyev, Aleksándr N.** (1826-71) famous as collector and publisher of Russian folk tales (1855-64).

**Aikhenvál'd, Yulii I.** (1872-1928) literary critic.

**Akhmátova, Anna A.** (1889-1966) poet; a founder of Acmeism in 1911; married the poet Gumilyov in 1910.

**Artsybáshev, Mikhaíl P.** (1878-1927) novelist and story-writer, specialising in themes of violence.

**Aséev, Nikolái N.** (1889-1962) poet and writer.

**Bal'mónt, Konstantín D.** (1867-1942) poet, Symbolist.

**Bátyushkov, Konstantin N.** (1787-1855) poet.

**Bédnyi, Demyán** (1883-1945) poet, writer of folk-style verse, propagandist for Communist Party.

**Bélyi** (pseudonym meaning 'White'), **Andréi** (1880-1934) poet, novelist and literary theorist; a leading Symbolist.

**Blok, Aleksándr A.** (1880-1921) poet; a leading Symbolist. Blok welcomed the Revolution and worked for institutions of the new government, but spent the last two years of his life in disappointment and decline.

'The Unknown Woman': a well-known poem of 1907.

*The Twelve*: Blok's most famous poem, written January 1918, in twelve parts, describing twelve Red Guards marching through Petersburg in the early days of the Bolshevik Revolution and unexpectedly led by Jesus Christ.

**Búnin, Iván A.** (1870-1953) story-writer with a high reputation by the turn of the century. Left Russia after the Revolution, lived in France. First Russian writer to receive the Nobel Prize (1933).

*The Village*: a novella written 1909-10.

**Chateaubriand, Francois- René de** (1768-1848) French writer and political figure.

**Chórnyi, Sásha** (pseudonym)(1880-1933) satirical poet.

**Demyán**, *see* **Bédnyi**

**Derzhávin, Gavriíl R.** (1743-1816) classical poet.

**Erenbúrg, Ilyá G.** (1891-1967) journalist and writer, a public figure; lived in Paris in the 1920s and 30s as foreign correspondent. 'His works served as weather vane for the political atmosphere of his time' (V. Terras).

**Esénin, Sergéi A.** (1895-1925) 'peasant' poet; called for a return to ideals of village life; in 1920s became 'bohemian' and alcoholic; doubted the value of his work; committed suicide.

'I'm the last poet of the village': opening of a poem of 1920.

**Gíppius, Zinaída N.** (1869-1945) poet and writer; organised an influential religious circle in Petersburg; left Russia 1919; lived in Paris.

**Goethe, Johann Wolfgang von** (1749-1832) Germany's greatest poet and writer,'the last of the great universal geniuses'. From 1775, Goethe was one of the principal ministers of the Duke of Weimar.

*Götz von Berlichingen*: play (1771-3 ).

*The Sufferings of Young Werther*: epistolary novel of 1774 in which the hero shoots himself as a result of disappointed love.

'The Erlking': one of Goethe's best- known poems.

*Roman Elegies*: 1788-90.

*Faust*, his most famous play: Part I published in 1808, Part II finished shortly before his death.

*Theory of Colours* and *Metamorphosis of Plants*: works containing his scientific theories.

**Gógol, Nikolái V.** (1809-52) one of the masters of Russian prose. Gogol gave up comic writing to work for the spiritual transformation of Russia. Ten days before his death he burnt the unpublished manuscript of Part II of his novel.

*Dead Souls*, for which Pushkin gave him the idea, was published in 1842: Part I ends with the description of a troika-ride, in which the fast reckless troika is identified with Russia careering through history.

**Goncourt, Jules** (1830-70) French writer. He suffered mental disintegration at the end of his life. Brother of Edmond Goncourt, also a writer.

**Gumilyóv, Nikolái A.** (1886-1921) poet, a founder of Acmeism; travelled in Africa; known as poet of romantic adventure and heroism. Executed for alleged counter-revolutionary activities.

'Tram that got lost': one of his later poems.

*Bonfire*: a volume of poems (1918).

**Heine, Heinrich** (1797-1856) German poet.

**Hölderlin, Friedrich** (1770-1843) German poet.

**Ivánov, Geórgii, V** (1894-1958) poet and critic; emigrated 1922.

**Ivánov, Vyacheslàv I.** (1866-1949) poet and scholar, principal theorist for the Symbolist movement; emigrated 1924.

**Khodasévich, Vladisláv, F.**(1886-1939) poet and critic; emigrated 1922.

**Kleist, Heinrich von** (1777-1811) German dramatist and story-writer.

**Kuzmín, Mikhaíl A.**(1875-1936) poet and prose-writer.

**Lenau, Nikolaus** (1802-50) German poet.

**Lérmontov, Mikhaíl Yu.** (1814-41) Romantic poet and novelist. Among his best-known short poems are 'The Angel' (1830) and 'The Sail' (1832).

**Leskóv, Nikolái S.** (1831-95) novelist and story-writer.

**Lunachársky, Anatolii V.** (1875-1933) critic and writer; became first People's Commissar for Enlightenment in 1917.

**Mandelstám, Osip E.** (1891-1938) poet, a founder of Acmeism; arrested in 1934 and 1938; died in captivity.

*Tristia* (1922): his second volume of verse (containing the poem 'Insomnia').

**Mayakóvsky, Vladímir V.** (1893-1930) poet, a founder of Russian Futurism, was an author of the 1912 manifesto 'A Slap in the Face of Public Taste', demanding that Pushkin, Dostoevsky and Tolstoy be thrown off the 'ship of modernity'. Committed suicide.

*Vladimir Mayakovsky*, a Tragedy, presents the author as a Christ-figure suffering for all city-dwellers.

'War and the World' (1916): fantasy poem about World War I.

*150,000,000*: a long satirical-political poem of 1919, its title the number of inhabitants of the Soviet Union.

**Mírsky (Svyatopólk-Mírsky), Prince Dmítrii P.** (1890-1939) literary historian and critic; emigrated 1920 to Greece, then to England.

Joined the British Communist Party in 1931, returned to Soviet Russia in 1932, was arrested and disappeared in 1937. His *History of Russian Literature* (1926) is still a standard work.

**Nádson, Semyón Ya.** (1862-87) a very popular writer of melodious, 'socially conscious' verse.

**Nekrásov, Nikolái A.** (1821-78) poet, writer, publisher, representative of the 'realist' school and of 'civic' poetry. His well-known poem 'The Pedlars' (1861) is an example of his ability to write in style of folksong.

**Pasternák, Borís L.** (1890-1960) poet and prose writer. His father was the well-known artist, Leonid Osipovich Pasternak (1862-1945). Studied philosophy in Marburg, Germany, in 1912. Was friend of Mayakovsky, also of Tsvetaeva with whom he conducted a passionate correspondence.

*Over the Barriers*: collection of verse published in 1917.

*My Sister Life*: written 1917, published 1922 – the collection that won him fame; it includes the poem 'About these Verses' with its lines, often quoted by Tsvetaeva: 'What millennium, my dears/is it out there?', as well as the poem 'Stars in summer', from which she often quotes the lines 'Silence, you are the best/of all I've ever heard'.

*The Childhood of Lyuvers*: written 1918, published 1922, a story about a girl's growing consciousness.

The long poems *The Year 1905* (1926) and *Lieutenant Schmidt* (1927) were attempts at writing about revolutionary history which many, including Tsvetaeva, saw as less than his best work.

**Púshkin, Aleksándr S.** (1799-1837) Russia's greatest poet, 'father of Russian literature' (greatly loved by Tsvetaeva: see her memoir 'My Pushkin', in *A Captive Spirit*). His best-known poems include 'To the Sea' (1824; starting with the line 'Farewell, free element'), 'The Poet and the Crowd' (1828), and 'Echo' (1831). In an intensely creative period while confined to his estate at Boldino in 1830, Pushkin wrote, *inter alia*, his *Little Tragedies*, which include *Mozart and Salieri*, *The Covetous Knight*, and *Feast in Time of Plague*. Killed in a duel with a Frenchman, D'Anthès.

*Evgenii Onegin*: a novel in verse, written 1823-31, published 1833.

*History of the Pugachov Rebellion*: a short piece of historical research about the eighteenth-century peasant leader, published 1833.

*The Captain's Daughter*: Pushkin's novel about the same events.

**Rémizov, Alekséi M.** (1877-1957) novelist and story-writer; left Russia 1921.

**Rilke, Rainer Maria** (1875-1926) German poet. Travelled to Russia, 1899 and 1900. After being put in touch with Tsvetaeva by Pasternak in 1926, he had a brief but intense correspondence with her. Greatly admired and loved by her.

*The Book of Hours* (1905) contains poems purportedly written by a monk (the 'prayers' mentioned in 'Art in the Light of Conscience').

**Rolland, Romain** (1866-1944) French novelist and dramatist.

**Sainte-Beuve, Charles** (1804-69) French critic and novelist.

**Savódnik, V.F.** (1874-1940) author of textbooks on the history of Russian literature.

**Schiller, Friedrich** (1759-1805) German poet and foremost dramatist of German classicism.

His poem 'Das Lied von der Glocke' (1799) starts with the lines 'Fest gemauert in der Erden/Steht die Form, aus Lehm gebrannt.'

**Severyánin, Ígor** (1887-1941) poet; wrote somewhat opulent and self-indulgent poems.

**Sologúb, Fyódor K.** (1863-1927) poet and prose-writer, important in the Symbolist movement, considered a 'decadent'; stayed in the Soviet Union although unable to publish after 1923; in his later work pessimism yields to a metaphysical optimism.

*The Reed-Pipe*. Russian Bergeries (1922).

**Svyatopolk** (*see* **Mirsky**)

**Tolstóy, Lev N.** (1828-1910) one of the great Russian novelists. *War and Peace* was written in the 1860s; *Anna Karenina* in the 1870s. In the 1880s and after, Tolstoy wrote predominantly works on religion, morality and education.

*What is Art?* (1898) argues for the promotion of only religious art or art with a clear moral.

**Tyútchev, Fyódor I.** (1803-73) poet.

**Vertínsky, Aleksándr N.** (1889-1957) poet, singer, variety actor.

**Villon, François** (1431- after1463) French poet.

**Volóshin, Maksimilián A.** (1877-1932) poet, associated with Symbolism; lived in Koktebel in the Crimea where his house became a refuge for many writers and artists.

**Vyacheslav** (*see* **Ivanov**)

**Zhukóvsky, Vasílii A.** (1783-1852) Romantic poet and translator. Famed for his translations of poetry, especially English and German.

*A singer in the camp of Russian warriors*: written in 1812 after he witnessed the Battle of Borodino.

Printed in the USA
CPSIA information can be obtained
at www.ICGtesting.com
JSHW012027140824
68134JS00033B/2906